For Our Parents

*

CALIFORNIA CIVIL PROCEDURE

By

David I. Levine
Professor of Law
University of California
Hastings College of the Law

Rochelle J. Shapell
Adjunct Professor of Law
University of California
Hastings College of the Law

THOMSON
WEST™

Mat #40604394

Sum & Substance Quick Review of California Civil Procedure is a publication of West

610 Opperman Drive
St. Paul, MN 55123
1–800–313–9378

Printed in the United States of America

ISBN: 978–0–314–18098–8

TEXT IS PRINTED ON 10% POST CONSUMER RECYCLED PAPER

Preface

As students go through law school, they sometimes wonder whether they should know more about the differences in civil practice in state and federal courts. Failing to act on this concern is risky. Students who start their professional careers assuming that civil procedure in California's state courts mirrors the federal system they encountered in their first procedure course are in for a surprise. It is especially perilous to presume that the systems are the same now that state civil procedure is eligible for testing on the California Bar Examination.

Readers who find their way to this Quick Review will probably fall into one of four groups. Some law students will have chosen to take an advanced course in California Civil Procedure and are now looking for a study guide. Other students will have elected not (or neglected) to take a state procedure course, but are nevertheless interested in learning about the differences between the two systems. Graduating students looking toward the California Bar Examination may find this outline a helpful supplemental study aid. New (or not so new) lawyers also may find this Quick Review to be a handy guide if they find themselves about to be cast into the unfamiliar territory of state court. Whichever group you find yourself in, we hope that this Quick Review will fill your needs.

This Quick Review provides a tour through the most important aspects of California civil procedure. The book focuses on topics not covered in the standard first course in procedure where California has taken a road not followed in federal practice. It also features topics where California procedural law has solved problems in somewhat different fashion than in federal courts. We frequently provide discussion in sections of the book entitled "Compare Federal Procedure," which expressly highlight the state/federal differences that are so crucial to this field of study. Finally, each chapter contains many illustrations and sample examination questions so you can test your understanding of the topics. (All such illustrations and questions throughout the Quick Review are placed in California state courts, unless specified otherwise.)

Nearly all of the state and federal statutes and rules cited in the Quick Review can be found in Mary Kay Kane & David I. Levine, Civil Procedure in California: State and Federal. Thomson/West publishes this paperback of supplemental materials annually. In Chapter 1 of the Quick Review, we cite to useful secondary sources for further understanding of or research in California Civil Procedure.

We express our sincere thanks to the following research assistants for their valuable assistance in the development of this Quick Review: Yoori Choi, Lynn Combs, Drew Elliott, Kevin McLaughlin, Nicholas Short, and J.J. Stein. Their help would not have been possible without the support of our home institution, University of California, Hastings College of the Law. Most of all, we thank William R. Slomanson of Thomas Jefferson School of Law, our co-author on Cases and Materials in California Civil Procedure (Thomson/West, 3d ed. 2008). Through our collaboration on that project, he has contributed mightily to our understanding of this complex field.

D.I.L.
R.J.S.

August 2008
San Francisco

TABLE OF CONTENTS

TABLE OF CONTENTS

TABLE OF CONTENTS

TABLE OF CONTENTS

CHAPTER 1

INTRODUCTION

I. SOURCES OF PROCEDURAL LAW

A. Primary Authorities

"Primary authorities" constitute "the law." See CCP §§ 1895–1899. All primary authorities have binding force in their respective jurisdictions.

1. Constitutions

a. Constitution of California

California's Constitution contains several procedural provisions. For example, the Constitution sets out the structure and hierarchy of the state's trial and appellate courts (art. VI), and it secures the right to a jury trial in civil and criminal cases (art. I, § 16). In contrast to the U.S. Constitution, the state Constitution explicitly provides an inalienable right to privacy (art. I, § 1), which affects such procedural matters as the scope of discovery (see Chapter 4).

b. Constitution of the United States

The federal Constitution impacts California procedure to the extent its provisions apply to the states. For example, the Due Process Clause of the Fourteenth Amendment is applicable to the exercise of personal jurisdiction in California. (See Chapter 2(II).) However, the Seventh Amendment's right to a jury trial in civil cases does not apply to the states. Dice v. Akron, C. & Y. R. Co., 342 U.S. 359, 72 S.Ct. 312, 96 L.Ed. 398 (1952). (See Chapter 6(III).)

2. Statutes

The California Code of Civil Procedure (CCP) is the repository for numerous provisions enacted by the California Legislature that govern state civil procedure. In addition to the CCP, several other California codes contain important procedural statutes, including the Civil, Evidence, and Government Codes.

3. Code of Regulations

Administrative agencies (which are part of the state's executive branch) are empowered to adopt regulations to aid in the implementation of statutory law. The California Code of Regulations (formerly called the California Administrative Code) is the compilation that contains California's regulatory law.

4. California Rules of Court

The Judicial Council of California is authorized by the California Constitution (art. VI, § 6) and statutes (e.g., CCP §§ 575, 901) to adopt statewide rules of court (CRC) governing many aspects of civil procedure and practice in the state's trial and appellate courts. The state Constitution (art. VI, § 6) requires that the CRC "not be inconsistent with statute." The main purposes of the CRC are to achieve statewide uniformity and to supplement statutory provisions contained in the CCP and other codes.

5. Cases

California appellate courts develop a body of legal precedent that is constantly evolving. Often, the courts interpret and apply statutory provisions and rules of court. Sometimes, in keeping with the common law tradition, the appellate courts "make" law.

a. Structure of California Courts

California has three levels of courts:

1) Superior Court

Each of California's 58 counties has a trial court called the Superior Court. In addition to conducting pretrial proceedings and trials, the superior courts are also authorized to review certain matters designated for hearing within the courts' Appellate Division. CCP § 77.

2) Court of Appeal

The California Court of Appeal hears cases in panels of three justices. The Court of Appeal is divided into six districts. The panels in the larger appellate districts are organized into divisions.

3) Supreme Court

The highest court of the state is the California Supreme Court. It has one Chief Justice and six Associate Justices.

CALIFORNIA COURT SYSTEM

CALIFORNIA SUPREME COURT

1 Chief Justice and 6 Associate Justices

Jurisdiction

Discretion to hear appeals from courts of appeal.

Must hear appeals directly from superior courts on death penalty matters.

Also hears appeals directly from decisions of Public Utilities Commission, recommendations of State Bar on attorney admission and discipline, and recommendations from Commission on Judicial Performance on discipline of judges.

CALIFORNIA COURT OF APPEAL

105 Justices in 6 Districts (19 Divisions)

First District: San Francisco
Second District: Los Angeles, Ventura
Third District: Sacramento
Fourth District: San Diego, Riverside, Santa Ana
Fifth District: Fresno
Sixth District: San Jose

Jurisdiction

Hears appeals and writ petitions from decisions of superior courts within appellate district.

Hears appeals and writ proceedings from decisions of Workers' Compensation Appeals Board, Agricultural Relations Appeals Board, and Public Employment Relations Board, and from certain decisions of Public Utilities Commission.

CALIFORNIA SUPERIOR COURT

1,500 Judges, 440 Commissioners and Referees
58 Counties, 450 court locations

Jurisdiction

Trial Departments: conduct trial proceedings in criminal (felony and misdemeanor) and civil (unlimited and limited) cases.

Small Claims Division: conducts civil proceedings.

Appellate Division: hears appeals from limited civil cases and criminal misdemeanor cases.

Source: David I. Levine, William R. Slomanson & Rochelle J. Shapell, Cases and Materials on California Civil Procedure (Thomson/West, 3d ed. 2008).

b. Publication and Citation of Judicial Decisions

All California Supreme Court opinions are officially published. No Superior Court decisions at the trial level are officially published. Decisions of the Court of Appeal or the Appellate Division of the Superior Court are officially published according to criteria contained in the CRC and implemented by the California Supreme Court.

1) Certification for Publication

Certification of a Court of Appeal or Superior Court Appellate Division decision for publication requires consideration of several factors, such as whether the opinion establishes a new rule of law or involves an issue of public interest. CRC 8.1105(b)–(c). Citation to nonpublished California Court of Appeal or Appellate Division decisions is prohibited. CRC 8.1115. However, a party may cite to unpublished decisions from the federal courts and courts of other states.

2) *Compare Federal Procedure*

Federal Rule of Appellate Procedure (FRAP) 32.1 permits citation of all federal opinions and dispositions issued after January 1, 2007, including those which have been designated as "unpublished" or "non-precedential." Ninth Circuit Rule 36–3 prohibits citation of most pre–2007 unpublished dispositions issued by courts within the circuit. Unpublished rulings are specifically deemed "not precedent" under the Ninth Circuit rule.

3) Illustration

Defendant Demi filed a motion for summary judgment against Plaintiff Park. In her memorandum of points and authorities in support of the motion, Demi included a citation to a California Court of Appeal decision that had not been certified for publication. Demi may not include the citation in her memorandum, and the court may not rely upon the unpublished decision when ruling on the motion. Schmier v. Supreme Court of California, 78 Cal.App.4th 703, 93 Cal.Rptr.2d 580 (2000).

6. Local Rules

The superior courts are empowered by CCP § 575.1 and Cal. Gov't Code § 68070 to adopt written rules applicable to an individual

Superior Court. The six districts of the Court of Appeal also are authorized to publish local rules. CRC 10.1030. Local rules are invalid if they are inconsistent with statute or the statewide CRC. Elkins v. Superior Court, 41 Cal.4th 1337, 63 Cal.Rptr.3d 483, 163 P.3d 160 (2007) (invalidating family court local rule requiring parties in dissolution matters to present their case by declarations because rule inconsistent with statute).

7. Local Policies and Practices

Sometimes, courts adopt procedures that apply to practice only within a single branch or district of a court, or even a particular judicial department or courtroom. Such local practices or policies are authorized as part of the inherent power of judges to control judicial proceedings. CCP §§ 128(a)(3), 187. Although these policies and practices are considered less formal, they must be published so litigants are on notice of their existence and requirements. CCP § 575.1(c). Local practices and policies may not conflict with state statutes or the CRC.

B. Secondary Authorities

Several secondary authorities exist to aid a California practitioner in interpreting and understanding civil procedural laws and practices contained in the primary authorities discussed above. Secondary authorities are not "the law" itself, but they can be very influential in gap-filling where primary authorities do not provide answers. Secondary authorities include legislative histories, opinions of the California Attorney General, scholarly publications, treatises, and practice guides. See, e.g., Bernard E. Witkin, California Procedure (5th ed. 2008); Robert I. Weil, Ira A. Brown, Jr. & William F. Rylaarsdam, California Practice Guide: Civil Procedure Before Trial (2008 ed.); William E. Wegner, Robert H. Fairbank & Norman L. Epstein, California Practice Guide: Civil Trials and Evidence (2007 ed.); Jon B. Eisenberg, Ellis J. Horvitz & Howard B. Wiener, California Practice Guide: Civil Appeals and Writs (2008 ed.); and John K. Hanft, Legal Research in California (6th ed. 2007).

II. CHOICE BETWEEN CALIFORNIA AND FEDERAL COURT

A. How Choice Arises

The many procedural distinctions that exist between the California and federal courts (noted throughout this outline) give rise to a key litigation question: Should an action be filed in state or federal court? Some elements of this choice are not flexible. For example, subject matter jurisdiction considerations may dictate that an action involving exclusive federal jurisdiction must be filed in federal district court, or that a federal forum is not available for cases not invoking diversity or federal question jurisdiction. But once those "givens" are resolved, several tactical and practical reasons may sway a litigant toward one court system over the other when a choice is available.

B. State/Federal Distinctions

Some areas in which state/federal distinctions are particularly noteworthy include:

- subject matter jurisdiction (Chapter 2)
- venue and choice of forum (Chapter 2)
- pleading and joinder (Chapter 3)
- attacks on pleadings (Chapter 3)
- discovery (Chapter 4)
- case management and diligent prosecution (Chapter 5)
- alternative dispute resolution (Chapter 5)
- summary judgment (Chapter 5)
- settlement and offer of judgment (Chapter 5)
- jury trials (Chapter 6)
- right to attorney's fees (Chapter 7)
- appellate review (Chapter 8)
- claim preclusion (Chapter 9)

Chapter 2

JURISDICTION, VENUE AND CONFLICT OF LAWS

I. SUBJECT MATTER JURISDICTION

Subject matter jurisdiction refers to the power of a trial court to hear or determine a cause of action. Subject matter jurisdiction of the California superior courts is broader than the limited subject matter jurisdiction available in the federal district courts.

A. Superior Courts as Courts of General Jurisdiction

The superior courts are trial courts of general jurisdiction. Unless jurisdiction resides exclusively in another court or tribunal, the superior courts have the power to decide any matter, whether it involves California law, federal law, or the law of other states or nations.

B. Structure of Superior Courts

1. Former Structure

Until 1998, all of the trial courts of California were divided into superior and municipal courts, with separate jurisdictional requirements, procedures, and administration.

2. Current Structure

With the passage of Proposition 220 by California voters in 1998, the two trial court systems began the process of consolidation or unification. Since 2001, every California county has had a unified Superior Court. The distinctions between the former Superior and Municipal Court systems are reflected in the jurisdictional classifications of unlimited and limited civil cases in the unified Superior Court.

C. Classification of Actions

1. Unlimited Civil Cases

A civil action other than a limited civil case is classified as an unlimited civil case. CCP § 88. Primarily, unlimited civil cases are those in which the amount in controversy exceeds $25,000. The full range of equitable relief is also encompassed in the subject matter jurisdiction of unlimited civil cases.

2. Limited Civil Cases

CCP § 86 sets out the subject matter jurisdiction of limited civil cases. Most commonly, a limited civil case is one in which the amount in controversy is $25,000 or less. The court hearing a limited civil case also has restricted equitable and declaratory jurisdiction. (Generally, a complaint praying for an equitable remedy must be classified as an unlimited civil case.) Economic Litigation procedures limit the number and types of pleadings, motions, and discovery requests that can be used in a limited civil case. See Chapter 3(III)(E); Chapter 4(III)(C).

3. Compare: Small Claims Cases

Small claims matters are limited civil cases that are adjudicated within the Small Claims Division of the Superior Court. A litigant may choose whether to maintain her action as a limited civil case or as a small claims case. Each Superior Court has a Small Claims Division with jurisdiction over cases in which the amount in controversy does not exceed $7,500 for a natural person and $5,000 for other types of plaintiffs. CCP §§ 116.221, 116.220(a)(1). Small claims cases are subject to several important restrictions. For example, small claims cases do not allow for discovery, and generally attorneys are not permitted to appear on behalf of parties. CCP §§ 116.310, 116.530. A small claims plaintiff may not appeal the judgment rendered, but a small claims defendant may appeal the judgment to the Superior Court and obtain a trial de novo before a judge. CCP § 116.710.

4. Cost Consequences of Incorrect Classification

If a plaintiff exaggerates the value of her case, she may be subject to cost consequences for incorrectly filing her case as an unlimited or a limited civil case. These consequences are intended to encourage plaintiffs to classify their actions appropriately. If the plaintiff files her action as an unlimited civil case, but she recovers a judgment within the jurisdiction of a limited civil case, the Superior Court in its discretion may deny an award of costs to the plaintiff. CCP § 1033(a). Similar cost consequences hold true for a plaintiff in a limited civil case that could have been filed as a small claims case. CCP § 1033(b)(1).

5. Amount in Controversy

a. Calculating the Amount

"Amount in controversy" means the amount of the demand, or the recovery sought, or the value of the property that is in controversy in the action, exclusive of interest, attorney's fees and costs. CCP § 85(a). Generally, the amount demanded in the prayer of the complaint determines the amount in controversy—and thus the classification—of the case, unless the prayer is fraudulent or fictitious on its face. A party may waive any portion of a demand that is in excess of $25,000 in order to retain limited civil case status. CCP § 403.040(f).

b. Aggregation of Claims

The amount in controversy may be influenced by the aggregation of claims:

- One Plaintiff v. One Defendant: All of the plaintiff's claims will be aggregated in determining the amount in controversy.

- One Plaintiff v. Multiple Defendants: All of the plaintiff's claims against any one defendant will be aggregated. Claims against multiple defendants will not be aggregated if they involve separate causes of action or obligations. If the claims against the defendants involve a joint obligation, they will be aggregated. If the plaintiff's claim against at least one of the defendants exceeds $25,000, the entire action may be treated as an unlimited civil case if the claims against the other defendants may be joined under CCP § 379 (i.e., they arise from the same transaction and occurrence and share a common question of law or fact).

- Multiple Plaintiffs v. One or More Defendants: Where the plaintiffs have suffered an indivisible harm or where their claims are otherwise necessarily joint, the claims of the plaintiffs will be aggregated. However, each separate claim—where each plaintiff will recover individually—will be assessed separately when determining the amount in controversy. If one plaintiff's separate claims exceed $25,000, all claims by the other plaintiffs also may be heard as unlimited civil cases as long as they satisfy the requirements for joinder under CCP § 378 (same transaction or occurrence and common question of law or fact).

6. *Compare Federal Procedure*

While the California superior courts are courts of general jurisdiction, federal district courts have limited jurisdiction. They can hear only those cases permitted by the U.S. Constitution and by statutes, such as those involving a federal question or where diversity of citizenship exists. 28 USC §§ 1331, 1332. The amount in controversy for diversity cases must exceed $75,000. There is no amount in controversy requirement for federal question actions. In calculating the amount in controversy in a diversity action, the district court will aggregate the claims of plaintiffs against defendants under the same aggregation rules as in a California state court.

7. Illustration

Page and Doon entered into a written agreement in Walnut Creek for Doon to purchase two sculptures from Page for $6,000 each. Page has delivered the first sculpture to Doon. Page believes that under the contract she is entitled to payment for the first half of the shipment. Doon believes that he must pay only after both of the sculptures have been delivered. Page has sued Doon in the Contra Costa County Superior Court for payment of the first $6,000. Her complaint also seeks revision of the contract to "clarify" the parties' intent. Although the amount in controversy requirement for a limited civil case is satisfied here, the court's equitable jurisdiction in a limited civil case is restricted under CCP § 86. However, revision of a contract (an equitable remedy) is permitted "where the relief is sought in an action upon the contract if the court action otherwise is a limited civil case." CCP § 86(a)(3). Therefore, this case is properly classified as a limited civil case.

D. Reclassification of Actions

1. Motion for Reclassification

A party or the court may move to reclassify an action if it is erroneously classified. CCP § 403.040. Notice and opportunity to be heard are required. If, before trial, it becomes clear that the verdict or judgment in an unlimited civil case will "necessarily" fall below the $25,000 jurisdictional dividing line, the court will reclassify it as a limited civil case. Stern v. Superior Court, 105 Cal.App.4th 223, 129 Cal.Rptr.2d 275 (2003). If a party seeks reclassification from a limited civil case to an unlimited civil case, the court will order reclassification if there is a possibility that the damages will exceed $25,000. Ytuarte v. Superior Court, 129 Cal.App.4th 266, 28 Cal.Rptr.3d 474 (2005). In evaluating the amount in controversy, the court may consider the prayer of the complaint, as well as evidence such as settlement or case management conference statements, and arbitration awards.

2. Reclassification by Amended Complaint or Cross–Complaint

A matter may be reclassified if the plaintiff files an amended complaint that alters the amount in controversy or the type of relief sought. CCP § 403.020. In a limited civil case, if a defendant files a cross-complaint against the plaintiff for an amount over $25,000, the filing will be sufficient to reclassify the entire action as an unlimited civil case. CCP § 403.030. In an unlimited civil case, a cross-complaint for an amount of $25,000 or less will not cause the case to be reclassified as limited—the court will have jurisdiction to dispose of the limited cross-complaint as part of the unlimited civil action. CCP § 403.040(e).

3. Compare: Challenge Based on Lack of Subject Matter Jurisdiction

In contrast to reclassification, a defendant who contends that the Superior Court lacks subject matter jurisdiction over the action (i.e., is without power to adjudicate) may file a demurrer (CCP § 430.10(a)) or motion for judgment on the pleadings (CCP § 438(c)(1)(B)) on that ground. See Chapter 3(IV).

4. *Compare Federal Procedure*

There is no federal equivalent to California's reclassification procedures.

5. Illustration

Pluto discovered that his accountant, Denzel, had falsely represented that he was a licensed certified public accountant. Pluto sued Denzel in Stanislaus County Superior Court for fraud and unfair business practices. Pluto's unlimited civil complaint prayed for

> $36,000 in damages. The court conducted a case management conference and referred the action to judicial arbitration, which resulted in an award for Pluto of $18,000. Upon receiving Pluto's request for a trial de novo, Denzel filed a motion to reclassify the action as a limited civil case on the ground that Pluto will not be able to obtain a verdict at trial within the jurisdictional level of an unlimited civil case. The court will reclassify the action as a limited civil case only if it determines that the verdict will necessarily fall below the $25,000+ required for unlimited jurisdiction. In making its determination, the court may consider the prayer of the complaint, the case management conference statements, and the judicial arbitration results. Stern v. Superior Court, 105 Cal.App.4th 223, 129 Cal.Rptr.2d 275 (2003).

II. JURISDICTION OVER PERSONS

A state court must have personal jurisdiction over the defendant to enter a binding judgment. Personal jurisdiction in California courts is defined by the Due Process Clause of the Fourteenth Amendment of the U.S. Constitution and by the state's "long arm" statute. California's broad long arm statute permits the exercise of personal jurisdiction on any "basis not inconsistent with the Constitution of [California] or of the United States." CCP § 410.10.

A. Traditional Bases of Personal Jurisdiction

California, like other states, routinely exercises personal jurisdiction over defendants in a number of traditional situations:

- The defendant is *domiciled* in California;
- The defendant is served while *physically present* in the state, even if the defendant's presence is transient;
- The defendant has *consented* to jurisdiction (e.g., appointment of agent for service of process, execution of contract containing a forum-selection clause); or
- The defendant has made a *general appearance* before the California court by participating in the action in a way that recognizes the authority of the court to adjudicate the merits. Typically, a defendant generally appears in an action by filing an

answer, but other motions and litigation conduct also may constitute a general appearance. See CCP § 1014 (filing a motion to strike, to transfer venue, or to reclassify an action considered general appearance). See also section IV(A)(1)(b), below.

B. Constitutional Limitations: Minimum Contacts

1. Background

To be subject to the personal jurisdiction of a state court, the Due Process Clause requires that a defendant who is not present in the state or has not consented to jurisdiction must "have certain minimum contacts with [the forum state] such that the maintenance of the suit does not offend 'traditional notions of fair play and substantial justice.' " International Shoe Co. v. Washington, 326 U.S. 310, 316, 66 S.Ct. 154, 158, 90 L.Ed. 95 (1945). California recognizes two categories of personal jurisdiction under the minimum contacts analysis: general jurisdiction and specific (limited) jurisdiction.

a. General Jurisdiction

California state courts may exercise general jurisdiction over a nonresident defendant if the defendant has conducted sufficiently extensive, continuous, and systematic activities in California. If general jurisdiction exists, the court has jurisdiction over the defendant for all causes of action against him, even those unrelated to the defendant's activities in the forum state.

b. Specific Jurisdiction

When a court has specific (or limited) jurisdiction over a defendant, the court may exercise personal jurisdiction only for causes of action arising out of the defendant's activities in the forum state. California courts have recognized three requirements for specific jurisdiction:

- The defendant must have purposefully availed himself of the forum by voluntarily directing his activities to California;
- There must be a substantial nexus between the plaintiff's causes of action and the defendant's activity in California; and
- Traditional notions of fair play and substantial justice require the court to balance the conveniences of the parties and interests of the forum state.

Cornelison v. Chaney, 16 Cal.3d 143, 127 Cal.Rptr. 352, 545 P.2d 264 (1976).

2. Compare: Personal Jurisdiction Via the Internet and the "Effects Test"

a. Internet Activities

Internet activities of nonresidents can be a possible basis of personal jurisdiction if the activities meet sufficient minimum contacts requirements. Merely posting information on a passive Internet site is insufficient to subject a nonresident defendant to California jurisdiction. However, operation of an interactive Internet site where the defendant knowingly makes repeated contacts with California residents may be sufficient to confer jurisdiction. Snowney v. Harrah's Entertainment, Inc., 35 Cal.4th 1054, 29 Cal.Rptr.3d 33, 112 P.3d 28 (2005).

b. Effects Test

The "effects test" requires a nonresident to expressly aim conduct toward California residents in order to impose personal jurisdiction over him for his Internet activities. Mere knowledge or foreseeability that the defendant's conduct might cause harm in California is not enough to confer personal jurisdiction under this test. A higher degree of purposefulness is required. Pavlovich v. Superior Court, 29 Cal.4th 262, 127 Cal.Rptr.2d 329, 58 P.3d 2 (2002).

3. *Compare Federal Procedure*

Federal law under the Due Process Clause generally recognizes the same traditional bases for and constitutional limitations on the exercise of personal jurisdiction as do the California courts.

4. Illustration

Pam was in the market for a car. She happened upon the Web site of Drivers' Dream, a company located in Miami, Florida. The Drivers' Dream Web site stated that it supplies cars "worldwide" and provided a telephone number. Drivers' Dream does not have an office or employees in California, and it has previously sold

> cars to only four other California residents. On the Web site, Pam saw an advertisement for a powder blue 1967 Ford Mustang. Pam negotiated with Drivers' Dream by phone and fax for the purchase of the Mustang. Pam made her own arrangements for shipping the car from Miami to her home in Ventura. When the car arrived, Pam was dissatisfied with its condition. She sued Drivers' Dream in Ventura County Superior Court. Drivers' Dream filed a motion to quash service of summons for lack of personal jurisdiction. The court will likely grant the motion on the basis of lack of either general or specific jurisdiction. Although Drivers' Dream operated an Internet site to advertise its cars, it did not target California residents and did not actually conduct business through the Web site. Therefore, Drivers' Dream did not purposefully avail itself of the California forum. The maintenance of the Web site alone is an insufficient basis for upholding jurisdiction. Shisler v. Sanfer Sports Cars, Inc., 146 Cal.App.4th 1254, 53 Cal.Rptr.3d 335 (2006).

C. Compare: In Rem Jurisdiction

In rem actions involve the adjudication of rights related to property. The exercise of jurisdiction is based on the presence of the property (res) in the state. The distinction between in personam and in rem jurisdiction is no longer sharply delineated because due process and minimum contacts are required for all exercises of jurisdiction by the court. Shaffer v. Heitner, 433 U.S. 186, 97 S.Ct. 2569, 53 L.Ed.2d 683 (1977). In rem jurisdiction arises in actions for quiet title, condemnation, civil forfeiture, probate, and marital dissolution, among others. See, e.g., People v. $25,000 United States Currency, 131 Cal.App.4th 127, 31 Cal.Rptr.3d 637 (2005).

III. SERVICE OF PROCESS

Upon commencing an action by filing a complaint with the court, the plaintiff must then notify the defendant of the lawsuit through the service of process (summons and complaint). Service of process on a defendant within California establishes personal jurisdiction over that defendant. Service on a defendant outside of California does not in itself create personal jurisdiction; the defendant must also have had sufficient minimum contacts with California. The plaintiff must use a proper method of service of process (CCP §§ 415.10–415.95) that accomplishes service on the appropriate "person to be served" (CCP §§ 416.10–416.90). California courts interpret the statutory requirements for service liberally in order to uphold service. If the defendant received actual notice of the lawsuit, service will likely be considered valid as long as the plaintiff substantially complied with the service statutes.

A. Summons

1. Purposes of Summons

The court clerk issues a summons to the plaintiff. The summons serves several purposes, including:

- providing notice to the defendant in English and Spanish of the filing of the lawsuit;

- warning that the defendant must respond to the lawsuit within 30 days or be subject to entry of default judgment; and

- suggesting that the defendant might wish to seek advice of counsel before the response is due.

CCP § 412.20.

2. Who May Serve Summons

The summons may be served by "[a]ny person who is at least 18 years of age, and not a party to the action." CCP § 414.10.

B. Manner of Service

California statutes authorize several methods of service of process, depending on the type of defendant and whether the defendant is located within California or outside the state.

1. Defendant Within California

a. Personal Delivery

Personal delivery of summons and complaint is the most reliable method of service. CCP § 415.10. As long as the process server states that the defendant is being served with process and leaves the papers in close proximity to the defendant, service will be deemed valid (even if the defendant refuses the papers). Service is complete upon delivery.

b. Substituted Service

Substituted service involves serving the defendant by leaving the summons and complaint with an authorized person in an authorized location, followed by mailing copies of the papers to the defendant or other "person to be served" at that location. Service is complete on the tenth day after the date of mailing. CCP § 415.20.

1) Substituted Service on Individual

If the defendant is an individual (or a representative of an individual, such as a conservator), the plaintiff must make a reasonably diligent effort to serve the defendant by personal delivery before using substituted service. CCP § 415.20(b); Espindola v. Nunez, 199 Cal.App.3d 1389, 245 Cal.Rptr. 596 (1988). Substituted service on an individual defendant may be made by leaving the papers with a person at least 18 years old who is a "competent member of the household" or a person "apparently in charge of [the defendant's] office or place of business."

2) Substituted Service on Entity

No prior attempt at personal delivery is required before substituted service may be made on a corporation or other entity. CCP § 415.20(a). Substituted service on an entity is accomplished by leaving the papers during "usual office hours" with a "person apparently in charge" of the office or, if the physical office address is unknown, the usual mailing address.

c. Service by Mail

This method involves mailing a copy of the summons and complaint to the defendant or "other person to be served," accompanied by two copies of a notice and acknowledgement of receipt of summons. CCP § 415.30. On the acknowledgement, the defendant merely notes the date and location of receipt of the summons and complaint. The notice informs the defendant that if she fails to return the acknowledgement to the plaintiff within 20 days, she may be liable for the expenses the plaintiff subsequently incurs in attempting to serve the defendant in another manner. Service by this method is deemed complete on the date the defendant executes the acknowledgement, as long as it is returned to the plaintiff.

d. Service by Publication

Service by publication is the method least likely to result in actual notice. For that reason, it is the only method requiring leave of court. It is used mostly when a defendant's address or whereabouts are unknown or if the defendant has evaded service. The plaintiff must demonstrate that he used reasonable diligence to locate the defendant and that attempts to accomplish service by other methods were unsuccessful. The court orders the summons to be published once a week for four successive weeks in a newspaper "most likely to give actual notice" to the defendant. Service is deemed complete on the 28th day following the first day of publication. CCP § 415.50.

2. Defendant Outside California

a. Interstate Service

A defendant outside California may be served by any of the methods available for in-state defendants or by a method permitted by the state in which the defendant is served. CCP § 413.10(b). In addition, out-of-state defendants may be served by mail. This manner of service requires mailing only a copy of the summons and complaint to the "person to be served." It does not require sending a notice and acknowledgement of receipt of summons. Service by mail is complete on the tenth day after the mailing. CCP § 415.40.

b. International Service

To serve a foreign defendant, a plaintiff may use any of the methods of service authorized under the CCP, as well as any method of service authorized by the place of service as long as that method is reasonably calculated to give actual notice. CCP § 413.10(c). Parties who are citizens of signatories to certain service treaties, such as the Hague Service Convention or the Inter–American Convention on Letters Rogatory, must use the methods of service described in those treaties.

C. Person to Be Served

In addition to utilizing a proper method of service, a plaintiff must accomplish service on a proper person. CCP §§ 416.10–416.90 describe the types of persons who may be served with process. For example, for corporations and unincorporated associations (including partnerships), the proper persons to be served include several specified categories of officers or employees (such as president, vice president, secretary, treasurer, or general manager), the person designated as agent for service of process, or a person authorized by the entity to receive service of process. CCP §§ 416.10–416.40. Individual defendants may be served personally, or through an authorized representative (such as a parent, guardian or other fiduciary). CCP §§ 416.60–416.90.

D. Proof of Service

Unless a defendant has already made a general appearance, proof of service of a summons must be filed with the court after completion of service. CCP § 417.30. Specific proof of service requirements apply depending on the manner of service and whether service occurred inside or outside of California. See CCP §§ 417.10–417.20. The filing of proof of service showing compliance with statutory requirements gives rise to a rebuttable presumption that service has been properly executed.

E. Abrogation of Immunity from Service of Process

California does not grant immunity from service of process to those nonresidents temporarily present in the state to participate in litigation. Silverman v. Superior Court, 203 Cal.App.3d 145, 249 Cal.Rptr. 724 (1988).

F. *Compare Federal Procedure*

The methods of service of process under FRCP 4 are largely similar to those authorized by the California statutes. Moreover, FRCP 4(e)(1) permits service of process to be implemented pursuant to the law of the state in which the federal district court sits.

G. Illustration

Leo Bloom filed suit in Lake County Superior Court against Roger DeBris for breach of contract. Leo's process server served the summons and complaint by leaving them with Roger's personal assistant, Carmen Ghia. Although Roger had received actual notice of the lawsuit, Roger's attorney advised him not to respond to the complaint because service on Carmen did not constitute valid substituted service on Roger under CCP § 415.20(b). A default judgment against Roger for failing to respond would be invalid because Roger had not been properly served. Carmen was not a person authorized by Roger "to receive service of process" under CCP § 416.90. Although courts are encouraged to liberally construe the service of process statutes, actual notice received by the defendant is not sufficient to relieve the plaintiff of the requirement of substantial compliance. Although Carmen is Roger's personal assistant, she is not necessarily authorized to accept service on behalf of Roger. Summers v. McClanahan, 140 Cal.App.4th 403, 44 Cal.Rptr.3d 338 (2006).

IV. CHALLENGING PERSONAL JURISDICTION AND SERVICE OF PROCESS

Several procedures exist for a defendant to challenge the propriety of service of process and the exercise of personal jurisdiction over her.

A. Special Appearance

A defendant may make a special appearance in the Superior Court to challenge service of processand jurisdiction without otherwise submitting to the court's jurisdiction.

1. Motion to Quash Service of Summons

a. Timing

A defendant may specially appear by moving to quash service of summons on the ground of lack of jurisdiction. CCP § 418.10(a)(1). The defendant must file this motion on or before the last day to respond to the complaint. CCP § 418.10(a). The defendant may move to quash and "simultaneously answer, demur, or move to strike the complaint or cross-complaint" without making a general appearance. CCP § 418.10(e). Failure to move to quash service at the same time as filing a separate answer, demurrer or motion to strike will be deemed to be a waiver of the jurisdiction objection. Roy v. Superior Court, 127 Cal.App.4th 337, 25 Cal.Rptr.3d 488 (2005). The burden of proof on a motion to quash is on the plaintiff to demonstrate proper service and minimum contacts.

b. General Appearance if Motion Denied

If the motion to quash is denied, the defendant will be deemed to have made a general appearance unless the defendant seeks immediate appellate court review via a writ petition. CCP § 418.10(c), (e)(2). A defendant who has moved to quash service of summons must also be careful not to unwittingly participate in the action in a way that could be deemed a general appearance. For example, a defendant who moves to quash service of summons but then initiates discovery unrelated to jurisdiction while the motion is pending will be found to have made a general appearance.

c. *Compare Federal Procedure*

Unlike California practice, a federal defendant may preserve the right to challenge the exercise of personal jurisdiction by including the objection as an affirmative defense in a responsive pleading (such as an answer). The defendant may also object to personal jurisdiction by a motion to dismiss under FRCP 12(b)(2). In contrast to California procedure, if a federal judge denies a defendant's challenge to personal jurisdiction, the defendant may defend the case on the merits and still raise the jurisdictional objection on appeal because the denial of a challenge to personal jurisdiction is not considered an appealable order. Stewart v. Ragland, 934 F.2d 1033 (9th Cir. 1991).

d. Illustration

Pisces Co. brought an action in Riverside County Superior Court against its largest competitor, Delights, Inc., for unfair competition. Before filing its answer, Delights filed an ex parte application to take early discovery regarding Pisces' unfair competition claims. Delights subsequently filed a motion to quash service of summons based on the lack of personal jurisdiction over it. Delights' attempt to obtain discovery on the merits of the action through the ex parte application constitutes a general appearance. Had the request for discovery been limited to the jurisdictional issues on the motion to quash, no general appearance would have resulted. Delights could not act in a way that constituted a general appearance, and then take the position that filing a motion to quash negated that action. Factor Health Management v. Superior Court, 132 Cal.App.4th 246, 33 Cal.Rptr.3d 599 (2005).

2. Motion to Dismiss for Failure to Serve Summons

A defendant may make a special appearance to file a motion to dismiss an action where service of process has not been completed within two years (discretionary dismissal) or three years (mandatory dismissal). CCP §§ 418.10(a)(3); 583.210–.250; 583.410–.420. See Chapter 5(III)(A).

3. Motion to Set Aside Default Judgment

If service of process was defective and did not result in actual notice to the defendant, and the plaintiff obtained a default judgment, the defendant may make a special appearance to set aside the default judgment. CCP § 473.5. Generally, the defendant must bring a concurrent motion to quash service of summons so the court can simultaneously rule on the defendant's jurisdictional objections.

B. Other Challenges

A defendant may decline to make an appearance in an action involving defective service or personal jurisdiction. Instead, the defendant may appeal from any default judgment entered against him and challenge the defective service and lack of jurisdiction at that time. Alternatively, the defendant may bring a separate Superior Court lawsuit in equity to attack the entry of default judgment for lack of jurisdiction.

V. VENUE

Venue in California refers to the county for the "trial of the action." CCP §§ 392(a), 395(a). The purpose of California's venue statutes is to ensure that a defendant is not compelled to defend in an unreasonably distant county. A defendant may move the court to transfer venue based on several grounds set out in CCP § 397.

A. Proper Court: Classification of Actions

Based on the allegations of the complaint, actions are classified for venue purposes as local or transitory. Each classification has its own set of rules governing the proper location of trial.

1. Local Actions

Local actions relate to real property. Examples include actions seeking recovery of real property, adjudication of the rights of the parties to real property, or recovery for injuries to real property. Venue in local actions is proper in the county or counties in which the real property or any part of it is located. CCP § 392(a).

2. Transitory Actions

Actions not classified as local are transitory. Under the general rule for transitory actions, venue is proper in the county in which the defendants or some of them reside at the commencement of the action. CCP § 395(a).

a. Expanded Venue Choices in Particular Actions

In addition to the general transitory venue rule, venue may be proper in other counties in certain types of actions:

- Personal injury or wrongful death actions: in the county in which the injury occurred.

- Contract actions: in the county in which the obligation is to be performed or the contract was entered.

CCP § 395(a).

b. Actions Against Corporations

In an action against a corporation, venue is proper in the county in which the contract was made or was to be performed, the obligation or liability arose, the breach occurred, or the corporation has its principal place of business. CCP § 395.5.

3. Mixed Actions

a. Application of General Transitory Venue Rule

In a mixed action, the defendants and/or causes of action might be subject to different venue rules. For example, a complaint may contain a local and a transitory cause of action, or it may include a cause of action or defendant subject to a special venue rule outside of the general transitory venue provisions contained in CCP § 395. Generally, venue in a mixed action is proper in a county in which any defendant resides. If a defendant is entitled to a change of venue to his or her residence county on one cause of action in a mixed action, the court must grant a change of venue on all causes of action in the complaint. Gallin v. Superior Court, 230 Cal.App.3d 541, 281 Cal.Rptr. 304 (1991).

b. Effect of Special Venue Rules

While the general transitory venue rule may apply to some causes of action, public policy or other compelling considerations may supersede the general rule, favoring venue in a location other than in defendant's county of residence. See Brown v. Superior Court, 37 Cal.3d 477, 208 Cal.Rptr. 724, 691 P.2d 272 (1984) (special venue rule under Fair Employment and Housing Act supplants general transitory venue rule governing mixed actions).

4. Main Relief Rule

If the complaint contains one cause of action but more than one form of relief, proper venue is determined by the main relief rule. Massae v. Superior Court, 118 Cal.App.3d 527, 173 Cal.Rptr. 527 (1981). For example, if a complaint seeks relief in the form of an adjudication of the rights to land (local) as well as specific performance of a land purchase contract (transitory), venue is proper according to the rule governing the main relief sought.

5. ***Compare Federal Procedure***

Under 28 USC § 1391, venue in a federal transitory action is proper in any district in which any defendant resides or where a substantial part of the events or omissions giving rise to the claim occurred. If no district satisfies either of these criteria, then venue is proper for actions based solely on diversity in the district in which any defendant is subject to personal jurisdiction, and, for actions not based solely on diversity, in the district in which any defendant may be found. Venue rules for local actions are almost identical to those under the California statute. See 28 USC §§ 1391, 1392.

6. **Illustration**

Parthy was a rabid fan of the rock group Broken Chain. Much to her distress, Parthy learned that the members of the group did not actually sing the lyrics. Rather, other singers performed without credit on Broken Chain's recordings. In concerts, members of Broken Chain "lip-synched" the words to recorded lyrics. Parthy sued the members of Broken Chain and their manager, Dodge, for fraud and for causes of action under the California Consumers Legal Remedies Act, alleging that she had attended two Broken Chain concerts and bought several Broken Chain CDs in Monterey. Parthy filed the complaint in Monterey County Superior Court, where she resides. Dodge brought a motion to transfer venue to Los Angeles County, the county of his residence, arguing that no defendant resides in Monterey County. Parthy contended that the Consumers Legal Remedies Act provided for additional venue choices, including the county in which a substantial portion of the transaction occurred. Parthy argued that the special venue rule for the Consumers Legal Remedies Act should govern all of her causes of action, making venue in Monterey County proper. Dodge asserted that in a mixed action such as this one, the defendant is entitled to transfer the action to the county of his residence. The court will likely order transfer to Los Angeles County. The Consumers Legal Remedies Act does not provide an exclusive statutory remedy for Parthy's claims, and there has been no violation of a fundamental right. Thus, there are no compelling policy reasons to supersede the general venue rule for a mixed action. Gallin v. Superior Court, 230 Cal.App.3d 541, 281 Cal. Rptr. 304 (1991).

B. Grounds for Transfer of Venue

1. Improper Court

If the plaintiff has filed the complaint in an "improper" court according to the rules discussed in section A, above, any defendant may move for a transfer of venue to a proper court. CCP §§ 396b, 397(a). If no defendant objects to improper venue, the original court has the power to conduct the trial and enter a valid judgment. A motion to transfer venue based on the ground of improper court must be brought within the time to responsively plead to the complaint. CCP § 396b(a).

a. *Compare Federal Procedure*

A federal party may challenge improper venue via either an affirmative defense or a motion. FRCP 12(b)(3). A challenge based on improper venue is waived unless timely raised. In addition, if venue is improper in the original district, the court may transfer venue in "the interest of justice" to a district or division where the action could have been brought, as an alternative to dismissal. 28 USC § 1406(a). The transferee court must have subject matter jurisdiction, personal jurisdiction and venue.

b. Illustration

Peet sued his supervisor Dylan for wrongful termination and intentional infliction of emotional distress in Shasta County Superior Court, the county where Peet lived and worked. Dylan moved to change venue to Trinity County, where she resided. Peet opposed the motion on the ground that the emotional distress claim constitutes a "personal injury" cause of action under CCP § 395, making Shasta County a proper venue. However, Peet's intentional infliction of emotional distress claim resulting from a wrongful termination is not considered a personal injury action within the statutory language of section 395. "Personal injury," in the context of the venue statutes, encompasses only physical injury. Therefore, Shasta County, based on the sole fact that it was the place of harm, is not a proper venue, and Dylan is entitled to a change of venue to Trinity County. Cubic Corp. v. Superior Court, 186 Cal.App.3d 622, 231 Cal.Rptr. 18 (1986).

2. Convenience of Witnesses

Even if venue is in a "proper" court, a defendant may move for a change of venue on the ground that "the convenience of witnesses and the ends of justice would be promoted by the change." CCP § 397(c). Generally, the court evaluates the convenience of nonparty witnesses only. The convenience of parties or attorneys is not considered. In addition to demonstrating how a change of venue would enhance witness convenience, the moving defendant must show how the ends of justice will be promoted (e.g., that material evidence is available only in the transferee county). A motion for transfer of venue on this ground must be brought within a reasonable time after the answer is filed.

a. ***Compare Federal Procedure***

The district court may transfer venue to a district or division where the action might have been brought for "the convenience of parties and witnesses, in the interest of justice." 28 USC § 1404(a).

b. Illustration

Pat and Drake worked at a branch of Digital Data, Inc., located in Fresno County. Digital Data's headquarters are in Kern County. After months of enduring sexually inappropriate conduct from Drake, Pat sued Digital Data in Kern County Superior Court for sexual harassment under California's Fair Employment and Housing Act (FEHA). Under the several venue options pursuant to the FEHA statutes, Kern County is a proper venue because it is the county where relevant records are maintained. However, Digital Data has moved to transfer venue to Fresno County because it is a more convenient county for the key nonparty witnesses. Digital Data has provided supporting affidavits with its motion. Even though the FEHA statutes evidence a strong policy of providing wide venue choices to plaintiffs, the Legislature did not preclude a defendant's motion to change venue based on the promotion of the convenience of witnesses and the ends of justice. Richfield Hotel Management, Inc. v. Superior Court, 22 Cal.App.4th 222, 27 Cal.Rptr.2d 161 (1994).

3. Additional Grounds

A defendant may move to change the place of trial "[w]hen there is reason to believe that an impartial trial cannot be had therein" (CCP § 397(b)), or "[w]hen from any cause there is no judge of the court qualified to act" (CCP § 397(d)). In addition, CCP § 394 authorizes transfer of venue to a "neutral" county in actions involving certain governmental plaintiffs and defendants.

C. Venue Selection Clauses

Generally, parties are not permitted to contractually designate venue. Venue is fixed by statute. Accordingly, venue selection clauses are invalid. Alexander v. Superior Court, 114 Cal.App.4th 723, 8 Cal.Rptr.3d 111 (2003). In contrast, parties are free to include forum selection clauses in their contracts. For example, a clause choosing the State of California as the forum for jurisdiction is permissible, but a clause specifying Sierra County Superior Court as the venue is not.

VI. FORUM NON CONVENIENS

A. Nature of Doctrine

Even if jurisdiction and venue are proper, a court may exercise its discretion to stay or dismiss an action under the doctrine of forum non conveniens. Originally a common law doctrine, forum non conveniens has been codified in state law. CCP §§ 410.30, 418.10. Under section 410.30(a), upon motion of any party or the court, the court may stay or dismiss an action when it "finds that in the interest of substantial justice an action should be heard in a forum outside this state," either in another state or a foreign nation. CCP § 418.10 sets out the procedure for a defendant's forum non conveniens motion. Forum non conveniens does not effect a transfer of the action to another forum. It is "an equitable doctrine invoking the discretionary power of a court to decline the exercise of jurisdiction it has over a transitory cause of action when it believes that the action may be more appropriately and justly tried elsewhere." Stangvik v. Shiley, Inc., 54 Cal.3d 744, 751, 1 Cal.Rptr.2d 556, 559, 819 P.2d 14 (1991).

B. Timing

Like a motion to quash service of summons, CCP § 418.10(a) authorizes a defendant's motion based on "inconvenient forum" to be brought within the time to file a responsive pleading to the complaint if the defendant has not already generally appeared in the action. If a defendant files a demurrer or motion to strike, she will be deemed to have made a general appearance unless she simultaneously brings a forum non conveniens motion. CCP § 418.10(e)(1), (3). However, in contrast to the motion to quash, a defendant who has filed an answer may still bring a forum non conveniens motion, as authorized by CCP § 410.30(b). Britton v. Dallas Airmotive, Inc., 153 Cal.App.4th 127, 62 Cal.Rptr.3d 487 (2007).

C. Court's Analysis

1. Two-Step Approach

The court applies a two-step analysis to decide a forum non conveniens motion:

Step 1: Suitability of Alternate Forum

This step involves little or no discretion. The court determines whether:

- the defendant is subject to personal jurisdiction in the alternate forum;
- a statute of limitations would bar the action in the alternate forum; and
- the alternate forum will provide basic due process and an impartial tribunal.

Chong v. Superior Court, 58 Cal.App.4th 1032, 68 Cal.Rptr.2d 427 (1997). The defendant may agree to waive personal jurisdiction and statute of limitations defenses in order to render the alternate forum suitable. The fact that the law of the alternate forum may disadvantage a party or provide a less favorable remedy does not make that forum unsuitable.

Step 2: Balancing of Private and Public Interest Factors

If the alternate forum is suitable, the court exercises its discretion in balancing a composite of factors. No one of these factors is in itself dispositive:

- <u>Private interests of the litigants</u>: These factors include ease of access to evidence and witnesses; the availability of procedures to compel attendance of unwilling witnesses; and expense.
- <u>Public interest in retaining the action</u>: These factors include the burden on the local court system, jurors and taxpayers; the difficulty of the application of foreign law in California courts; and a comparison of the interest of the alternate forum with California's interest.

2. Discretion to Dismiss or Stay Action

If the forum non conveniens motion survives the two-step analysis, the court determines whether to stay or dismiss the litigation. If the court stays the action, the court retains jurisdiction and can order the action tried in California if the plaintiff's rights turn out to be seriously compromised in the alternate forum. Stays are more commonly granted than dismissals. A dismissal is likely only if the balance of all factors clearly points to the superiority of the proposed forum over the California forum. If the court orders dismissal, the California court no longer has jurisdiction over the matter. If the plaintiff is a California resident, great deference is given to her choice of forum. In that case, the court will not dismiss the action—it will only consider a stay. If the plaintiff is not a California resident, little deference is given to her choice of a California forum.

3. *Compare Federal Procedure*

The federal common law forum non conveniens doctrine is substantially similar. The doctrine is applied in federal court where the alternate forum is a foreign country. Piper Aircraft Co. v. Reyno, 454 U.S. 235, 102 S.Ct. 252, 70 L.Ed.2d 419 (1981). Where another federal district is a more appropriate forum, the original federal court will instead transfer the action under 28 USC § 1404(a). In either context, the plaintiff's choice of forum will not be disturbed unless the defendant makes a strong showing of public and private interest factors favoring litigation in another country or district. A distinction between the common law and statutory doctrines is that in a transfer under section 1404(a), the substantive law of the transferor district will apply in the transferee district, whereas under the forum non conveniens doctrine, the law of the original forum will not carry over to the alternate forum.

4. Illustration

Pang sued Don in Sonoma County Superior Court for breach of a contract entered in Hong Kong for the shipment of goods to a California company. Pang and Don are both residents of Hong Kong. Don filed a motion to stay or dismiss the action on the ground of forum non conveniens, arguing that Hong Kong was a more convenient forum. Pang objected to the motion because of concern about the independence of the judiciary in Hong Kong

> under the current control of China. The court must conduct a two-step analysis. In the first step, the court must find that Hong Kong is a suitable alternate forum, there is jurisdiction over Don in Hong Kong, and there is no statute of limitations bar. The court will examine the due process issues surrounding Hong Kong's judiciary as part of the first step. If the foreign forum is found to be suitable, in the second step the court must balance the private interests of the parties and the interests of the public in maintaining the action in California. If the court is inclined to grant the motion, it likely will stay the action rather than dismiss it so that it can retain jurisdiction while monitoring the Hong Kong judiciary issues. Because Pang is not a California resident, the court gives relatively little deference to her choice of a California forum. Chong v. Superior Court, 58 Cal.App.4th 1032, 68 Cal.Rptr.2d 427 (1997).

VII. CONFLICT OF LAWS

Ordinarily, California courts apply the substantive law of California to the causes of action being litigated. However, a party may raise a conflict of laws issue when the law of another state or country potentially also applies to the causes of action. California, like many states, once followed the "lex loci" approach to conflict of laws, applying the law of the place of the wrong. Since 1967, a California court's approach to resolving conflict of laws issues has involved a broader set of considerations. See, e.g., Reich v. Purcell, 67 Cal.2d 551, 63 Cal.Rptr. 31, 432 P.2d 727 (1967); Bernhard v. Harrah's Club, 16 Cal.3d 313, 128 Cal.Rptr. 215, 546 P.2d 719 (1976).

A. Governmental Interest Approach in Tort Actions

Applied by CA

In tort actions, the court uses a three-part analysis to choose the law of the state whose interest will be more significantly impaired if its law is not applied:

- The court first determines whether the laws of each state are materially different.
- If they are, the court then assesses whether each state has an interest in the application of its law. If only one state has such an interest, there is a "false conflict," and the law of the only interested state is applied. If each state has such an interest, a "true conflict" exists.
- If a true conflict exists, the court then evaluates the "comparative impairment" to each state's interest if a different state's law is applied, and it chooses the law of the state whose interest would be more impaired.

Kearney v. Salomon Smith Barney, Inc., 39 Cal.4th 95, 45 Cal.Rptr.3d 730, 137 P.3d 914 (2006).

B. Choice of Law Approaches in Contract Actions

1. Enforceable Choice of Law Clause in Contract

In contract actions, the court analyzes whether a choice of law clause in a contract is enforceable by applying the approach set forth in Nedlloyd Lines B.V. v. Superior Court, 3 Cal.4th 459, 11 Cal.Rptr.2d 330, 834 P.2d 1148 (1992):

- The court first ascertains whether the choice of law clause encompasses all of the causes of action of the complaint.
- If so, the court determines whether the clause is enforceable by applying the test in section 187(2) of the Restatement (Second) of Conflict of Laws:
  - Does the chosen state have a substantial relationship to the parties or their transaction; or
  - Is there any other reasonable basis for the parties' choice of law?
- If either Restatement test is met, the court will enforce the parties' choice of law unless:
  - The chosen state's law is contrary to a fundamental California policy; and
  - California has a materially greater interest than the chosen state in the determination of the specific issue.

Washington Mutual Bank, FA v. Superior Court, 24 Cal.4th 906, 103 Cal.Rptr.2d 320, 15 P.3d 1071 (2001).

2. No Enforceable Choice of Law Clause in Contract

If a choice of law clause in a contract is unenforceable, or if the parties' contract does not contain such a clause, the court generally applies the governmental interest approach to determine which state's law will apply to the causes of action. The court might alternatively employ the factors set forth in Restatement (Second) of Conflict of Laws § 188 to determine which state's law would apply in the absence of a choice of law clause. The court examines such contacts as where the contract was negotiated, entered, and performed. Expansion Pointe Properties Ltd. Partnership v. Procopio, Cory, Hargreaves & Savitch, LLP, 152 Cal.App.4th 42, 61 Cal.Rptr.3d 166 (2007).

C. *Compare Federal Procedure*

Choice of law rules are considered substantive under *Erie* principles. Klaxon Co. v. Stetnor Electric Manufacturing Co., 313 U.S. 487, 61 S.Ct. 1020, 85 L.Ed. 1477 (1941). Thus, a federal court sitting in diversity will apply the choice of law rules of the state in which the federal court sits.

D. Illustration

Pablo, a resident of Tijuana, Mexico, was injured on a highway in Tijuana when his car was struck by a car driven by Daniel, a resident of El Centro, California. Pablo sued Daniel for damages in Imperial County Superior Court. California's law did not limit the amount of damages a personal injury plaintiff could recover, but Mexico's law limited personal injury damages to $2,000. Daniel argued that Mexico's law of damages applied. Applying the governmental interest test, Mexico's law will apply. While the laws of California and Mexico are different, California does not have an interest in the application of its law because Daniel's conduct took place in Mexico. In addition, since Pablo is a resident of Mexico, California does not have an interest in extending its more generous damages rule to him. Mexico, on the other hand, has an interest in the application of its law, even though Daniel is not a resident of Mexico. Attracting California tourists to Tijuana is a legitimate interest of Mexico, and applying Mexico's damages cap to nonresident motorists might foster that interest. Because only Mexico has an interest in applying its damages law, there is a false conflict and the law of Mexico, the only interested jurisdiction, will govern. Hernandez v. Burger, 102 Cal.App.3d 795, 162 Cal.Rptr. 564 (1980).

SAMPLE EXAM QUESTIONS

OBJECTIVE QUESTIONS

The questions in this section are based on the following hypothetical:

Joe filed a complaint in San Mateo County Superior Court for injuries he sustained when he slipped on the shiny marble floor of his friend Andy's house (located in San Mateo County) during a Super Bowl party. Joe is also a resident of San Mateo County. The defendants are Andy and his co-owner Lily, who bought the house with Andy as an investment but who actually resides in Maricopa County, Arizona.

---

(1) The total demand of Joe's complaint is $6,000, which is within the jurisdictional limit of the Small Claims Division of the Superior Court. If Joe brings his case in the Small Claims Division:

a. Joe may appeal the small claims judgment to the Superior Court for a trial de novo, but Andy and Lily may not;

b. Andy and Lily may appeal the small claims judgment to the Superior Court for a trial de novo, but Joe may not;

c. No lawyers are permitted to appear;

d. Both b and c.

(2) Assume that the total demand of Joe's complaint is $26,000, making it an unlimited civil case. The action might be reclassified from an unlimited civil case to a limited civil case:

a. At any time by the court on its own motion without a hearing;

b. During the pretrial stage, if it is clear that the matter will necessarily result in a verdict below the jurisdictional amount for an unlimited civil case;

c. If, at a jurisdictional hearing, clear and convincing evidence establishes that the action was classified as unlimited due to mistake or inadvertence;

d. During the pretrial stage, when there is a possibility that the matter will result in a verdict below the jurisdictional amount for an unlimited civil case.

(3) True or False: Joe's unlimited civil case must be reclassified as a limited civil case if Andy files a cross-complaint against Joe for $15,000 in damages.

(4) Joe hired a process server to serve Andy with the summons and complaint. The process server has tried unsuccessfully to personally deliver the papers to Andy at Andy's office (three times) and at Andy's house (once). The process server delivered a copy of the summons and complaint to Andy's office, leaving the documents with the secretary of the Vice President of Andy's company, with instructions to give the documents to Andy. If Andy files a timely motion to quash service of summons, the court will likely rule that service is improper because:

a. The process server did not mail a copy of the summons and complaint to Andy after leaving the documents at Andy's office;

b. The process server did not exercise reasonable diligence to deliver the papers to Andy before leaving them at his office;

c. Substituted service may be effected only at Andy's dwelling place, not at his office;

d. The process server should have attempted service by mail before leaving the papers at Andy's office.

(5) If Lily wishes to challenge the California Superior Court's exercise of personal jurisdiction over her, she:

a. May file a motion to strike the complaint for lack of personal jurisdiction;

b. Must file a separate motion to quash service of summons before or at the same time she files her answer;

c. May assert lack of personal jurisdiction as a defense in her answer and bring a motion to dismiss the action at a later time;

d. May file a general demurrer on the ground of lack of personal jurisdiction.

(6) True or False: Andy may not challenge the exercise of personal jurisdiction over him after Joe has obtained a default judgment against him.

(7) San Mateo County is a proper venue for Joe's action because it is the county:

a. Where Joe, the plaintiff, resides;

b. Where Andy, one of the defendants, resides;

c. Where the injury occurred;

d. Both b and c.

(8) After Lily answered the complaint, she decided that she would like venue to be transferred to Los Angeles County because it would be more convenient for her, her architect, and her contractor (who designed and installed the marble floor, respectively, but are not parties to the action) to attend trial as witnesses. Lily's motion for transfer of venue:

a. Is untimely because she has already filed her answer;

b. Will be granted based on Lily's showing of greater convenience to her, the architect and the contractor by conducting the trial in Los Angeles County;

c. Will be granted based on Lily's showing of greater convenience to the architect and the contractor of conducting the trial in Los Angeles County;

d. Will be granted based on Lily's showing that justice will be promoted by the greater availability of evidence located in Los Angeles;

e. Both c and d.

(9) Assume that Lily believes that the trial should proceed in Maricopa County, Arizona, instead of in San Mateo County. Lily's most appropriate alternative is to make a motion before the San Mateo County Superior Court to:

a. Transfer venue to Maricopa County;

b. Transfer the action to Maricopa County on the ground of inconvenient forum;

c. Stay the California action in favor of the action proceeding in Maricopa County;

d. Dismiss the California action in favor of the action proceeding in Maricopa County.

(10) Assume that Joe has also sued Marvelous Marble, Inc. (MM), the manufacturer and supplier of the marble floor at Andy's house. MM's principal place of business is in Ohio, where the marble for Andy's house was fabricated and from where it was shipped. MM believes that the law of Ohio should apply to Joe's suit against it. Assume that Ohio's law limits liability of manufacturers and suppliers of household

goods to $50,000, while California's law has no limit. In ruling on MM's request to apply the law of Ohio, the California court will:

a. Apply the test set out in § 187 of the Restatement (Second) of Conflict of Laws;

b. Apply the governmental interest test;

c. Apply the lex loci test;

d. Apply the law of California because it is the forum state.

Answers to Objective Questions

(1) **d.** Both b and c are correct. Only defendants may appeal a small claims judgment to the Superior Court. No attorneys are permitted to appear at a proceeding in the Small Claims Division.

(2) **b.** The court applies the pre-unification standard to reclassify the action to a limited civil case.

(3) **False**. A limited civil cross-complaint filed in an unlimited action does not reclassify the action as a limited civil case. Joe's action will remain an unlimited civil case.

(4) **a.** Substituted service at Andy's place of business is not complete unless the process server mails a copy of the summons and complaint to Andy at the same address where he left the documents.

(5) **b.** Lily must file a separate motion to quash service of summons before or at the same time as she files her answer in order to preserve her jurisdictional objection. CCP § 418.10. Lily may not merely include an affirmative defense in her answer, proceed to litigate, and subsequently raise the lack of personal jurisdiction. Lack of personal jurisdiction is not a ground for a motion to strike or a general demurrer.

(6) **False**. Andy may permit a default judgment to be entered against him, and then challenge personal jurisdiction in a special appearance via a simultaneous motion to set aside the default judgment and motion to quash service of summons.

(7) **d.** Both b and c. The general venue rule for transitory actions is that venue is proper in the county of residence of at least one of the defendants. An additional venue choice in personal injury actions such as this one is the county where the injury occurred.

(8) **e.** Both c and d. Transfer of venue is permitted on the ground that the convenience of witnesses (not parties or attorneys) *and* the ends of justice will be promoted by the change of venue. CCP § 397(c). The motion to transfer on this ground is brought after the answer has been filed.

(9) **c.** The doctrine of forum non conveniens applies to these facts. The court does not transfer the action to the alternate forum. It either stays or dismisses the action to permit the plaintiff to refile it in the other jurisdiction. Because Joe is a California plaintiff, the court will likely stay the action rather than dismiss it.

(10) **b.** California applies the governmental interest test in tort actions.

ESSAY QUESTIONS

A. Denny Drinker was at the weekly "Beer on the Beach" party with his friends one Thursday afternoon at California State University, Chico. Denny had too much to drink, but he decided to drive home anyway. On his way home, Denny reached down to change a CD. The car swerved to the right and jumped onto the sidewalk, running into three pedestrians—Athena, Bruce and Conan.

Athena sustained the most serious injuries. She spent nearly a month in the hospital, after which she underwent extensive rehabilitation. She has spent $150,000 on hospital and medical bills. She has sustained $40,000 in lost wages and has experienced significant pain and suffering.

Bruce escaped with only scrapes and bruises. He spent $700 in medical bills to cover his brief trip to the emergency room.

Conan sustained a sprained ankle and a concussion. He recovered quickly and missed no time from work. Conan incurred $8,000 in medical bills.

Athena, Bruce and Conan have each filed separate lawsuits against Denny Drinker in Butte County Superior Court.

(1) Discuss the jurisdictional classification of each plaintiff's action.

(2) Assess how these classifications might be affected should the plaintiffs join together to file a single action against Denny.

(3) Discuss whether and how Conan's case might be reclassified if he amends his complaint to seek $33,000 due to additional medical expenses and pain and suffering damages.

B. Annabelle is a graphic designer. She worked at Jessie Jones Stationery Corporation (JJSC), located in Seattle, Washington. As part of her employment contract, Annabelle agreed not to disclose JJSC's confidential information, including its trade secrets. After working at JJSC for nearly ten years, Annabelle resigned. Two years later, she began working at the Seattle, Washington office of Rainbow Papers, one of JJSC's competitors.

During Annabelle's unemployment, Mel, a former JJSC employee, relocated to join Rainbow Papers' San Francisco office. Since Annabelle began working at Rainbow Papers, she has exchanged e-mails and telephone calls with Mel two to three times a month. She has made two phone calls to distribution warehouses located in San Francisco.

Shortly after she began working for Rainbow Papers, Annabelle attended two one-day business-related meetings in California. Other than those meetings, she has been in California one time, on a layover at the San Francisco airport on her way to her sister's wedding in Hawaii.

JJSC filed suit against Annabelle in San Francisco County Superior Court, alleging breach of her contractual non-disclosure duty and misappropriation of JJSC's trade secrets. Annabelle was served with process by Federal Express delivery at her office address in Seattle.

Annabelle's attorney has filed a timely motion to quash service of summons based on lack of personal jurisdiction and invalid service of process. Assess the strengths and weaknesses of Annabelle's position regarding personal jurisdiction and the validity of service of process.

C. Carol Consulting, Inc. (CC) specializes in consulting with companies wishing to expand their operations into additional geographical locations. CC is incorporated in Delaware, with its headquarters in Connecticut. It has recently opened an office in San Diego, California.

Bruno Publications, Inc. (Bruno) hired CC to assist it in expanding its production facilities to several California counties. Bruno is incorporated in Delaware, with its headquarters in Missouri.

Bruno and CC signed a contract for CC's services. Under the terms of the contract, CC was supposed to help Bruno with all stages of its industrial expansion into Alameda and Santa Cruz counties, including overseeing the actual construction of the new plants. The contract was negotiated by telephone and email by the vice presidents of operations for each company from their respective company headquarters in Connecticut and Missouri. After the vice presidents had reached agreement on terms, they had a final face-to-face meeting in Santa Cruz County to sign the contract.

Unfortunately, CC was unable to provide the level of service required by the contract, and Bruno filed suit against CC in Alameda County Superior Court for breach of contract. CC has filed a motion to transfer venue to San Diego County, arguing that San Diego County is the proper venue.

(1) Discuss whether Alameda County is a proper venue for this action.

(2) Assess whether there are grounds to transfer the action to a different California county or counties.

D. Fit & Fab, a gym in Santa Barbara, California, has a long-term contract with ShapeUp, Inc., for the purchase of exercise equipment and the replacement of machines as new models become available. Fit & Fab has purchased 12 treadmills from ShapeUp, all of the same design. ShapeUp is incorporated and located in Illinois. About one-third of its clients are gyms in Illinois and another one-third are gyms in California. The contract was executed by Fit & Fab and ShapeUp in California. It contains a clause stating: "This Agreement is governed by the laws of the State of Illinois."

Fit & Fab had recently experienced three incidents where customers were injured using the ShapeUp treadmills when the speed suddenly increased, causing the customers to lose their balance. Fit & Fab filed a lawsuit against ShapeUp in Santa Barbara County Superior Court, alleging negligence, breach of contract, and breach of warranty. Fit & Fab seeks both compensatory damages and punitive damages for ShapeUp's "egregious" conduct in selling dangerous equipment for use by the public. Assume that California law permits an award of punitive damages for actions involving the sale of dangerous consumer goods, but Illinois law does not.

ShapeUp has filed a motion to strike Fit & Fab's punitive damages claim on the ground that under the parties' choice of law (Illinois), there is no entitlement to punitive damages. Describe the analysis you would use to determine whether Illinois or California law applies to Fit & Fab's punitive damages demand, and reach a conclusion as to which state's law should govern.

Essay Answers

Essay A

(1) Jurisdictional Classifications

- Athena v. Denny:
    - This case will be classified as an unlimited civil case because the amount in controversy exceeds $25,000 ($150,000 in hospital bills + $40,000 in lost wages + general damages for pain and suffering).
    - Advantages of unlimited classification include access to full discovery, motions, pleadings and relief.

- Bruce v. Denny:

  - This case is arguably classified as a small claims case because Bruce only sustained $700 in damages. The jurisdictional limit for small claims cases is $7,500 or less for an individual. Bruce may pursue his case either in the Small Claims Division or as a limited civil case. If Bruce chooses to maintain his action as a limited civil case instead of bringing it in the Small Claims Division, the court may deny Bruce recovery of his costs even if he is the prevailing party, if he recovers less than $7,500.

  - If Bruce files his action in the Small Claims Division, Bruce and Denny will not be allowed to have attorneys appear on their behalf, and they will not be entitled to discovery. If Bruce loses his case, he is not permitted to appeal.

- Conan v. Denny:

  - This case should be classified as limited civil case because the amount in controversy does not exceed $25,000. Conan's case will be subject to the Economic Litigation procedures.

(2) Aggregation

- If Athena, Bruce and Conan file a single lawsuit against Denny, they may not aggregate their claims because they are not suing for indivisible harm. However, because Athena's case qualifies as an unlimited civil case, Bruce and Conan's cases may be heard as unlimited cases if the requirements for joinder (CCP § 378) are satisfied.

(3) Amended Complaint

- If Conan amends his complaint to seek damages within the jurisdiction of an unlimited civil case, Conan would pay a reclassification fee at the time of filing his amended complaint, and the clerk of the court will reclassify his action as an unlimited civil case. No motion or hearing is required. CCP § 403.020(a).

Essay B

- California's long arm statute, CCP § 410.10, provides that California courts may exercise personal jurisdiction to the extent consistent with the U.S. and California Constitutions.

  - Thus, the only significant restrictions placed on California courts' exercise of personal jurisdiction are constitutional in nature.

- Personal jurisdiction over Annabelle in California:
    - No general jurisdiction because Annabelle's contacts with California are not pervasive and systematic.
    - Specific jurisdiction via minimum contacts with California: analysis should focus on the three-part test for specific jurisdiction.
        - Factors in favor of jurisdiction:
            - Annabelle works for a company with offices and a warehouse in California.
            - Annabelle exchanged e-mails and phone calls with a coworker in the California office two to three times per month.
            - Annabelle made two phone calls to the California warehouses.
            - Annabelle attended two work-related meetings in California.
            - On her way to her sister's Hawaii wedding, Annabelle had a layover in a California airport.
        - Factors weighing against jurisdiction:
            - Her physical presence in California has been limited and only tangentially related to the lawsuit in question.
            - Her contacts with California have mostly been by phone and email from Seattle, rather than via her physical presence.
            - She was present in California for only one day at a time (at most).
            - Her layover at the airport for the wedding trip was unrelated to her work.
            - While her previous employer and current employer both have offices in California, neither company is incorporated nor has its primary place of business in California.
    - While there are persuasive arguments for and against exercising personal jurisdiction in this case, the court is likely to conclude that

Annabelle's motion to quash the service of summons should be granted due to lack of personal jurisdiction.

- Service of Process:
  - Annabelle may be served with process in the State of Washington by any of the methods of service available for service under California or Washington law. CCP § 413.10(b).
  - Alternatively, she may be served by first-class mail, postage prepaid, requiring a return receipt. CCP § 415.40.
  - The California statutes make no provision for service by Federal Express or other private mail service. Even if Rainbow Papers argues that the Federal Express delivery is an acceptable form of substituted service (leaving the summons and complaint with a person apparently in charge of Annabelle's office), the requirements of that method of service have not been satisfied. CCP § 415.20(b). Service via a private mail service will be valid if permitted under Washington law.
  - Annabelle's motion to quash based on invalid service of process will probably be granted.

Essay C

(1) Alameda County as Proper Court

- This is a transitory action. CCP § 395.5 provides several venue alternatives for suits against a corporation: the county where the contract is made or is to be performed; where the obligation or liability arises; where the breach occurs; or where the corporation's principal place of business is located.
- Is Alameda County a proper venue?
  - The parties intended to perform the contract partially in Alameda County, so Alameda County may be a proper venue on this basis.
  - Alameda County may also be where the contractual liability partially arises or where the breach partially occurs.
  - The contract was not made in Alameda County, so this basis for venue does not apply.
  - Alameda County is not the principal place of business of CC, so this ground for venue does not apply.

- CC's choice of venue, San Diego County, would not be a proper venue under any of the provisions of CCP § 395.5.

(2) Grounds for Transfer

- Improper court:
  - The court may transfer the action to another county that meets the requirements of CCP § 395.5 if Alameda County is not a proper venue. CCP § 397(a).
  - CC must bring a motion to transfer on this ground within the time to respond to the complaint.
- Convenience of witnesses:
  - The court may transfer the action if CC can show that the transfer will promote the convenience of witnesses and the ends of justice. CCP § 397(c).
  - CC must have already filed its answer in order to bring a motion to transfer on this ground.
  - CC must provide:

    Names of witnesses;

    Nature of testimony expected from each witness;

    Reasons why attendance of each witness would be inconvenient; and

    Reasons why the ends of justice would be promoted by the change.
  - The facts in this case do not indicate that CC will be able to make this showing, so the motion will be denied.

Essay D

- The applicable conflict of laws test is from *Nedlloyd* and the Restatement (Second) of Conflict of Laws.
  - The court first ascertains whether the choice of law clause encompasses all of the causes of action of the complaint.

- If so, the court determines whether the clause is enforceable by applying the test in section 187(2) of the Restatement (Second) of Conflict of Laws:

    - Does the chosen state have a substantial relationship to the parties or their transaction; or

    - Is there any other reasonable basis for the parties' choice of law?

- If either test is met, the court will enforce the parties' choice of law unless:

    - The chosen state's law is contrary to a fundamental California policy; and

    - California has a materially greater interest than the chosen state in the determination of the specific issue.

- Application:

    - The choice of law clause encompasses all of the causes of action in the complaint.

    - The clause is enforceable because Illinois has a substantial relationship to the parties and their transaction. It is the state of ShapeUp's incorporation, the location of the manufacture and distribution of the equipment, and the location of one-third of its clients.

    - The court will enforce the clause unless Fit & Fab can establish that the punitive damages limitations under Illinois law is contrary to a fundamental California policy to punish out-of-state companies and deter them from sending defective consumer goods into the state.

    - If California has a materially greater interest than Illinois in the application of its law on this issue, the court will apply California law despite the parties' choice of law clause.

- If the choice of law clause were unenforceable, the court would likely apply the governmental interest test to determine which state's law to apply. Alternatively, the court might apply the factors in Restatement (Second) of Conflict of Laws § 188, examining where the contract was negotiated, entered, and performed.

CHAPTER 3

PARTIES, PLEADINGS AND JOINDER

I. PARTIES (WHO MAY SUE AND BE SUED)

The ability to sue or be sued is a central procedural requirement. A plaintiff must have standing *and* capacity to sue, and a defendant must have the capacity to be sued.

A. Standing

1. Real Party in Interest

"Every action must be prosecuted in the name of the real party in interest . . . ." CCP § 367. A person has standing to bring the action when he is the real party in interest. (These terms are often used interchangeably.) The standing doctrine is intended to "ensure that the courts will decide only actual controversies between parties with a sufficient interest in the subject matter of the dispute to press their case with vigor." Common Cause v. Board of Supervisors, 49 Cal.3d 432, 439, 261 Cal.Rptr. 574, 577, 777 P.2d 610 (1989). If standing is not granted by a specific statutory provision, the real party in interest is usually considered to be the person to whom the substantive law grants the right to sue for relief. Lack of standing is a jurisdictional defect. It is not waived even if the opposing party fails to object.

2. *Compare Federal Procedure*

FRCP 17(a) also requires that an action be prosecuted in the name of the real party in interest. Principles of standing in federal court are based in the U.S. Constitution. Article III's "case or controversy" language has been interpreted to require that a party bringing suit in federal court must have suffered an "injury in fact," that the injury is traceable to the defendant's conduct, and that there is a likelihood that a favorable decision will redress the injury. Massachusetts v. Environmental Protection Agency, 549 U.S. 497, 127 S.Ct. 1438, 167 L.Ed.2d 248 (2007). In addition, federal courts have developed "prudential considerations" that affect standing. Those considerations include whether the plaintiff's claims fall within the "zone of interests" sought to be protected, and whether the injury is reasonably confined to an individual or small group as opposed to constituting a "generalized grievance." Elk Grove Unified School District v. Newdow, 542 U.S. 1, 12, 124 S.Ct. 2301, 2309, 159 L.Ed.2d 98 (2004).

3. Illustration

In the past, Phil had been a victim of domestic abuse by his wife. Phil decided that if his wife ever physically harmed him again, he would seek help from a domestic violence shelter. Phil phoned two state-funded shelters in the Los Angeles area to find out if they accepted men. He was told that they did not. Phil sued both shelters in Los Angeles County Superior Court under a California civil rights statute on the ground of gender discrimination. Phil does not have standing to sue the shelters. His complaint did not allege that he was a victim of domestic violence at the time he made his telephone calls. Therefore, he had not suffered an actual injury. Blumhorst v. Jewish Family Services of Los Angeles, 126 Cal.App.4th 993, 24 Cal.Rptr.3d 474 (2005).

B. Capacity

1. Right to Come to Court

Capacity to sue is a separate concept from that of standing. For plaintiffs, both are required: a person with standing (a right to relief) must also have capacity (the right to come to court). Defendants must have capacity to defend. Persons and entities generally have capacity to sue or be sued. Typical exceptions are minors and incompetent persons (who must appear in court through a guardian), and corporations whose powers have been suspended under the California tax laws for failure to pay state franchise (income) taxes.

2. *Compare Federal Procedure*

Capacity of an individual to sue or be sued in federal court is determined by the law of the individual's domicile. A corporation's capacity is determined by the law of the state of its incorporation. FRCP 17(b).

3. Illustration

Pod Corp. sued Dolores in Lassen County Superior Court for failure to pay for the delivery of building materials to a home site in Susanville. Dolores answered the complaint. Dolores then discovered that a month before filing its complaint, Pod Corp.'s corporate powers had been suspended by the state for failure to pay franchise taxes. Dolores sought leave of court to amend her answer to include a defense of Pod Corp.'s lack of capacity. The motion will likely be granted. Although Pod Corp. has standing to sue, it lacks capacity to sue because of its suspension for nonpayment of franchise taxes. Color–Vue, Inc. v. Abrams, 44 Cal.App.4th 1599, 52 Cal.Rptr.2d 443 (1996).

II. INITIATING A LAWSUIT

An action usually commences with the filing of the complaint. CCP § 411.10. Sometimes, a petition, rather than a complaint, is the document that initiates an action (e.g., petition to compel arbitration under CCP § 1281.2). Under some circumstances, a party must take additional steps before initiating an action.

A. Prior Notice of Lawsuit

In some cases, a plaintiff must provide early notice of a claim. For example, a plaintiff who intends to sue a governmental agency must file notice of the claim with the appropriate public office within six months of the accrual of the claim. Cal. Gov't Code § 945.4. In addition, a plaintiff who seeks to sue a health care provider for professional negligence must first serve the defendant with a notice 90 days prior to commencement of the litigation. CCP § 364. Where multiple statutes require pre-filing of notice of a plaintiff's claims, the plaintiff must be careful to satisfy the requirements of each statute. Wurts v. County of Fresno, 44 Cal.App.4th 380, 51 Cal.Rptr.2d 689 (1996) (notice of claim filed with a governmental agency pursuant to Cal. Gov't Code § 945.4 does not also constitute a notice of intent to sue under CCP § 364).

B. Certificate of Merit

Certain actions require a plaintiff to obtain, file and serve a certificate of merit in connection with a lawsuit. Failure to do so when required subjects the complaint to attack by demurrer or motion to strike. See, e.g., CCP § 411.35 (action for malpractice of architect, engineer or land surveyor); Cal. Health & Safety Code § 25249.7(d) (private action to enforce Safe Drinking Water and Toxic Enforcement Act).

C. Court Order

In order to discourage certain lawsuits, some statutes require a court order before the plaintiff may file an action or a particular claim. Examples include claims for punitive damages against health care providers (CCP § 425.13) and religious organizations (CCP § 425.14), claims against attorneys for conspiracy with a client (Cal. Civ. Code § 1714.10), and actions filed by parties designated as vexatious litigants (see section VIII(B), below).

D. *Compare Federal Procedure*

Some federal statutes have pre-filing requirements. For example, a plaintiff who intends to sue an employer for employment discrimination under federal anti-discrimination statutes, such as Title VII of the Civil Rights Act of 1964, must first file the claim with the Equal Employment Opportunity Commission (EEOC) and obtain a "right to sue" letter. See, e.g., 42 USC § 2000e–16. Claims under the Federal Tort Claims Act are also subject to pre-lawsuit claims requirements. 28 USC § 2675.

E. Illustration

Pierce was incarcerated at Pelican Bay State Prison. Officials of the prison failed to diagnose and treat Pierce's lung cancer. After Pierce was ultimately diagnosed, he sued the California Department of Corrections in Del Norte County Superior Court for violation of a federal civil rights statute (42 USC § 1983) and for state common law negligence. Because Pierce's attorney failed to comply with the pre-filing requirements of California's Government Claims Act, Cal. Gov't Code § 945.4, the State filed a general demurrer. While a claim arising under federal law is not subject to the pre-filing requirement of Cal. Gov't Code § 945.4, the state negligence claim is. Since Pierce failed to allege facts sufficient to establish compliance with Cal. Gov't Code § 945.4 or show why noncompliance should be excused, his complaint is subject to a general demurrer for failure to state facts sufficient to constitute a cause of action. State v. Superior Court, 32 Cal.4th 1234, 13 Cal.Rptr.3d 534, 90 P.3d 116 (2004).

III. COMPLAINTS

The complaint is one of the four documents characterized as "pleadings" in California civil actions. CCP § 422.10. (The others are the demurrer, answer and cross-complaint, all discussed later in this Chapter.) The complaint contains two principal components: factual allegations constituting the cause or causes of action, and a demand for judgment.

A. Pleading Factual Allegations

A complaint (or cross-complaint) filed in a California court must contain a "statement of the facts constituting the cause of action, in ordinary and concise language." CCP § 425.10(a)(1). The standard in California for pleading factual allegations is called "fact" or "code" pleading (as compared to the federal "notice pleading" standard). In interpreting the factual allegations of a complaint (or other pleading), the court must liberally construe the allegations "with a view to substantial justice between the parties." CCP § 452. This liberal construction often obscures the formal distinctions between fact pleading and notice pleading.

1. Cause of Action

"Cause of action" is a slippery concept in California procedure. The term has taken on varied meanings depending on the context in which it is used. In the pleading context, cause of action is often used to mean a legal theory or claim for relief. It has a different meaning in the context of compulsory cross-complaints (see section VI(A), below) and claim preclusion (see Chapter 9(II)(A)).

2. Fact Pleading

a. Ultimate Facts

Fact pleading requires that the plaintiff plead ultimate facts in the complaint. Ultimate facts are those upon which the defendant's liability or the plaintiff's right to recovery depends. They address each element of each cause of action included in the complaint. Neither evidentiary details nor bare legal conclusions are to be pleaded, but a court may disregard their inclusion as long as each cause of action contains sufficient allegations of ultimate fact. The liberal availability of discovery makes more detailed pleading less essential than in the past. Committee on Children's Television, Inc. v. General Foods Corp., 35 Cal.3d 197, 197 Cal.Rptr. 783, 673 P.2d 660 (1983).

b. Stating Factual Allegations

Ultimate facts may be pleaded directly (based on the plaintiff's personal knowledge of the facts) or on information and belief ("Plaintiff is informed and believes, and based on that information and belief alleges that . . . "). In addition, attachments to the complaint are considered a part of the pleading if they are properly incorporated by reference. Plaintiffs may plead facts or legal theories inconsistently or in the alternative. (Exception: inconsistent facts may not be pleaded in a verified complaint; see section III(D)(2), below.)

c. **Heightened Pleading Standard**

Certain causes of action must be pleaded with greater particularity than is required under normal fact pleading. The most typical examples of this heightened pleading standard are causes of action for fraud and certain statutory violations (such as those under the Government Claims Act). The complaint must contain detailed factual allegations supporting each element of these causes of action.

3. ***Compare Federal Procedure***

In contrast to California's fact pleading standard, the federal rules merely require notice pleading. FRCP 8(a)(2) requires a "short and plain statement of the claim showing that the pleader is entitled to relief." Federal notice pleading is generally considered to require less detail than state fact pleading. Bell Atlantic Corp. v. Twombly, 550 U.S. ___, 127 S.Ct. 1955, 167 L.Ed.2d 929 (2007). The federal complaint must simply provide the defendant with adequate notice of the nature of the claim against him. A claim may be implied from the facts, and conclusions of law are acceptable. Particularity is required only in limited circumstances, such as pleading fraud under FRCP 9(b), or for certain statutory claims.

4. **Illustration**

After a double mastectomy, Petra underwent a surgical procedure to insert breast implants. Almost immediately, she experienced extreme pain and other symptoms. She consulted several other specialists who recommended that she have the implants removed. Over the year following the removal, she had several reconstructive surgeries. Petra then sued Denali, Inc., the manufacturer of the implants, in Kings County Superior Court for product liability, negligence, and fraud. In the fraud cause of action, Petra pleaded that Denali had falsely represented that "its product was safe for use by the public, that it posed no dangerous risk, and that it would not require removal." These allegations are insufficient to meet the

> heightened pleading requirement for fraud. Petra failed to plead every element of the fraud cause of action with specificity. She did not plead "what was said or to whom or in what manner." Petra may not merely recast her negligence cause of action as one for fraud without providing additional supporting facts. Goldrich v. Natural Y Surgical Specialties, Inc., 25 Cal.App.4th 772, 31 Cal.Rptr.2d 162 (1994).

B. Demand for Judgment

A complaint must contain a "demand for judgment for the relief to which the pleader claims to be entitled." CCP § 425.10(a)(2).

1. Damages

If the plaintiff seeks damages or other monetary relief, the general rule is that "the amount demanded shall be stated" in the complaint. CCP § 425.10(a)(2). There are several exceptions to this requirement:

a. Exception: Personal Injury and Wrongful Death Actions

In a personal injury or wrongful death action, the plaintiff may not state the amount of actual or punitive damages in the complaint. CCP § 425.10(b). In order to reveal the amount the plaintiff seeks, the plaintiff may serve on the defendant, or the defendant may request from the plaintiff, a separate "statement setting forth the nature and amount of damages being sought." CCP § 425.11(b). No default judgment may be entered against the defendant unless the plaintiff has served a statement of damages.

b. Exception: Claims for Punitive Damages

A plaintiff is prohibited from including in any complaint the amount of punitive damages sought. Cal. Civ. Code § 3295(e). If the plaintiff intends to seek an award of punitive damages, she preserves that right by serving on the defendant a statement of punitive damages under CCP § 425.115. The plaintiff must serve the defendant with this statement if she seeks a default judgment that includes an award of punitive damages. CCP § 425.115(f). If a personal injury or wrongful death plaintiff seeks punitive damages, she must also serve a statement of punitive damages, either as a separate document or as a part of the statement of damages. CCP § 425.115(e).

2. *Compare Federal Procedure*

The prayer of a federal complaint must contain "a demand for the relief sought." FRCP 8(a)(3). The Rule does not explicitly require a party to state the actual amount of monetary damages in the complaint. As a matter of practice, however, federal plaintiffs in diversity actions typically demand a particular amount or at least plead that the amount in controversy exceeds the $75,000 minimum for diversity jurisdiction. In contrast to California law, there are no special federal rules regarding the pleading of damages in particular kinds of actions or for demanding punitive damages.

3. Illustration

Prosper, Inc. sued Dharma Co. in Napa County Superior Court for misappropriation of trade secrets, requesting damages in the complaint "in excess of $50,000." Prosper subsequently served a statement of damages on Dharma claiming $8 million in compensatory damages. As a discovery sanction for destroying evidence, the judge entered a default judgment against Dharma and awarded Prosper $8 million in compensatory damages. The trial court may not award this amount. Because Prosper's action is not one for personal injury or wrongful death, it was required to state the amount of damages in the complaint and not in the purported statement of damages. Consequently, Prosper is entitled to only $50,000 in compensatory damages, the amount stated in the complaint. Levine v. Smith, 145 Cal.App.4th 1131, 52 Cal.Rptr.3d 197 (2006).

C. Subscription

Every pleading must be "subscribed" (i.e., signed) by an attorney or unrepresented party. CCP § 446(a). The signature serves as a representation to the court that the pleading is warranted under law and fact and is not submitted for an improper purpose. CCP § 128.7 (see section VIII(A)(1), below).

D. Types of Complaints

1. Form Complaints

Instead of filing a "custom" drafted complaint, a plaintiff may use an official form complaint developed by the Judicial Council of California for certain types of actions (including personal injury, breach of contract, and fraud). CCP § 425.12. The form complaint must still allege ultimate facts sufficient to state a cause of action or it is subject to attack by demurrer. People ex rel. Dept. of Transportation v. Superior Court, 5 Cal.App.4th 1480, 7 Cal.Rptr.2d 498 (1992).

2. Verified Complaints

a. Verification by Party

A verified complaint contains a declaration signed by the plaintiff under penalty of perjury attesting that the facts alleged in the complaint are true of the plaintiff's personal knowledge, except as to those facts stated on information and belief, and as to those matters the plaintiff believes them to be true. CCP § 446(a). Most of the time, the plaintiff has the option of filing either a verified or an unverified complaint. In some actions, however, a verified complaint is required (e.g., quiet title actions, Family Code pleadings, petition for writ of mandate). A pleading verified by the plaintiff has heightened evidentiary value because it is considered a sworn affidavit and can be cited as such when the plaintiff files a motion with the court. Except in limited civil cases, an answer to a verified complaint must itself be verified by the defendant, and it must include specific denials instead of a general denial (see section V(A)(4), below).

b. Verification by Attorney

The plaintiff's attorney may verify the pleading if the plaintiff is absent from the county where the attorney has his office, or if the facts in the complaint are within the attorney's personal knowledge. CCP § 446(a).

c. Verification by Corporation or Governmental Party

Any corporate officer may verify a complaint filed by a corporation. The complaint of a governmental plaintiff is deemed to be verified. A nongovernmental defendant must file a verified answer in response to a governmental complaint. A governmental defendant need not file a verified answer, even if the complaint was verified. CCP § 446(a).

3. *Compare Federal Procedure*

Forms containing examples of pleading for a variety of claims are included in the Appendix to the Federal Rules. See, e.g., Forms 10–21. These forms "suffice under these rules and illustrate the simplicity and brevity that these rules contemplate." FRCP 84. A federal complaint is generally not required to be verified. FRCP 11(a). Even if a complaint is verified, the defendant is not obligated to file a verified answer.

4. Illustration

Prawn filed a complaint in Amador County Superior Court that included a verification stating that he is "familiar with the matters alleged in the complaint and based thereon knows that the allegations of said complaint are meritorious." The verification falls unacceptably short of the language of CCP § 446, which requires that the verification must state that the pleading is true of the plaintiff's own knowledge, except as to the matters which are stated on his information or belief, and as to those matters that he believes it to be true. "Meritorious" is not synonymous with "true." The verification must state the truthfulness of the allegations so that sanctions for perjury might apply if the facts stated to be true are actually not. Ancora–Citronelle Corp. v. Green, 41 Cal.App.3d 146, 115 Cal.Rptr. 879 (1974).

E. Limited Civil Cases

Limited civil cases are subject to Economic Litigation Procedures that restrict the types of pleadings, motions and discovery permitted in that category of actions. CCP §§ 90–100. The pleadings allowed in a limited civil case are complaints, answers, cross-complaints and general demurrers. No special demurrers are allowed. An answer to a limited civil case complaint need not be verified, even if the complaint is verified. CCP § 92.

IV. ATTACKING THE COMPLAINT

Several types of responses may be filed by a defendant objecting to various aspects of the plaintiff's complaint. These devices may also be used to attack an answer or cross-complaint.

A. Demurrers

A demurrer is a form of pleading that attacks the allegations of the complaint on a number of alternate grounds. CCP § 430.10. A defendant may file a demurrer instead of or at the same time as filing the answer. CCP § 430.30(c). A demurrer may also be filed against a defendant's answer. CCP § 430.20.

1. Types of Demurrers

a. General Demurrer

A defendant may object on the ground that the "pleading does not state facts sufficient to constitute a cause of action." CCP § 430.10(e). This response, known as a general demurrer, may be addressed to the entire complaint or to any individual cause of action within it. If the complaint states *any* legitimate cause of action, even if it is not the one intended by the plaintiff, the general demurrer addressed to the entire complaint may not be sustained. If a defendant objects to the complaint on the ground that the court lacks subject matter jurisdiction, that objection is usually considered to be a general demurrer rather than a special demurrer. CCP § 430.10(a). A plaintiff may bring a demurrer on the ground that the defendant's answer fails to state facts sufficient to constitute a defense. CCP § 430.20(a).

b. Special Demurrer

In addition to the two general demurrer grounds, a defendant may also bring a special demurrer on the grounds that:

- the person filing the complaint lacks the legal capacity to sue (see section I(B), above);
- there is another action pending between the same parties on the same cause of action;
- there is a defect or misjoinder of parties;
- the pleading is uncertain; or
- in a contract action, it cannot be determined from the pleading whether the contract is written, oral or implied by conduct.

CCP § 430.10. A plaintiff may bring a special demurrer on two grounds: (1) the answer is uncertain; or (2) it cannot be ascertained from the answer whether a contract pleaded in the answer is written or oral. CCP § 430.20(b)–(c).

2. Court's Consideration of Demurrer

The demurrer does not test the truth of the facts contained in the pleading. Rather, when a court considers a demurrer, it assumes the truth of any material allegations of fact that have been properly pleaded. The court restricts its consideration to defects on the face of the complaint (and attachments that have been incorporated by reference), and to matters subject to judicial notice under Cal. Evid. Code §§ 450–460. A judge may sustain a demurrer either with or without leave to amend the complaint. The court should grant leave to amend if there is a reasonable probability that an amendment will cure the defect. If the court overrules the demurrer, the defendant must file an answer to the complaint.

3. *Compare Federal Procedure*

The grounds for demurrer have several counterparts in FRCP 12. These grounds may be raised either in a FRCP 12(b) motion to dismiss, or alternatively may be asserted as defenses in a responsive pleading. The federal equivalent of a general demurrer is a motion under FRCP 12(b)(6) for "failure to state a claim upon which relief can be granted." A party may also attack the court's subject matter jurisdiction (FRCP 12(b)(1)), and may object on ground of "failure to join a party under Rule 19" (FRCP 12(b)(7)). In addition, a party may bring a motion for a more definite statement if the pleading "is so vague or ambiguous that the party cannot reasonably prepare a response." FRCP 12(e). This motion is similar to a special demurrer for uncertainty in California practice. There is no federal equivalent of the California special demurrer based on the inability to ascertain from the pleading whether a contract is oral or written.

4. Illustration

Primo Makeup Supplies (PMS) sells beauty products to the public. PMS signed a contract with Daily Beauty Regime (DBR) to sell DBR products. By oral contract, DBR agreed to supply its products to PMS as long as PMS employees attending training classes and agreed to market DBR products. PMS fulfilled its obligations under the contract, and DBR supplied its products. One year later, after PMS had developed a loyal clientele for DBR products, DBR refused to continue to supply its products to PMS. PMS filed suit in Sutter County Superior Court, alleging breach of the oral contract. PMS alleged in the complaint that in reliance on the representations of DBR, it had attended training sessions, set aside shelf space, and developed a committed clientele. DBR filed a special demurrer to the complaint on the grounds that the factual allegations for the cause of action for breach of oral contract were

> uncertain. The court is likely to overrule the demurrer. Demurrers based on uncertainty are disfavored and are strictly construed. Although the cause of action may be pleaded somewhat ambiguously, the process of discovery can clarify the allegations. PMS is not required to allege the exact wording of the oral contract. Khoury v. Maly's of California, Inc., 14 Cal.App.4th 612, 17 Cal.Rptr.2d 708 (1993).

B. Motions to Attack Complaint

1. General Procedural Requirements for Motions

A motion is an application to the court for an order. CCP § 1003. The rules governing pretrial motion practice are found in the CCP, CRC, case law and local court rules.

a. Papers

The moving party files and serves the following papers: (1) the motion (request) itself; (2) a notice of the time and place of the hearing ("notice of motion"); (3) a statement of the grounds for the motion and the relief sought; (4) evidence in support of the requested order; (5) a memorandum of points and authorities; and (6) a proposed order. The responding party may file a memorandum of points and authorities, evidence, and a proposed order in opposition to the motion. The moving party usually has the opportunity to file reply papers.

b. Service of Moving Papers and Timing of Hearing

For most pretrial motions, the hearing date set forth in the notice of motion must be at least 16 court days after service by personal delivery of the moving papers (with longer notice periods if service is by mail, fax, overnight delivery, or email). CCP § 1005(b). Some motions require lengthier notice periods (such as motions for summary judgment or for discretionary dismissal under the diligent prosecution statutes). The moving papers must be served on all parties who have appeared in the action, usually through the parties' respective attorneys of record.

c. Hearing

In many superior courts, judges issue tentative rulings before the hearing on the motion. Depending on the tentative ruling, the parties may or may not decide to appear at the hearing for oral argument. At a hearing, the judge may enter a final ruling on the motion in open court, or she may take the matter "under submission" for determination at a later date. The judge's ruling is entered into the court minutes. The judge may also sign a formal written order, but it is not always required.

d. Motions to Reconsider Prior Rulings or Renew Prior Motions

If the trial court enters an interim or final order following a motion, a party may move the court to reconsider and perhaps modify or revoke the order. CCP § 1008(a). A party may also renew a motion previously brought before the court. CCP § 1008(b). A party's motion for reconsideration or renewal is subject to strict statutory requirements under CCP § 1008.

1) Party's Motion for Reconsideration

Any party affected by a trial court's ruling on a motion may request the court to reconsider the ruling and enter a different order. CCP § 1008(a). The statute contains several requirements:

- The party must seek reconsideration within ten days after service of notice of entry of the order.
- The motion for reconsideration must be made to the same judge or court that entered the order.
- The motion for reconsideration must be based on new or different facts, circumstances or law.

CCP § 1008(a). If the party's application for reconsideration does not meet the above requirements, the court has no jurisdiction to consider it. CCP § 1008(e).

2) Party's Motion for Renewal

A party who previously made a motion and who is dissatisfied with the outcome may renew the motion with the court. The moving party must show new or different facts, circumstances or law as a basis for the motion. CCP § 1008(b). The statute does not set out a time deadline for a renewal motion, and it does not require that the renewal motion be made to the same judge or court.

3) Reconsideration on Court's Own Motion

The strict requirements of CCP § 1008 apply only to party applications for reconsideration or renewal. The trial court possesses inherent authority to reconsider its prior rulings even in the absence of new or different facts, circumstances or law. A court may exercise its inherent authority even if a party has suggested that the court reconsider its prior ruling. Le Francois v. Goel, 35 Cal.4th 1094, 29 Cal.Rptr.3d 249, 112 P.3d 636 (2005).

4) *Compare Federal Procedure*

There is no exact counterpart to California's motion for reconsideration or renewal in the FRCP, but several rules address the district court's ability to revise or set aside orders. FRCP 54(b) authorizes the district court to revise a nonfinal order at any time before final judgment is entered. A federal party may move under FRCP 60(b) for relief from final orders under similar grounds as found in California's CCP § 473(b). (See Chapter 6(V)(E).) FRCP 60(d) also acknowledges that the rule does not limit the district court's power to "entertain an independent action to relieve a party from a[n] . . . order."

5) Illustration

Pauline instituted dissolution of marriage proceedings against her husband, Drew, in Tehama County Superior Court. Under the couple's marital settlement agreement, Pauline was entitled to remain in the family home until the end of the school year in June. Pauline did not move out until August. At that point, Drew sought an order from the court that Pauline pay him a fair market rental for the period between June and August. The court granted the order. Pauline then moved the court to reconsider its order. In support of the motion, Pauline filed all of the same papers she filed in response to Drew's original motion, including a declaration stating the text of an oral conversation she and Drew had in June in which Drew told Pauline that he would allow her to remain in the home until August. Pauline's application for reconsideration will be denied on the ground that it does not meet the strict requirements of CCP § 1008 (because it did not include new or different facts, circumstances or law). The defective application may nevertheless prompt the court to exercise its inherent authority to reconsider its earlier order on its own motion and to change its ruling. In re Marriage of Barthold, 158 Cal.App.4th 1301, 70 Cal.Rptr.3d 691 (2008).

2. Motion for Judgment on the Pleadings

a. Grounds for Motion

A motion for judgment on the pleadings has several similarities to a general demurrer. A defendant may bring this motion when the court lacks subject matter jurisdiction (CCP § 438(c)(1)(B)(i)), or when the complaint fails to state facts sufficient to constitute a cause of action (CCP § 438(c)(1)(B)(ii)). A plaintiff may also move for judgment on the pleadings as to the defendant's affirmative defenses in the answer. CCP § 438(c)(1)(A). Material facts properly pleaded are deemed true, and the grounds for the motion must appear on the face of the pleading or be based on matters subject to judicial notice. CCP § 438(d). Like a demurrer, a motion for judgment on the pleadings may be granted with or without leave to amend. CCP § 438(h)(1).

b. Timing

A motion for judgment on the pleadings is sometimes referred to as a "delayed demurrer." A defendant may bring the motion after filing an answer and the time to file a demurrer has expired. CCP § 438(f)(2).

c. *Compare Federal Procedure*

FRCP 12(c) provides for a motion for judgment on the pleadings "[a]fter the pleadings are closed—but early enough not to delay trial."

d. Illustration

Paloma sued Derry Co. in Mariposa County Superior Court for the wrongful death of her husband. Paloma's complaint

> did not allege an employment relationship between Derry Co. and her husband. Derry Co.'s answer, however, alleged that Paloma's husband had been an employee. It raised the affirmative defense that Paloma's remedy was exclusively through the worker's compensation system. Derry Co. then brought a motion for judgment on the pleadings on this ground. Although a motion for judgment on the pleadings is brought after the defendant has filed its answer, the motion cannot be based on matters raised via the answer. The court must view the complaint on its own to determine if its allegations state a cause of action. Thus, Paloma's failure to negate Derry Co.'s defense is not a ground to grant the motion. Hughes v. Western MacArthur Co., 192 Cal.App.3d 951, 237 Cal.Rptr. 738 (1987).

3. Motion to Strike

A motion to strike may be used to attack a complaint on grounds not reachable through a demurrer or a motion for judgment on the pleadings.

a. Grounds for Motion

Within the time to file a responsive pleading to the complaint, a party may move to "[s]trike out any irrelevant, false, or improper matter inserted in any pleading," or "[s]trike out all or any part of any pleading not drawn or filed in conformity with the laws of this state, a court rule, or an order of the court." CCP §§ 435(b)(1), 436. The grounds for the motion to strike must appear on the face of the pleading or come from matters subject to judicial notice. CCP § 437. For example, a defendant might move to strike a demand for punitive damages in a typical contract action because punitive damages normally are not an available remedy for this type of claim.

b. Compare: Demurrer

A motion to strike has several characteristics in common with a demurrer: (1) each is brought during the pleading stage; (2) each constitutes a general appearance if the defendant has not previously appeared; (3) each may be granted with or without leave to amend; and (4) the court's consideration of each is restricted to the face of the challenged pleading and to matters subject to judicial notice. While a demurrer resembles a motion, it is actually considered a pleading. CCP § 422.10. One important manifestation of this distinction is that the court may bring its own motion to strike (CCP § 438(b)(2)), whereas only a party may file a pleading, such as a demurrer, in an action.

c. Compare: Anti–SLAPP Motion to Strike

A defendant or cross-defendant may bring a special motion to strike known as an anti-SLAPP motion. See section VIII(C), below.

d. *Compare Federal Procedure*

A federal district court may strike from a pleading any "redundant, immaterial, impertinent, or scandalous matter." FRCP 12(f). Generally, a defendant must file a motion to strike within the time to respond to the complaint. The court may also strike matter from a pleading on its own motion.

e. Illustration

Larry is a lawyer representing Priya in her lawsuit against Darth. Larry drafted a complaint for Priya and filed it in Plumas County Superior Court. Larry neglected to sign the complaint, as required by CCP § 128.7(a). Larry discovered the omission, but he did not promptly file an amended complaint with a proper signature. Darth moved to strike the entire complaint because it was "not drawn or filed in conformity with the laws of this state" under CCP § 436(b). The court will likely grant the motion to strike with leave to amend. It is an abuse of discretion to grant the motion without leave to amend because the defect is easily cured by amendment. Vaccaro v. Kaiman, 63 Cal.App.4th 761, 73 Cal.Rptr.2d 829 (1998).

V. ANSWERS

The answer is the defendant's substantive response to the factual allegations of the complaint. The filing of an answer places all unadmitted material facts in the complaint "at issue." The defendant may not request affirmative relief in the answer; she must file a cross-complaint for that purpose. Unless the defendant chooses to file a motion or demurrer attacking the complaint, or the parties stipulate to an extension, an answer must be filed within 30 days after service of the complaint on the defendant. CCP § 412.20(a)(3). An answer normally contains two components: denials and affirmative defenses.

A. Denials

Denials dispute the truth of the allegations of the complaint. Any material allegation that the defendant does not adequately deny in the answer will be deemed admitted. CCP § 431.20(a). A "material allegation" is "one essential to the claim or defense and which could not be stricken from the pleading without leaving it insufficient as to that claim or defense." CCP § 431.10(a). Denials may be either general or specific. CCP § 431.30(b)(1).

1. General Denials

A general denial is a blanket statement that the defendant denies each and every allegation of the complaint. The general denial is effective to deny all material allegations of an unverified complaint. A general denial is not permitted if the complaint is verified or deemed to be verified. CCP § 431.30(d).

2. Specific Denials

Specific denials take several forms. A defendant may deny certain paragraphs or parts of the complaint, or she may admit certain allegations and deny the remainder. The defendant may specifically deny an allegation: (a) directly, based on her personal knowledge; (b) based on information and belief; or (c) based on lack of information or belief sufficient to enable the defendant to answer. CCP § 431.30(e)–(f).

3. Subscription

The defendant's attorney must sign the answer. CCP § 446(a). If the defendant is not represented by counsel, the defendant may sign.

4. Verification

A defendant must respond to a verified complaint with a verified answer containing specific denials. Exceptions include answers filed in limited civil cases (CCP § 92), and answers filed by a governmental entity (CCP § 446(a)).

5. *Compare Federal Procedure*

FRCP 8(b)(3) allows both general and specific denials. A general denial denies all allegations, including those on jurisdictional grounds, and must be made in good faith. All allegations, not only material allegations, are admitted by failure to deny. The only exception is for allegations relating to the amount of damages. FRCP 8(b)(6). A defendant may deny based on lack of information sufficient to form a belief about the truth of an allegation. FRCP 8(b)(5).

6. Illustration

Pew filed suit in Alpine County Superior Court against Daw for specific performance of a real estate contract. Pew's complaint alleged that the consideration stated in the contract was the fair market value of the property. Daw's answer, consisting of many specific denials, did not deny Pew's allegation about the consideration. Pew's allegation constituted a material fact that will be deemed admitted and taken as true if not denied. Consequently, the admission relieves Pew of proving the reasonableness of the consideration at trial and precludes Daw from introducing contrary evidence. Hennefer v. Butcher, 182 Cal.App.3d 492, 227 Cal.Rptr. 318 (1986).

B. Affirmative Defenses

1. New Matter

Affirmative defenses do not respond directly to the elements of the plaintiff's prima facie case, as denials do. Nor do they seek affirmative relief. Instead, affirmative defenses raise new independent matter that would prevent the plaintiff from recovering, even if all allegations of the complaint were proven true. The defendant has the burden of proof on all affirmative defenses, which must be pleaded according to the standards of fact pleading applicable to complaints. Some of the most commonly pleaded affirmative defenses are statute of limitations, comparative negligence, fraud, waiver, estoppel, assumption of risk, and release. Most affirmative defenses will be deemed waived if the defendant fails to plead them in the answer.

2. *Compare Federal Procedure*

FRCP 8(c)(1) sets out a list of 19 potential affirmative defenses. A defendant must affirmatively assert these or any other applicable affirmative defenses in response to the complaint or they will be waived.

3. Illustration

Pia sued her insurance company, Dorsey Insurance Co., alleging breach of the implied covenant of good faith and fair dealing in handling her insurance claim. Dorsey answered with a general denial and no affirmative defenses. At trial in Calaveras County Superior Court, Dorsey attempted to introduce evidence that it relied on advice of counsel in handling Pia's claim. Pia moved to exclude all such evidence on the grounds that Dorsey had not pleaded advice of counsel as an affirmative defense in its answer. Dorsey responded that such evidence is not "new matter constituting a defense" within the meaning of CCP § 431.30(b)(2). The trial judge will likely agree and deny Pia's motion. Pia's complaint alleged bad faith on the part of Dorsey, and Dorsey's evidence of good faith reliance on the advice of counsel tends to negate the allegations of bad faith by showing that it acted reasonably. It does not introduce new matter into the proceeding and thus does not need to be pleaded as an affirmative defense. State Farm Mutual Automobile Insurance Co. v. Superior Court, 228 Cal.App.3d 721, 279 Cal.Rptr. 116 (1991).

C. Example of Common Affirmative Defense: Statute of Limitations

The statute of limitations is a frequently asserted affirmative defense in actions seeking damages or other forms of legal relief. It contends that the untimeliness of the filing of the complaint bars the plaintiff from recovery, regardless of the truth of the allegations or the plaintiff's ability to prove them.

1. Accrual of Cause of Action

Statutes of limitations set out time limits that require a complaint to be filed within a statutorily prescribed period starting from the date of the "accrual" of the cause of action. CCP § 312. The point of accrual is determined according to two main principles: the general rule and the discovery exception.

a. General Rule

Generally, a cause of action accrues when a plaintiff suffers "actual and appreciable harm." The moment of accrual is often stated to be when the "last element essential to the cause of action" has occurred. Norgart v. Upjohn Co., 21 Cal.4th 383, 397, 87 Cal.Rptr.2d 453, 463, 981 P.2d 79 (1999). The CCP contains a collection of statutes setting out statutes of limitations under the general rule for a variety of causes of action: e.g., two years for a personal injury or wrongful death action (CCP § 335.1(a)); three years for a fraud action (CCP § 338); and four years for an action based on a written contract (CCP § 337).

b. Exception: Discovery of Injury

Accrual of a cause of action may be delayed when a party has not discovered that he has been injured. Under these circumstances, the statute of limitations starts to run "when the plaintiff suspects or should suspect that her injury was caused by wrongdoing." Jolly v. Eli Lilly & Co., 44 Cal.3d 1103, 1110, 245 Cal.Rptr. 658, 662, 751 P.2d 923 (1988). The plaintiff may discover the cause of action even if he or she does not know the identity of the defendant. In this situation, the plaintiff may file a complaint containing fictitious "Doe" defendants and subsequently amend the complaint when the defendant's identity becomes known. (See section VII(B)(3), below.)

2. Tolling

The running of the statute of limitations may be tolled (halted) for a variety of reasons.

a. Statutory Tolling

The statute of limitations is tolled, for example, during the time the plaintiff is affected by war (CCP § 354), the plaintiff is a minor or insane (CCP § 352(a)), or the plaintiff is incarcerated (CCP § 352.1(a)).

b. Equitable Tolling

Equitable tolling is a judge-made doctrine that suspends the running of a statute of limitations in the interests of practicality and fairness, as long as the suspension would not prejudice the defendant. Lantzy v. Centex Homes, 31 Cal.4th 363, 2 Cal.Rptr.3d 655, 73 P.3d 517 (2003). The doctrine requires the court to balance the injustice to the plaintiff from the imposition of the limitations period against the public interest or policy embodied in the limitations statute.

c. Continuing Violation Doctrine

The "continuing violation doctrine" deems subsequent events to be new violations that "re-start" the running of the limitations period. Howard Jarvis Taxpayers Association v. City of La Habra, 25 Cal.4th 809, 107 Cal.Rptr.2d 369, 23 P.3d 601 (2001).

3. Compare: Laches

In actions for equitable relief, the judicial doctrine of laches may apply. A defendant must prove "unreasonable delay plus either acquiescence in the act about which plaintiff complains or prejudice to the defendant resulting from the delay." Johnson v. City of Loma Linda, 24 Cal.4th 61, 68, 99 Cal.Rptr.2d 316, 321, 5 P.3d 874 (2000). If the defendant prevails, the plaintiff will be prevented from recovering equitable relief even if the applicable statutory period has not expired.

4. Compare: Statutes of Repose

Unlike statutes of limitation, which are calculated under concepts of accrual based on the date of injury or its discovery, statutes of repose bar "all suits after the expiration of a specified time from the manufacture or delivery of a product or a transaction. It does not cut off an existing right of action, but rather provides that nothing which happens thereafter can *be* a cause of action." Inco Development Corp. v. Superior Court, 131 Cal.App.4th 1014, 1020, 31 Cal.Rptr.3d 872, 875 (2005). For example, CCP § 337.15, which sets out a ten-year period after substantial completion of construction projects in which a plaintiff may sue for damages for latent defects, is considered a statute of repose. It contains an absolute deadline to bring the action, regardless of when the injury was or could have been discovered. Lantzy v. Centex Homes, 31 Cal.4th 363, 2 Cal.Rptr.3d 655, 73 P.3d 517 (2003).

5. Compare: Revival Statutes

The Legislature may enact statutes that revive civil causes of action barred by the applicable statute of limitations. For example, CCP § 340.9 provided for a one-year revival in 2001 of time-barred claims against insurers arising out of the Northridge earthquake. CCP § 340.1 provided a one-year revival in 2003 of certain causes of action based on childhood sexual abuse.

6. *Compare Federal Procedure*

Civil actions arising under a federal statute enacted or amended after December 1, 1990 are subject to a four-year statute of limitations, unless otherwise provided in the federal statute in question. 28 USC § 1658. For suits arising under federal statutes containing no express limitation period and which were enacted prior to December 1, 1990, federal courts "borrow" comparable state law for the applicable statute of limitations. The accrual of a cause of action for statute of limitations purposes in diversity actions is considered "substantive" under *Erie* principles and thus directly subject to the applicable state law.

7. Illustration

Poppy suffered injury to her ankle when an examination chair malfunctioned during a routine eye exam performed by Daria, an optometry student serving an internship. Almost two years later, when her ankle had not healed, Poppy filed a lawsuit against Daria in Solano County Superior Court. Daria responded by filing a demurrer to the complaint based on the expiration of the statute of limitations. Daria contended that the action was barred by the one-year statute under CCP § 340.5, which governs actions against health care providers. Poppy contended that the two-year statute of limitations for negligence causes of action governed. Even though Daria was not a licensed optometrist, the one-year statute applied to her because, as a supervised student, she was legally authorized to practice optometry. Therefore, Poppy's complaint was not timely filed. Chosak v. Alameda County Medical Center, 153 Cal.App.4th 549, 63 Cal.Rptr.3d 184 (2007).

D. Pleas in Abatement

Certain categories of objections to the complaint must be specifically pleaded at the earliest opportunity or they are waived. These "pleas in abatement" (which are also called dilatory pleas to reflect their disfavored status) may be raised via an affirmative defense in the answer, or via a special demurrer if the defect appears on the face of the complaint. CCP §§ 430.30, 430.80. Examples include: (1) lack of capacity to sue; (2) nonjoinder or misjoinder of parties; and (3) other action pending. See CCP § 430.10(b)–(d).

VI. CROSS-COMPLAINTS

The cross-complaint is a pleading that allows a defendant to assert a cause of action against the plaintiff, a co-defendant, or one not yet a party to the suit. (Since the defendant may not seek affirmative relief in the answer, a cross-complaint against the plaintiff is the appropriate vehicle.) For most purposes, the cross-complaint is treated as an independent action severable from the original complaint. Cross-complaints serve the policy of judicial economy by resolving all disputes among the parties in one proceeding.

A. By Defendant Against Plaintiff

A cross-complaint filed by the defendant against the plaintiff is either compulsory or permissive.

1. Compulsory Cross-Complaint

A cross-complaint is compulsory when it alleges a cause of action that is related to the plaintiff's cause(s) of action. "Related" means that the causes of action arise from the "same transaction, occurrence, or series of transactions or occurrences" as those pleaded in the plaintiff's complaint. CCP § 426.10(c). (Some exceptions may apply. For example, a related cause of action that arises after the defendant has answered the complaint is treated as permissive.) Failure to plead a compulsory cross-complaint by the time of judgment will bar any assertion of the related cause of action in a later suit. CCP § 426.30(a). Because of this bar, the court liberally grants leave to file a compulsory cross-complaint at any time during the action.

2. Permissive Cross-Complaint

All other cross-complaints against the plaintiff are considered permissive, including those alleging any causes of action unrelated to the plaintiff's complaint. CCP § 428.10(a).

B. By Defendant Against Co-Defendant or Third Party

Cross-complaints filed by a defendant against any party other than the plaintiff are always permissive, never compulsory. A common use of a permissive cross-complaint is to seek indemnity. The cause of action in the cross-complaint must arise out of the same transaction, occurrence, or series of transactions or occurrences, or relate to the same property or controversy, that is the subject of the cause of action brought by the plaintiff against the cross-complaining defendant. CCP § 428.10(b). If those requirements are satisfied, that party may also bring unrelated causes of action, and even join new parties. If a cross-complaint involving third parties or unrelated causes of action unduly complicates the action, CCP § 1048(b) permits the court to order a separate trial of the cross-complaint. (See section IX(D)(1)(b), below.)

C. Timing and Statute of Limitations

A defendant's cross-complaint against the plaintiff may be filed as a matter of right before or at the time of filing the answer to the complaint. Similarly, no leave of court is required to file a complaint for indemnity against a cross-defendant or third party before a trial date is set. In all other circumstances, leave of court is required, which is liberally granted in the interest of justice. CCP § 428.50. Because it is an independent action, a permissive cross-complaint is subject to its own applicable statute of limitations. However, a compulsory cross-complaint will "relate back" to the date plaintiff filed the original complaint.

D. *Compare Federal Procedure*

California uses the single term "cross-complaint" to refer to three devices that are kept distinct in federal court:

1. Counterclaims

The counterclaim is a claim for relief asserted by a defendant against the plaintiff. FRCP 13(a)–(f). Counterclaims may be either compulsory or permissive, and the tests for determining the nature of the counterclaim are nearly identical to those under California law. Similar rules to California's also govern "relation back" for compulsory counterclaims.

2. Cross-Claims

A claim by one defendant against a co-defendant is called a cross-claim. FRCP 13(g). As under California law, cross-claims are never compulsory. The claims asserted must relate to the same transaction or occurrence, or the same property, that is the subject matter of the initial complaint.

3. Third-Party Complaints

A claim for indemnity by a defendant against a third party is called an impleader or third-party complaint. FRCP 14. As under California law, a third-party complaint is permissive.

E. Illustration

On July 4, 2006, Paley was swimming in Surprise Lake. Dixon accidentally ran into Paley with her jet ski, causing Paley a number of injuries. On July 2, 2008, Paley filed a complaint against Dixon for his injuries in Tuolumne County Superior Court. Two weeks later, Dixon answered Paley's complaint. Dixon simultaneously filed a cross-complaint for whiplash that she suffered in the accident, alleging that Paley was negligently swimming in a boats-only part of the lake. The cross-complaint is compulsory, as it arises from the same occurrence as that alleged in the initial complaint. Although filed more than two years after the accident, Dixon's cross-complaint is not barred by the two-year statute of limitations for personal injuries in CCP § 335.1. As a compulsory cross-complaint, it relates back to the date of the filing of Paley's initial complaint. K.R.L. Partnership v. Superior Court, 120 Cal.App.4th 490, 15 Cal.Rptr.3d 517 (2004).

VII. AMENDED PLEADINGS

Amendments to pleadings may occur at many points during a lawsuit, including during the pleading and discovery stages, after settlement negotiations, and during trial. Some amendments are permitted as a matter of right, and some require a court order. An amended complaint generally supersedes the original pleading if it makes material substantive changes. The amended complaint must then be served on all opposing parties, who must file new responsive pleadings.

A. Amendments as of Right

A party may amend a pleading once as a matter of right before a responsive pleading (answer or demurrer) is filed, or after a demurrer and before the trial. CCP § 472. The statute does not restrict the kinds of amendments a party may make as a matter of right.

1. *Compare Federal Procedure*

In federal practice, a plaintiff may amend the complaint once as a matter of course before the defendant serves a responsive pleading. FRCP 15(a)(1)(A). Otherwise, a party must obtain leave of court (which is liberally granted) or the consent of the opposing party in order to amend. FRCP 15(a)(2).

2. Illustration

Portnoy was a shareholder and an employee of Drenka Corporation. Portnoy sued Drenka Corp. and two of its officers, Roth and Zuckerman, in San Bernardino County Superior Court. Portnoy's complaint alleged Labor Code violations against Drenka Corp. and breach of fiduciary duty against the two corporate officers. In response to the complaint, Drenka Corp. filed an answer, and the officers filed a demurrer. Three days before the hearing of the officers' demurrer, Portnoy filed a first amended complaint without leave of court to address the issues raised by the demurrer. Portnoy's amended complaint is properly filed as of right under CCP § 472. Although Portnoy could no longer amend the complaint as of right as to Drenka Corp., since it had already filed its answer, he could amend without leave of court the breach of fiduciary duty cause of action because the officers' demurrer had not yet been heard. Drenka Corp.'s answer did not preclude Portnoy from amending the complaint as to Roth and Zuckerman. Barton v. Khan, 157 Cal.App.4th 1216, 69 Cal.Rptr.3d 238 (2007).

B. Amendments by Court Order

All other amendments not covered by CCP § 472 require leave of court. The court ordinarily grants leave to amend liberally.

1. After Demurrer or Motion to Strike

When a court sustains a demurrer or grants a motion to strike, it often grants leave to amend the pleading. The pleader normally has ten days to amend the pleading unless the court specifies a different time. CRC 3.1320(g).

2. Adding, Deleting or Correcting Parties

The court may grant leave to amend a pleading to add or remove parties, or to correct a mistaken name of a party. CCP § 473(a)(1). The addition of parties may run afoul of the statute of limitations unless the doctrine of "relation back" applies. (See section C, below).

3. Amendments Related to Doe Defendants

When a plaintiff is "genuinely ignorant" of a defendant's "name," the plaintiff may state that fact in the complaint and name the defendant as a fictitious "Doe." CCP § 474. The complaint must contain charging allegations against the Doe defendants. When the plaintiff discovers the defendant's true name, the complaint must be amended to substitute the true name for the Doe designation. The plaintiff may amend the complaint, even after the limitations period has expired, so long as the plaintiff was actually ignorant of the defendant's identity, or the facts giving rise to a cause of action against that defendant, at the time of filing the complaint. The plaintiff has three years under the diligent prosecution statutes (see Chapter 5(III)(A)(1)) to amend the complaint and make the Doe substitution. Fuller v. Tucker, 84 Cal.App.4th 1163, 101 Cal.Rptr.2d 776 (2000). If the amended complaint satisfies the requirements in section C, below, it will relate back to the date of the filing of the original complaint.

a. *Compare Federal Procedure*

Doe defendants generally are not allowed in federal court pleadings. The district court will ignore fictitious defendants when a state court complaint is removed to federal court. 28 USC § 1441(a).

b. Illustration

Peggy visited her regular dentist, Dr. Dray, in his office in Lee Vining for tooth pain. At two-thirty, Dr. Dray extracted two teeth. Two weeks later, Dr. Dray's associate, Dr. Flay, extracted one more tooth in the same area of the mouth as the

> first extractions. Peggy had not previously met Dr. Flay, who introduced himself just before the procedure. Several weeks later, Peggy experienced fever, listlessness and pain that did not go away. She consulted her physician, who hospitalized her for a severe bacterial infection that was likely caused by the dental procedures. When Peggy recovered, she filed a lawsuit (after satisfying all pre-filing requirements but just before the statute of limitations expired) in Mono County Superior Court, in which she named Dr. Dray as a defendant and included Does 1–10. When she attempted to amend the complaint one year later to substitute Dr. Flay's true name for Doe 1, the court did not allow the amendment to relate back to the filing of the original complaint. Peggy was not genuinely ignorant of Dr. Flay's identity and his association with Dr. Dray and her tooth extraction at the time she filed her complaint. Hazel v. Hewlett, 201 Cal.App.3d 1458, 247 Cal.Rptr. 723 (1988).

4. Other Court-Ordered Amendments

The court has broad discretion to order an amendment to "any pleading or proceeding in other particulars." CCP § 473(a)(1).

C. Statute of Limitations and Relation Back for Amended Pleadings

Amendments to pleadings to add new causes of action or new parties (named or Doe) may be subject to the bar of an applicable statute of limitations unless the doctrine of "relation back" applies. This doctrine allows the filing of an amended pleading to relate back to the date of the filing of the timely original complaint, thus making the amended pleading timely as well. An amended pleading must satisfy three requirements in order for the relation back doctrine to apply. It must:

- rest on the same general set of facts as the original pleading;
- seek recovery for the same injury or injuries as in the original pleading; and
- refer to the same accident and same offending instrumentality as in the original pleading.

Barrington v. A. H. Robins Co., 39 Cal.3d 146, 216 Cal.Rptr. 405, 702 P.2d 563 (1985).

1. *Compare Federal Procedure*

An amended pleading will relate back to the date of the filing of the original pleading if: (1) "the law that provides the applicable statute of limitations allows relation back" (FRCP 15(c)(1)(A)); or (2) "the amendment asserts a claim or defense that arose out of the conduct, transaction, or occurrence set out—or attempted to be set out—in the original pleading" (FRCP 15(c)(1)(B)). FRCP 15(c)(1)(A) appears to open the door to expanding Doe practice in federal court, at least for claims brought in diversity. While FRCP 15(c)(1)(C) provides a stricter relation back standard for a pleading that amends the "naming of the party against whom a claim is asserted," federal courts apply the more liberal standard of FRCP 15(c)(1)(A) when the claims are based on California substantive law. Motley v. Parks, 198 F.R.D. 532 (C.D. Cal. 2000).

2. Illustration

Pram worked for the University of California, Merced. Pram's workload was consistently heavy, causing her to work overtime hours for which she was not paid. The University terminated her employment. Pram filed a timely complaint against the University in Merced County Superior Court for overtime pay violations. After the statute of limitations had expired, she filed an amended complaint seeking to add a cause of action for age discrimination. Even though the amended complaint names the same employer and addresses the same employment, the amended complaint will not relate back to the filing of the original complaint because the age discrimination claim does not arise out of the same general facts as the claim for overtime pay. Kim v. Regents of University of California, 80 Cal.App.4th 160, 95 Cal.Rptr.2d 10 (2000).

VIII. TRUTH IN PLEADING

A. Frivolous Pleadings

1. Sanctions Under CCP § 128.7

Section 128.7 is the California equivalent of FRCP 11. It applies to actions in which the complaint was filed on or after January 1, 1995. CCP § 128.7(i). The statute imposes several requirements on parties and attorneys who present papers to a California court.

a. Signature of Papers

An attorney (or the party if not represented by an attorney) must sign every "pleading, petition, written notice of motion, or other similar paper." CCP § 128.7(a).

b. Certification

Section 128.7 requires that any paper presented to the court, either by signing, filing, submitting, or later advocating, must meet four requirements:

- The paper must not be presented primarily for an improper purpose, such as to harass or cause unnecessary delay;
- The claims, defenses, or other contentions in the paper must be warranted by existing law or by a nonfrivolous argument for extending or modifying the law;
- The factual allegations must have evidentiary support or be likely to after a reasonable opportunity for discovery; and
- The denials of factual contentions must be warranted by the evidence or be reasonably based on lack of information or belief.

CCP § 128.7(b). Sanctions are available, by motion of a party or the court, for violation of these requirements (except in discovery matters). CCP § 128.7(c), (g). The party seeking sanctions must have exercised due diligence in bringing the motion. CCP § 128.7(c).

c. Sanctions

1) Purpose and Types of Sanctions

The purpose of the sanctions is to "deter repetition of this conduct or comparable conduct by others similarly situated." CCP § 128.7(d). The court is authorized to issue both monetary and nonmonetary sanctions. Possible sanctions include payment of a penalty to the court, or a payment to the moving party of its reasonable attorney's fees and expenses incurred as a direct result of the violation of the statute. CCP § 128.7(d). A party who prevails on a sanctions motion under CCP § 128.7 may also be entitled to reasonable expenses and attorney's fees for presenting or opposing the motion. CCP § 128.7(c)(1). A motion for sanctions brought for an improper purpose may itself be the subject of a motion for sanctions. CCP § 128.7(h).

2) Safe Harbor Provision

The party seeking sanctions must serve the moving papers on the opposing party and allow the opponent to have 21 days to withdraw or correct the offending paper. If this "safe harbor" period expires without such withdrawal or correction, the moving party may proceed to file the motion with the court. CCP § 128.7(c)(1). The 21–day safe harbor period also applies to sanctions motions made by the court.

d. ***Compare Federal Procedure***

Because CCP § 128.7 was modeled on FRCP 11, California courts often rely on federal case law construing Rule 11 in applying that statute. Although the federal rule and the California statute are largely identical, some key distinctions exist:

- The California court assesses whether the moving party exercised due diligence in bringing a sanctions motion; FRCP 11 does not contain this requirement.
- The 21–day safe harbor provision in section 128.7 applies to motions by a party or by the court; under FRCP 11, the safe harbor period applies only to party motions.
- There is no provision in FRCP 11, as there is in section 128.7, authorizing sanctions for a motion for sanctions that was brought for an improper purpose.

e. **Illustration**

Paniz filed a complaint against Darcy in Modoc County Superior Court seeking recovery for fraud. The case went to trial, and the jury found for Darcy. Three months after the court entered judgment, Darcy served on Paniz a motion under CCP § 128.7, seeking an award of sanctions on the ground that Paniz's complaint was "frivolous and totally without foundation." More than three weeks after serving the motion on Paniz, Darcy filed it with the court. The sanctions motion is not timely. Under the safe harbor provision of CCP § 128.7(c)(1), Paniz must be given 21 days to correct or withdraw the pleading before the sanctions motion is filed with the court. By serving and filing the motion after the conclusion of the case, Darcy has not given Paniz the required opportunity to avoid sanctions by correcting the offending pleading. Darcy should not be permitted to circumvent the statutory requirements by waiting until after judgment to bring her sanctions motion. Barnes v. Department of Corrections, 74 Cal.App.4th 126, 87 Cal.Rptr.2d 594 (1999).

2. Sanctions Under CCP § 128.5

For actions filed prior to January 1, 1995, CCP § 128.5 is the applicable sanctions statute. Section 128.5 permits the court to order a party or attorney to "pay any reasonable expenses, including attorney's fees, incurred by another party as a result of bad-faith actions or tactics that are frivolous or solely intended to cause unnecessary delay." CCP § 128.5(a). " 'Actions or tactics' include, but are not limited to, the making or opposing of motions or the filing and service of a complaint or cross-complaint." CCP § 128.5(b)(1). " 'Frivolous' means . . . totally and completely without merit or . . . for the sole purpose of harassing an opposing party." CCP § 128.5(b)(2). Section 128.5 is not restricted to the presenting of papers, as is CCP § 128.7. Although few pre–1995 cases remain pending in the superior courts, the standards of section 128.5 have been imported to sanctions provisions of other statutes. See, e.g., CCP § 425.18(f); Cal. Fam. Code § 273.

B. Vexatious Litigants

1. Designation as Vexatious Litigant and Security Requirement

A defendant may move the court to designate the plaintiff as a vexatious litigant. A person is considered a vexatious litigant if he meets any of the following requirements:

- He has commenced or maintained in propria persona at least five lawsuits in the last seven years, and those suits have been resolved adversely to him;
- He has repeatedly attempted to relitigate a matter that previously had been finally determined against him;
- He has repeatedly filed unmeritorious motions, pleadings, or discovery requests, or has engaged in other frivolous or delaying tactics; or
- A court has previously designated him as a vexatious litigant in a matter based on the same or similar facts or transaction.

CCP § 391(b). If the plaintiff is designated a vexatious litigant and if there is no reasonable probability that the plaintiff will prevail in the action, the defendant may move the court to require the plaintiff to furnish security in order to bring his lawsuit. CCP § 391.1. If the vexatious litigant fails to post the required security, the court will dismiss the action. CCP § 391.4.

2. Leave of Court to File Lawsuit

In addition to the above procedure, the court may prohibit a vexatious litigant from filing any new litigation in the state in propria persona without first obtaining leave of court. CCP § 391.7.

3. *Compare Federal Procedure*

Federal courts have inherent power to issue narrowly tailored orders to limit the ability of a vexatious litigant to bring a lawsuit without leave of court. Johns v. Town of Los Gatos, 834 F.Supp. 1230 (N.D. Cal. 1993). Some courts have sanctioned vexatious litigants under FRCP 11, fashioning a sanction that requires such litigants to seek leave of court or comply with other conditions before filing an action in propria persona. DePonceau v. Bush, 2004 WL 1574621 (W.D.N.Y. 2004).

4. Illustration

Puneet, an attorney, was employed by Firm X in Washington, D.C. When he found out that Firm X would not make him a partner, Puneet left the firm and moved to California. Puneet sued Firm X in propria persona in California state court on 20 causes of action. Puneet brought numerous unmeritorious motions and writ petitions, all of which were denied. The court then dismissed Puneet's suit on personal jurisdiction grounds. Puneet became an associate at Firm Z in San Diego. When Firm Z declined to make him a partner, Puneet, this time represented by counsel, filed suit against Firm Z. The litigation against Firm Z was marked by the same pattern of repeated motions and writ petitions as occurred against Firm X. Puneet could be appropriately designated as a vexatious litigant under CCP § 391(b)(4), even though some of his litigation activity was performed on his behalf by counsel and not in propria persona. If he were designated a vexatious litigant, CCP § 391.7(b) would prohibit Puneet from filing a suit in California, whether in propria persona or through an attorney, without obtaining leave of the presiding judge. In re Shieh, 17 Cal.App.4th 1154, 21 Cal.Rptr.2d 886 (1993).

C. Anti–SLAPP Motion to Strike

Spurred by "a disturbing increase in lawsuits brought primarily to chill the valid exercise of the constitutional rights of freedom of speech and petition," the California Legislature in 1992 authorized a special motion to strike lawsuits characterized as SLAPP (Strategic Litigation Against Public Participation). CCP § 425.16(a). Anti–SLAPP motions are a mechanism for defendants to dispose of such lawsuits at the pleading stage, thereby avoiding the costs and delays of litigation. In order to encourage participation in matters of public importance, the anti-SLAPP statute is construed broadly. CCP § 425.16(a).

1. Features of Anti–SLAPP Motion

a. Burdens of Parties

A defendant bringing an anti-SLAPP motion to strike has the initial burden to make a prima facie showing that the plaintiff's cause of action arises from an act of the defendant in furtherance of the exercise of free speech or petition rights in connection with a public issue. The defendant is not required to demonstrate that the plaintiff intended to chill his constitutional rights. Equilon Enterprises, LLC v. Consumer Cause, Inc., 29 Cal.4th 53, 124 Cal.Rptr.2d 507, 52 P.3d 685 (2002). Once the defendant makes the initial showing, the burden shifts to the plaintiff to establish a probability of prevailing on the merits of the claim. CCP § 425.16(b)(1). To carry this burden, the plaintiff must demonstrate that the complaint is legally sufficient and supported by enough admissible evidence to sustain a favorable judgment.

1) Acts "In Furtherance"

An act of the defendant in furtherance of the right of petition or free speech includes:

- any statement or writing made before a legislative, executive, judicial or other official proceeding;
- any statement or writing made in connection with an issue under consideration or review by a legislative, executive, or judicial body, or any other legally authorized official proceeding;
- any statement or writing made in a place open to the public or in a public forum, in connection with an issue of public interest; or
- any other conduct in furtherance of the exercise of the constitutional right of petition or free speech in connection with an issue of public interest.

CCP § 425.16(e)(1)–(4). Activity that is illegal as a matter of law does not constitute a protected exercise of First Amendment rights. Novartis Vaccines & Diagnostics, Inc.

v. Stop Huntingdon Animal Cruelty USA, Inc., 143 Cal.App.4th 1284, 50 Cal.Rptr.3d 27 (2006).

2) Public Issue

The requirement that the defendant's speech be connected to a public issue is interpreted liberally. Public issues include not only governmental matters, but also conduct of private persons or institutions that affects communities or definable groups of people. Du Charme v. International Brotherhood of Electrical Workers, 110 Cal.App.4th 107, 1 Cal.Rptr.3d 501 (2003).

b. Timing

An anti-SLAPP motion generally must be filed within 60 days after service of the complaint or amended complaint. However, a court may in its discretion consider an anti-SLAPP motion filed after this deadline. The court is required hear the anti-SLAPP motion within 30 days of service of the motion unless the condition of the court's docket requires a later hearing. CCP § 425.16(f).

c. Discovery Stayed

Unless the court orders otherwise for good cause, the filing of an anti-SLAPP motion stays all discovery until the court rules on the motion. CCP § 425.16(g). The effect of this stay is to protect a defendant from the expense of discovery while the motion is pending.

d. Fees and Costs

A prevailing defendant on an anti-SLAPP motion is entitled to recover attorney's fees and costs. CCP § 425.16(c). The term "fees and costs" is ambiguous, but the legislative history indicates that the statute was intended to allow for the fees and costs associated with the motion and not with the entire litigation.

e. Appealability

An order granting or denying an anti-SLAPP motion under CCP § 425.16 is appealable. CCP §§ 425.16(i), 904.1(a)(13). See Chapter 8(III)(A)(3).

2. When Anti–SLAPP Motion Is Not Available

In response to what it found to be a "disturbing abuse" of the anti-SLAPP procedures, the California Legislature in 2003 exempted two categories of lawsuits from an anti-SLAPP motion:

a. Public Interest

Suits brought solely in the public interest or on behalf of the general public are not subject to an anti-SLAPP motion, as long as all of the following requirements are met:

- The plaintiff does not seek relief greater than or different from the relief sought for the general public;
- The lawsuit, if successful, would enforce an important right affecting the public interest and would confer a significant public benefit; and
- Private enforcement is necessary and places a disproportionate financial burden on the plaintiff.

CCP § 425.17(b).

b. Commercial Speech

Anti–SLAPP protections do not apply to lawsuits based on statements or conduct by persons or entities engaged primarily in the business of selling or leasing goods or services when:

- The statement or conduct at issue consists of representations of fact about that person's or a competitor's business;
- The statement or conduct occurred in connection with a commercial transaction; and
- The intended audience is an actual or potential customer or a person likely to influence an actual or potential customer, or the statement or conduct arose in connection with a regulatory approval process, proceeding or investigation.

CCP § 425.17(c).

3. SLAPPback Action

In 2005, the Legislature declared that a "SLAPPback" was distinguishable in character and origin from an ordinary malicious prosecution action. CCP § 425.18(a). A SLAPPback arises from a previous lawsuit dismissed pursuant to an anti-SLAPP motion. CCP § 425.18(b)(1).

A defendant who previously prevailed on the anti-SLAPP motion may bring a SLAPPback suit against the former plaintiff to recover damages beyond the attorney's fees and costs awarded to the former prevailing defendant. CCP § 425.18(b)(1). The defendant in the SLAPPback suit (the former plaintiff) may bring an anti-SLAPP motion against the SLAPPback, but many of the procedural protections for an anti-SLAPP movant are not available in the SLAPPback context. For example, the SLAPPback plaintiff may conduct discovery to oppose the anti-SLAPP motion. CCP § 425.18(c), (e).

4. *Compare Federal Procedure*

Federal procedure does not authorize an anti-SLAPP motion. Several potential conflicts between federal procedure and the anti-SLAPP procedures exist. For example, the burden on a plaintiff to establish a probability of prevailing on the merits at the pleading stage may run counter to FRCP 8(a)(2), which requires that the plaintiff merely provide a short and plain statement showing the pleader is entitled to relief. In addition, FRCP 56 allows a defendant to defeat meritless claims via summary judgment, but only later in the litigation (most notably after broad discovery has occurred). In contrast, an anti-SLAPP motion is filed much earlier in the litigation, and, once the motion is filed, discovery is stayed. Conflicts between California's anti-SLAPP provisions and federal procedures can lead to interesting *Erie* dilemmas. See Swierkiewicz v. Sorema N.A., 534 U.S. 506, 122 S.Ct. 992, 152 L.Ed.2d 1 (2002) (refusing to apply the discovery-limiting aspects of CCP § 425.16 because they directly collided with the discovery-allowing aspects of FRCP 56).

5. Illustration

During a contentious gubernatorial election, incumbent Prescott found himself battling against challenger Damon for the Governor's seat in Sacramento. In a former life, Prescott was a professional baseball player. Toward the end of his career, he admitted using illegal, performance-enhancing drugs. During the campaign, Damon released a commercial that referred to Prescott as "an admitted drug user" and a "cheater." After losing the election, Prescott brought suit against Damon in Sacramento County Superior Court for defamation. Damon filed an anti-SLAPP motion, arguing that he was merely exercising his constitutionally protected right to free speech and that his comments addressed a

> matter of public concern—Prescott's qualifications to be Governor. When the burden shifted to Prescott, he could not show that Damon made the comments with the knowledge that they were false or with reckless disregard as to whether they were false. As such, he could not establish a probability that he would prevail on his defamation claim. The court will thus strike Prescott's complaint as a SLAPP. Conroy v. Spitzer, 70 Cal.App.4th 1446, 83 Cal.Rptr.2d 443 (1999).

IX. JOINDER

California applies liberal rules of joinder of causes of action and of parties.

A. Joinder of Causes of Action

Subject to the application of the doctrine of claim preclusion (see Chapter 9(II)(A)), a California plaintiff who brings a cause of action against one or more defendants is permitted to join any other causes of action she has against those defendants. CCP § 427.10(a). There is no requirement that the causes of action must involve a common question of law or fact.

B. Permissive Joinder of Parties

1. Permissive Joinder of Defendants

The plaintiff may join several defendants in a single action if the action asserts against them: (a) a right to relief arising out of the same transaction, occurrence, or series of transactions or occurrences, *and* a question of law or fact common to all; or (b) an adverse claim, right or interest in the subject matter of the action. CCP § 379(a).

2. Permissive Joinder of Plaintiffs

CCP § 378(a) permits joinder of plaintiffs under the same liberal standard as that for permissive joinder of defendants.

3. *Compare Federal Procedure*

Permissive joinder of defendants and plaintiffs is liberally allowed under FRCP 20 under similar grounds as those found in the California statutes, as long as the requirements of subject matter jurisdiction are satisfied.

4. Illustration

Two hundred employees, as well as their spouses and children, sued Allen Adhesives Co. in Colusa County Superior Court for injuries to the employees from continuous exposure to toxic chemicals in Allen Adhesives' main plant in Williams. Allen Adhesives filed a special demurrer on the ground of misjoinder of parties, contending that each plaintiff should have filed separate complaints because of the significant differences in length of exposure and resulting injuries. The court will likely overrule the demurrer and allow all of the plaintiffs to be joined. CCP § 378(a) would permit joinder of the employees and their families because the employees were all exposed to the chemicals at the same location during the same series of transactions and occurrences. There also were common questions of exposure and injury among the plaintiffs, even though the exposure and injuries were not identical for each employee or family member. Anaya v. Superior Court, 160 Cal.App.3d 228, 206 Cal.Rptr. 520 (1984).

C. Compulsory Joinder of Parties

1. Necessary Parties

A court must order joinder of a person who is subject to service of process and whose joinder will not deprive the court of subject matter jurisdiction, if that person's joinder satisfies at least one of the conditions set forth in CCP § 389(a):

- In his absence complete relief cannot be accorded among those already parties; or

- He claims an interest in the subject matter of the action, and the disposition of the action in his absence may:

  - as a practical matter impair or impede his ability to protect his interest; or

  - subject existing parties to substantial risk of double, multiple or inconsistent obligations because of his claimed interest.

2. Indispensable Parties

If joinder of a necessary party is not possible, the court must determine whether the action "in equity and good conscience" should proceed in the absence of the person, or whether it should be dismissed without prejudice because the person is considered "indispensable." CCP § 389(b). The inability to join an indispensable party does not render the court without jurisdiction (power) to proceed. Rather, the court decides in equity and good conscience w*hether* it should proceed.

3. *Compare Federal Procedure*

CCP § 389 is taken nearly verbatim from FRCP 19.

4. Illustration

Dion owns a home in a housing development in Porterville that is governed by covenants, conditions and restrictions (CC & Rs). The homeowners' association is responsible for enforcing the CC & Rs. Dion wanted to build a patio cover that would block the view of his neighbors, the Millers. The Millers complained to the homeowners' association. The association filed an action against Dion and the Millers in Tulare County Superior Court for a declaratory judgment regarding whether the construction of the patio cover violates the CC & Rs. The Millers contend that they should be dismissed from the action, but the homeowners' association argues that the Millers are indispensable parties because the court's ruling on the patio cover affects the Millers' interests. The court likely will find that the Millers are not indispensable parties. No relief is sought against the Millers, and their participation in the lawsuit is not essential to achieve a complete determination of the dispute between the homeowners' association and Dion. Duffey v. Superior Court, 3 Cal.App.4th 425, 4 Cal.Rptr.2d 334 (1992).

D. Special Joinder Devices

Several special procedures exist in California to join (or, in some cases, separate) parties and claims.

1. Consolidation and Bifurcation

a. Consolidation

When two or more actions are pending before a court, and the actions involve a common question of law or fact, the court may order a joint hearing of any or all issues in the actions, or it may consolidate the actions. CCP § 1048(a). If consolidation would create confusion, conflict or prejudice, the court may exercise its discretion to deny consolidation.

1) **Complete Consolidation**

Complete consolidation unites two or more lawsuits into a single action. The pleadings are combined into one set, and the allegations and affirmative defenses are treated in tandem. The court enters a single judgment. Because of the total merging of the actions, complete consolidation is ordered only when the parties in each action are identical and the causes of action could have been joined in a single lawsuit.

2) **Partial Consolidation**

An order of partial consolidation combines two actions in the same court for the purpose of trial. Partial consolidation promotes judicial economy and prevents duplication and inconsistency. Partial consolidation maintains the separate nature of each set of pleadings; the court makes separate findings and judgments in each action.

3) **Consolidation and Coordination of Actions in Different Courts**

Noncomplex cases involving common questions that are pending in different courts may be ordered transferred to one court and consolidated with each other. CCP § 403. Complex cases in different courts may be coordinated under a more cumbersome procedure set forth in CCP § 404.

b. **Bifurcation**

A court may order separate trials of any causes of action or issues in a lawsuit if doing so would further convenience, avoid prejudice, or foster judicial economy. CCP § 1048(b). A common example is a court order of separate trials on the issues of liability and damages. An order of separate trials is often referred to as "bifurcation." The former label "severance" is no longer used.

c. ***Compare Federal Procedure***

CCP § 1048 is largely modeled on FRCP 42.

d. Illustration

Abbott, Baker, and Cass individually brought product liability suits alleging that cough syrup made by Drugsafe Co. was unsafe. In assessing whether the three actions should be consolidated, the Glenn County Superior Court found: (1) all plaintiffs had to use extensive expert testimony and scientific findings about the same product; (2) the jury would not be confused with only three plaintiffs; and (3) it is not likely that jury would be prejudiced against Drugsafe just because there were three plaintiffs alleging the same side effects. On these facts, it was proper to consolidate the three cases. Todd–Stenberg v. Dalkon Shield Claimants Trust, 48 Cal.App.4th 976, 56 Cal.Rptr.2d 16 (1996).

2. Interpleader

a. Conflicting Claims

Interpleader permits a person or entity—known as the stakeholder—who is subject to multiple and inconsistent claims to the same property or funds to join all of the claimants in a single suit to resolve the controversy. CCP § 386(b). A defendant to an existing claim or claims may file an interpleader action as a cross-complaint, or may, before answering the complaint, apply to the court to deposit the property in question with the court. A party may also initiate an action in interpleader as a plaintiff when that party faces conflicting claims to the same property. Once the right to interplead has been granted and the deposit has been made, the stakeholder is discharged from liability to the claimants. CCP § 386(a), (b).

1) Stakeholder Interest

Traditionally, interpleader actions could be brought only where the stakeholder explicitly disavowed any interest in the subject property. These actions were known as strict interpleader. It is not clear whether California continues to require that stakeholders disavow any interest in the interpleaded property. By permitting the stakeholder to deny liability "in part" to any of the claimants under CCP § 386(b), the stakeholder might impliedly be asserting an interest in the property.

2) Additional Claims Against Stakeholder

In an interpleader action, the claimants to the subject property should raise only issues related to the interpleader action. Although claimants should not also raise independent claims against the stakeholder, the court may consider such claims. Claimants are not required to assert causes of action that would otherwise constitute a compulsory cross-complaint.

b. ***Compare Federal Procedure***

Conceptually, federal interpleader under FRCP 22 and under 28 USC § 1335 is similar to California practice. In contrast to the ambiguity in the California law, federal law is clear that interpleader is available even if the stakeholder is not completely disinterested. In federal court, a stakeholder may deny liability in whole or in part to any of the other claimants, and may also claim a share of the subject property "in the nature of interpleader." FRCP 22; 28 USC § 1335. There is no limitation on additional claims against the stakeholder. Indeed, under FRCP 13, a claimant might be required to raise them.

c. Illustration

Julia was a partner in her law firm. Julia represented the City of Placerville. Julia became embroiled in a dispute with her partners, and she ended up leaving the firm. Julia attempted to collect her fees from the City for the legal services she had rendered while at the firm. The firm simultaneously attempted to collect its fees from the City. The City filed an action in interpleader in El Dorado County Superior Court because it was subject to conflicting claims for money. This is not a proper action in interpleader, because the City is not actually subject to conflicting claims between Julia and the firm. Julia performed her work in her capacity as a partner in the firm, and therefore she has no direct claim against the City for the fees. The City owes the fees to the firm, and Julia must make a claim against the firm for her fees. City of Morgan Hill v. Brown, 71 Cal.App.4th 1114, 84 Cal.Rptr.2d 361 (1999).

3. Intervention

a. Types of Intervention

Intervention allows a nonparty to an action to join as a party (either as a plaintiff or a defendant) if the nonparty has a sufficient interest in the subject matter of the litigation. There are two types of intervention: intervention of right and permissive intervention.

1) Intervention of Right

The court will order intervention if a nonparty establishes that:

- a statute entitles the nonparty to intervene in an action; or
- the nonparty satisfies all of the following criteria for intervention of right:
  - a showing of an interest in the subject matter of the action;
  - a showing that the disposition of the action may impede or impair the nonparty's ability to protect that interest; and
  - a timely application for intervention.

CCP § 387(b). If the requirements are met, the court must order intervention unless the nonparty's interest is already adequately represented by an existing party.

2) Permissive Intervention

a) Requirements

Intervention may be allowed in the court's discretion, upon timely application, where a nonparty has an "interest in the matter in litigation" or in the "success of either of the parties." CCP § 387(a). This provision has been interpreted to permit intervention when:

- the proper procedures have been followed;
- the nonparty has a direct and immediate interest in the action;
- the intervention will not enlarge the issues in the litigation; and
- the reasons for the intervention outweigh any opposition by the parties presently in the action.

City and County of San Francisco v. State, 128 Cal.App.4th 1030, 27 Cal.Rptr.3d 722 (2005).

b) Direct and Immediate Interest

The moving party's interest in the litigation must be direct and immediate. A consequential interest is not sufficient. It is not always easy to tell the difference. An interest is sufficiently direct where that party will benefit or suffer by the direct effect of the judgment, or where the judgment in itself adds to or diminishes that party's legal rights.

c) Liberal Construction

California follows a policy of liberal construction underlying the court's exercise of discretion for permissive intervention. Even if a party establishes the necessary interest for permissive intervention, however, the court may exercise its discretion to deny intervention where it would cause significant delay, reopen evidence, or enlarge the issues in the case.

b. Timeliness

The party seeking to intervene (both of right and permissively) must seek leave of court. The timeliness of the application for intervention depends on the circumstances of the case. The court will exercise its discretion to deny the motion to intervene where the moving party has not been diligent or there otherwise has been unreasonable delay.

c. *Compare Federal Procedure*

Federal intervention may be either mandatory (FRCP 24(a)) or permissive (FRCP 24(b)). While the federal and California provisions for intervention as of right are virtually identical, the standard for permissive intervention in FRCP 24(b) differs from that encompassed by CCP § 387(a). The federal court may permit a party to intervene when a federal statute grants a conditional right to intervene, or when a common question of law or fact exists between the main action and a claim or defense of the person seeking intervention. FRCP 24(b).

d. Illustration

Slippery Oil Corp. leased a parcel of land with the intent of extracting any oil under the surface. Ed brought a quiet title action against Slippery in Trinity County Superior Court, alleging that, under the terms of the deed to the parcel, he is entitled to extract any subsurface oil. Ione, who owns an adjacent parcel, fears that any oil extraction will cause subsidence in her parcel, and she timely moves for permission to intervene in the action between Ed and Slippery. Ione's motion will be denied, as the quiet title action between Ed and Slippery does not have a direct and immediate effect on Ione's interest. Lindelli v. Town of San Anselmo, 139 Cal.App.4th 1499, 43 Cal.Rptr.3d 707 (2006).

4. Class Actions

a. Purpose of Class Action Device

The class action device allows a person to bring a lawsuit on behalf of herself and others similarly situated. CCP § 382. Class actions are favored in California because they can provide effective relief to plaintiffs where the claim of any one individual plaintiff is too small to pursue individually. Because class actions involve the litigation of many claims at once, it is essential that a lead plaintiff fairly represent the class, that the class be well defined, and that adequate notice be given to class members. Although CCP § 382 authorizes class actions in California, it provides little instruction. As a result, FRCP 23 has long been used for guidance, as has Cal. Civ. Code §§ 1780 et seq. (pertaining to consumer class actions). Additionally, a substantial body of case law regarding class actions has developed in California.

1) Requirements

The essential requirements for a California class action are an ascertainable class and a community of interest among the class. Richmond v. Dart Industries, Inc., 29 Cal.3d 462, 174 Cal.Rptr. 515, 629 P.2d 23 (1981).

a) Ascertainable Class

Without a precisely framed class, capable of some objective definition, it becomes impossible for potential plaintiffs to receive notice of the action. The class definition must allow identification of those who fit within the class, and allow persons learning of the definition to determine whether or not they are members of the class.

b) **Community of Interest**

The community of interest requirement has three factors: (1) predominant questions of law or fact; (2) class representatives whose claims are typical of the class members; and (3) class representatives who will adequately represent the class. Typicality does not require that a representative's claims be identical to those of the class members—only that the representative be similarly situated and similarly motivated. Adequacy requires that a representative vigorously seek all relief the class would seek.

2) **Number of Plaintiffs**

There is no requirement as to the size of the class except that the class members must be "numerous." CCP § 382. Unlike the rule of thumb in federal practice, where a minimum of 40 plaintiffs is generally required for sufficient numerosity, there is no minimum number of plaintiffs required in California. However, where a class is extremely small, the benefits of the class action procedure may give way to individual adjudication.

b. **Grounds for Class Certification**

California follows federal procedure in allowing for three general types of class actions: (1) class actions where plaintiffs might be prejudiced if their claims are handled separately; (2) class actions where declaratory or injunctive relief is appropriate; or (3) class actions where common questions predominate and a class action is more appropriate than any other method. FRCP 23(b). A class member may not opt out of the first two types of class actions, but may opt out of the more general "common question" class. In considering a motion for class certification, a court must analyze only whether the requirements of class certification have been met. Any inquiry into the merits of the underlying claims is improper. Linder v. Thrifty Oil Co., 23 Cal.4th 429, 97 Cal.Rptr.2d 179, 2 P.3d 27 (2000). An order denying class certification on all causes of action is immediately appealable. Conley v. Pacific Gas & Electric Co., 131 Cal.App.4th 260, 31 Cal.Rptr.3d 719 (2005).

c. Notice

Because the resolution of the class action will bind all class members and preclude any further action on the same claims, it is essential that class members be given adequate notice of the pendency of the action. However, in expansive classes involving small losses, California courts have recognized that "class actions should be permitted to proceed, where the economic realities involved in giving 'adequate' notice, compared to the small individual losses of class members, would effectively negate any class action." Cartt v. Superior Court, 50 Cal.App.3d 960, 971, 124 Cal.Rptr. 376, 384 (1975). CRC 3.766(f) authorizes notice via publication where personal notification is "unreasonably expensive" or where class members have an "insubstantial" stake in the action. This standard is more lenient than the federal standard, which requires the best practicable notice possible under the circumstances, including individual notice to all members of the class who can be reasonably identified. FRCP 23(c)(2)(B). The court has discretion to shift some or all of the burden of the cost of notice onto the defendant.

d. Settlement

In determining whether a settlement is fair to the class members, the trial court considers a variety of factors on a case-by-case basis, including "(1) the strength of plaintiffs' case, (2) the risk, expense, complexity and likely duration of further litigation, (3) the risk of maintaining class action status through trial, (4) the amount offered in settlement, (5) the extent of discovery completed and the stage of the proceedings, (6) the experience and views of counsel, . . . and (7) the reaction of the class members to the proposed settlement." 7–Eleven Owners for Fair Franchising v. Southland Corp., 85 Cal.App.4th 1135, 1146, 102 Cal.Rptr.2d 777, 784 (2000).

e. *Compare Federal Procedure*

Federal class action practice, governed by FRCP 23, follows the same general principles as California class action practice. Indeed, FRCP 23 has long been used for guidance by California courts. However, there are some subtle distinctions. For example, a federal order denying class certification is subject to immediate appeal only at the discretion of the appellate court. FRCP 23(f). Notice procedures constitute another distinction: in federal practice, initially the plaintiff must bear the entire cost of providing notice to potential class members.

f. Illustration

Peyton lived near Dorke Corp., a manufacturer of machine parts located in Chowchilla. Peyton and several other residents of the area near the Dorke Corp. manufacturing plant filed suit in Madera County Superior Court against the company for damages from the discharge of dangerous chemicals and contamination of the local drinking water. The plaintiffs sought class certification for a "medical monitoring class" that would require Dorke Corp. to fund a court-supervised program for the medical monitoring of the class members. Although common issues exist among the potential class members, the individual issues actually predominate because of the presence of different levels of exposure and different monitoring needs among the class members. Therefore, class certification is not appropriate. Lockheed Martin Corp. v. Superior Court, 29 Cal.4th 1096, 131 Cal.Rptr.2d 1, 63 P.3d 913 (2003).

SAMPLE EXAM QUESTIONS

OBJECTIVE QUESTIONS

The questions in this section are based on the following hypothetical:

George had surgery at City Hospital, a governmental entity. When he awakened from the surgery, he experienced numbness in his arm and hand. George's lawyer filed a malpractice action 11 months after George's surgery, seeking damages for George's personal injuries. In the verified complaint, the attorney named City Hospital, Dr. Jones (George's surgeon), and a number of Doe defendants.

(1) True or False: George may sue City Hospital for his personal injuries as long as he files his lawsuit within the relevant statute of limitations period.

(2) George's complaint must include:

a. A short and plain statement of the claim showing that he is entitled to relief;

b. A statement of facts sufficient to constitute a cause of action in ordinary and concise language;

c. A demand for judgment specifying the amount of damages sought;

d. Both b and c.

(3) City Hospital's answer to George's complaint:

a. Must be verified because verified pleadings are required in personal injury actions;

b. Must be verified because verified answers are required of all defendants responding to a verified complaint;

c. Need not be verified because City Hospital is a governmental defendant;

d. Need not be verified because verified answers are always optional under California law.

(4) True or False: In George's personal injury action, George is required to serve Dr. Jones with a statement of damages at the same time as serving the complaint.

(5) Which of the following would be an appropriate ground for a demurrer by City Hospital to George's complaint:

a. The allegations of the complaint show that George has another action pending on the same causes of action against City Hospital and Dr. Jones;

b. The prayer requests relief that is not supported by the allegations of the complaint;

c. George stated in the complaint the amount of damages he seeks;

d. None of the above.

(6) True or False: A demurrer filed by City Hospital is timely if it is filed at the same time as the Hospital's answer.

(7) Which of the following is NOT an appropriate ground for Dr. Jones to file a motion to strike George's complaint:

a. The complaint includes irrelevant matter;

b. The complaint does not state facts sufficient to constitute a cause of action;

c. The complaint contains false allegations;

d. The complaint includes allegations prohibited by a previous court order.

(8) True or False: Dr. Jones may not file a general denial to George's complaint.

(9) The statute of limitations for a personal injury action like George's:

a. Begins to run only from the date on which the wrongful act was done to George (i.e., the date of the surgery);

b. Is actually a statute of repose;

c. May be tolled only for statutorily-permitted reasons;

d. Might not begin to run until George discovers or has reason to discover the harm.

(10) About 18 months after the complaint was filed, George and his attorney learned during Dr. Jones' deposition that George's injury was the likely result of the

anesthesia. George learned that Dr. Wall was the anesthesiologist. George's attorney promptly moved to amend the complaint to substitute Dr. Wall's true name for one of the Doe defendants. Should the court permit the amendment?

a. Yes, because the amendment is part of the same transaction or occurrence as that pleaded in George's complaint;

b. No, because the statute of limitations has expired as to George's cause of action against Dr. Wall;

c. Yes, because George filed the amendment substituting Dr. Wall for one of the Doe defendants as soon as he had actual knowledge that Dr. Wall contributed to George's injury;

d. No, because George failed to investigate Dr. Wall's involvement before George filed his complaint.

(11) George files a motion to amend the complaint to add a cause of action for fraud against Dr. Jones. If the trial court denies George's motion to amend the complaint, George may:

a. Make an ex parte application to the court to reconsider its ruling;

b. Within ten days of the court's order denying the motion to amend, move the court to permit renewal of the motion to amend;

c. Refile all of the papers he presented to the court on the motion to amend and move thc court to reconsider its denial of the motion;

d. Suggest to the court that it reconsider, on its own motion, the denial of the motion to amend.

(12) Which of the following complaints is most appropriately challenged by an anti-SLAPP motion to strike?

a. A college football player files a libel suit against a blogger for a series of postings about the football player's alleged gambling addiction;

b. A group of homeowners concerned about noise and safety file a class action seeking an injunction against a group that protests the United States' dependence on oil by erecting human barricades across intersections in their neighborhood;

c. A plaintiff sues the manufacturer of a "miracle" cure for baldness for false advertising;

d. George's complaint against Dr. Jones.

(13) George wishes to bring a class action against City Hospital for injuries suffered by dozens of patients allegedly caused by poor sanitation practices. If George seeks certification to proceed as a class action, he must show:

a. An ascertainable class;

b. A class representative who can adequately represent the class and whose claims are typical of the entire class;

c. Common questions of law or fact that predominate;

d. All of the above.

The questions in this section are based on the following hypothetical:

Earl owns a piece of real property near San Juan Bautista to which he believed he had full and clear title. At one time the property was owned by three individuals, Lan, Mia and Noa. Earl bought the property from Lan, and only afterward discovered that Mia and Noa were still owners. Earl sued Lan in San Benito County Superior Court for damages for failure to disclose, alleging that Lan knew of the existence of Mia and Noa when Lan sold the property to Earl.

(14) True or False: After Lan has answered the complaint, she may file a motion for judgment on the pleadings on any of the grounds available for a demurrer.

(15) True or False: Any amendments Earl may wish to make to his complaint require leave of court, which is granted liberally.

(16) Mia and Noa wish to intervene in the lawsuit between Earl and Lan. The court will order intervention:

a. Only if all parties in the action stipulate to Mia and Noa's intervention;

b. Even if Mia and Noa's intervention would substantially expand the issues in the lawsuit;

c. If Mia and Noa make a showing that their interests with respect to the property will be affected as a direct result of the judgment rendered in Earl's lawsuit;

d. As long as such a motion would be granted under the standards of FRCP 24(b).

(17) True or False: Lan may file a cross-complaint against Earl for damages arising out of a separate and unrelated business deal gone awry.

(18) Lan has filed an anti-SLAPP motion against Earl's complaint, which the court denied. Earl wants to bring a motion for sanctions under CCP § 128.7 on the ground that the motion was presented primarily to harass Earl and cause him unnecessary expense. The court:

a. Will deny the motion for sanctions because section 128.7 is not applicable to anti-SLAPP motions;

b. Is authorized to award Earl both deterrence sanctions as well as Earl's costs and attorney's fees if he is the prevailing party on the motion;

c. Will not require a 21–day safe harbor period because that requirement only applies when the court brings its own motion for sanctions;

d. Will consider sanctions only against Lan's attorney because the attorney actually filed the anti-SLAPP motion.

Answers to Objective Questions

(1) **False**: Cal. Gov't Code § 945.4 states that a plaintiff may not file suit against a government entity until she has filed a claim with the relevant government agency. In addition, a notice of intention to sue a health care provider is required by CCP § 364.

(2) **b.** CCP § 425.10(a) requires that a complaint must contain: (1) a statement of the facts constituting the cause of action, in ordinary and concise language; and (2) a demand for judgment for the relief to which the pleader claims to be entitled. CCP § 425.10(b), however, provides that the amount of monetary damages shall not be pleaded in a personal injury action. Answer "a" sets out the federal standard in FRCP 8(a)(1).

(3) **c.** CCP § 446(a) does not require a governmental defendant to file a verified answer, even if the complaint is verified.

(4) **False**. George is not required to serve a statement of damages simultaneously with his complaint. He must serve the statement upon request of City Hospital or Dr. Jones. Additionally, the court may not enter a default judgment against either defendant unless George has previously served the statement of damages. CCP § 425.11.

(5) **a.** This is a ground for special demurrer. CCP § 430.10(c). Answers "b" and "c" are not grounds for demurrer. They are more appropriately addressed via a motion to strike.

(6) **True**. CCP § 430.30(c) provides "a party objecting to a complaint or cross complaint may demur and answer at the same time."

(7) **b.** CCP § 436 states that a party may move the court to strike out "any irrelevant, false, or improper matters inserted in any pleading" or "all or any part of a pleading not drawn or filed in conformity with . . . an order of the court." Answer "b" states a ground for a general demurrer.

(8) **True**. Dr. Jones may not file a general denial under CCP § 431.30(b)(1) because George's complaint is verified. Dr. Jones is required to file a verified answer containing specific denials.

(9) **d.** Under the general rule for defining the accrual of a cause of action, the statute of limitations starts to run when the wrongful act has been done or the liability arises. However, the discovery rule delays the accrual of the cause of action until the plaintiff discovers or has reason to discover the cause of action. Answer "b" is incorrect because a statute of repose provides that a defendant is liable only for certain periods of time, regardless of when the plaintiff has actually sustained an injury. Answer "c" is incorrect because there are also equitable principles that may toll the running of the statute of limitations.

(10) **c.** George must amend the complaint to substitute Dr. Wall for one of the Doe designations once he is no longer genuinely ignorant of the identity of the defendant or of the facts giving rise to a cause of action against that defendant. CCP § 474. For practical purposes, George generally would have three years from the date he commenced his action to substitute Dr. Wall and accomplish service of process. CCP § 583.210. Shorter deadlines would apply under Fast Track rules.

(11) **d.** If George applies to the court for reconsideration of its order or renewal of his motion, he must adhere to the jurisdictional requirements of CCP § 1008. However, George is not precluded from suggesting to the court (e.g., in a case management conference) that the court might reconsider its ruling, and the court then may exercise its inherent power to grant reconsideration or renewal on its own motion.

(12) **a.** The football player's lawsuit appears to be a SLAPP because it arises from the blogger's posting in furtherance of his right to freedom of speech. Answer "b" arguably meets the requirements of a suit brought solely in the public interest or on behalf of the general public and therefore is exempt from an anti-SLAPP motion. CCP § 425.17(b). Answer "c" involves defendants who are engaged primarily in the

business of selling goods and are likewise prohibited from bringing an anti-SLAPP motion. CCP § 425.17(c). Answer "d" is incorrect because George's lawsuit does not arise from any act of Dr. Jones in furtherance of Dr. Jones' free speech rights.

(13) **d.** All of these requirements must be satisfied for class certification. CCP § 382; Cal. Civ. Code § 1781.

(14) **False**. The only grounds for a motion for judgment on the pleadings that overlap with a demurrer are those based on lack of subject matter jurisdiction and on failure to state facts sufficient to constitute a cause of action or defense.

(15) **False**. Earl may amend his complaint without leave of court once before the answer or demurrer of a defendant is filed, or after demurrer and before trial. CCP § 472.

(16) **c.** The court will require a showing of a direct and immediate interest in the action such that the judgment will add to or diminish Mia's or Noa's rights. Answer "a" is incorrect because parties may not stipulate for intervention; a court order is required. Answer "b" is incorrect because intervention will be denied if it would substantially expand the issues in the lawsuit. Answer "d" is incorrect because the standard for permissive intervention under FRCP 24(b) is somewhat different than that under California law.

(17) **True**. Lan's permissive cross-complaint against Earl may allege any causes of action she has against Earl, even if they do not arise out of the same transaction or occurrence as those pleaded in Earl's complaint. CCP §§ 428.10(a), 428.30.

(18) **b.** Sanctions under CCP § 128.7(d) are intended to deter repetition of the conduct by Lan or by others similarly situated. In addition, CCP § 128.7(c)(1) permits an award of costs and attorney's fees to the prevailing party incurred in making or opposing the sanctions motion. Answer "a" is incorrect because there is no express exemption of anti-SLAPP motions. Answer "c" is incorrect because the safe harbor period required under California law applies to motions brought either by the court or by a party. Answer "d" is incorrect because section 128.7(c) permits an award of sanctions against parties as well as attorneys.

ESSAY QUESTIONS

A. Sally was riding a bus operated by Santa Clara County to her doctor's appointment. While on the bus, a young man punched her, knocked out two of her teeth, grabbed her purse, and jumped off the bus. Concerned passengers chased the man down the street and held him until the police arrived. While criminal charges are currently pending against the attacker, Sally's attorney filed a lawsuit against the attacker and the County in Santa Clara County Superior Court. In the cause of action against the attacker, Sally has described the facts of the incident, and she has sought damages on a number of intentional tort theories. In the cause of action against the County, the complaint pleads only that the County was negligent in failing to prevent the attack. Sally is demanding $10,000 for her medical and dental expenses, $25,000 for her pain and suffering, and $500,000 in punitive damages.

(1) Discuss the response(s) each of the defendants might file to Sally's complaint. Include a discussion of any timing issues that may be involved in the defendants' response(s).

(2) Assume that Santa Clara County wishes to sue the bus manufacturer for indemnity because a mechanism on the bus that would have allowed the driver to alert the police failed. Via which vehicle(s) may the County sue the bus manufacturer for indemnity?

B. Citizens Respecting Animals' Rights (CRAR), is a nonprofit organization whose mission is to prevent cruelty toward animals throughout California. The group's large infrastructure targets the employees of public and private organizations that conduct research and testing on animals. CRAR's members have directed their protest efforts toward thousands of employees of university laboratories, pharmaceutical manufacturers and cosmetics companies throughout the state.

Preston is a researcher at the University of California, Santa Barbara. CRAR members have vandalized his house, yelled at his children as they waited for their school bus, and called Preston's house at all hours. CRAR members have gone to the homes of other UCSB employees, vandalized their property, set off alarms late at night, broken windows, spray-painted cars, left threatening telephone messages, and publicized the employees' private information on the Internet.

Preston has filed a lawsuit against CRAR in Santa Barbara County Superior Court, seeking to enjoin the group from engaging in further harassing activity and seeking compensation for property damage and emotional distress the group inflicted on Preston and his family. Preston's attorneys suggest turning Preston's complaint into a class action.

(1) Discuss the potential for class certification and any barriers Preston might face.

(2) Identify and analyze the possible response(s) CRAR might file to Preston's lawsuit.

Essay Answers

Essay A

(1) Defendants' Responses

- Santa Clara County's responses:
    - Failure to file a notice of claim:
        - When suing a governmental agency, Sally must first file a notice of the claim with the appropriate agency. Once the County has denied Sally's claim, she may proceed to file her complaint.
        - The County might attempt to file a demurrer to challenge the court's subject matter jurisdiction, Sally's failure to state sufficient facts to constitute a cause of action, or Sally's lack of legal capacity to sue. CCP § 430.10(a), (b). But these grounds must be present on the face of the complaint or by matters subject to judicial notice.
        - The County might alternatively file a motion to strike the complaint because it was not filed in conformity with the laws of the state requiring Sally to file a claim. CCP § 436(b). The same limitations as to the face of the complaint and judicial notice apply.
        - If a demurrer or motion to strike are not proper ways to challenge the failure to file a pre-lawsuit claim, the County may later bring a motion for summary judgment or summary adjudication. (See Chapter 5(VII)(A).)
    - Failure to plead sufficient facts to constitute a cause of action:
        - The County may file a general demurrer on the ground that Sally has not met her burden under California's fact pleading requirement. CCP § 430.10(e). The complaint alleges negligence without any facts supporting the elements of the cause of action.
        - The County might alternatively file a motion for judgment on the pleadings on this ground after it has filed its answer. CCP § 438(c)(1)(B).
    - Amount of damages:
        - The County may file a motion to strike the prayer of the complaint. No amount of damages may be stated in a personal injury unlimited civil case. CCP § 425.10(b).

- Attacker's responses:
  - The attacker probably has no ground to challenge the sufficiency of the complaint. The complaint appears to set out ultimate facts in support of the intentional tort causes of action.
  - Unlike the County, there is no pre-lawsuit claim requirement Sally must satisfy as to the attacker.
  - The attacker may bring a motion to strike the prayer of the complaint because it states an amount of damages.

(2) Indemnity

- The County may file a permissive cross-complaint against the bus manufacturer under CCP § 428.10(b). The indemnity cause of action against the manufacturer arises out the same transaction or occurrence as the negligence cause of action in Sally's complaint.
- Alternatively, the County may bring a separate lawsuit against the manufacturer. The statute of limitations does not start to run until after a judgment against the County is entered.

Essay B

(1) Class Certification

- On a class certification motion, Preston must establish:
  - An ascertainable class in which common questions of law or fact predominate;
  - Numerosity;
  - Class representatives with claims typical of the class; and
  - Class representatives who can adequately represent the class.
- Ascertainable class, common questions of law or fact:
  - The CRAR campaign has resulted in damage to the property and disruption to the lives of many university employees. Although common questions exist, the differences in the experiences and injuries of the employees may indicate that the common questions do not predominate.
  - Members of the class appear to be ascertainable.

- Numerosity:
  - It is not known how many potential class members there are, but it appears that the class would be sufficiently numerous to make the class action device appropriate.
- Class representatives with claims or defenses typical of the class:
  - Preston's claim is that CRAR's vandalism campaign resulted in property damage and harassment of his family.
  - Other members of the class have similar claims, although some might have had different experiences or degrees of injury.
- Class representatives who can adequately represent the class:
  - Preston's interests are likely congruent with other potential class members such that Preston will be motivated to vigorously litigate the issues.

(2) CRAR's Responses

- CRAR's principal response: anti-SLAPP motion to strike.
  - CRAR may contend that Preston's lawsuit has been brought to chill CRAR'S First Amendment right of freedom of speech, and that an anti-SLAPP motions is the appropriate response.
  - Two-step process:
    - CRAR must show that Preston's lawsuit arises out of CRAR's acts in furtherance of its free speech right.
    - Then the burden shifts to Preston to establish a likelihood of success on the merits.
  - CRAR will not be able to satisfy its burden if the activity in question is illegal.
    - In this case, CRAR has committed trespassing and vandalism while engaging in the protesting they claim is protected speech.

    - The court will likely deny the anti-SLAPP motion before the burden would be shifted to Preston.

- If defects in Preston's complaint appear on the face of the pleading, CRAR might file a general or special demurrer, a motion to strike, or a motion for judgment on the pleadings.

CHAPTER 4

DISCOVERY

I. DISCOVERY IN CALIFORNIA

A. Philosophy

Discovery is the formal information-gathering portion of a lawsuit. The California discovery statutes are construed in favor of a liberal exchange of information. Discovery is intended to put the prospective evidence of the case out in the open, to narrow the issues, to promote settlement, and to prevent surprise at trial. Greyhound Corp. v. Superior Court, 56 Cal.2d 355, 15 Cal.Rptr. 90, 364 P.2d 266 (1961). The California discovery system is intended to be self-executing—implemented by the parties with minimal court intervention. In an action pending in state court, each party is entitled to discovery through properly propounded requests, but parties are not obligated to make any automatic disclosures.

B. *Compare Federal Procedure*

California's discovery statutes are far more detailed than their federal rule counterparts. In marked contrast to California procedure, federal parties are obligated, independent of any request, to automatically disclose certain information at the outset of the action, including the identity of witnesses and copies of documents that may support the disclosing party's claims or defenses. FRCP 26(a)(1).

II. DISCOVERY SCOPE

A. Broad Scope

California's liberal philosophy of discovery is manifested in the expansive scope of discovery. A matter is discoverable as long as it is: (1) relevant to the subject matter of the action; (2) admissible or reasonably calculated to lead to the discovery of admissible evidence; and (3) not subject to a privilege or other protection from discovery. CCP § 2017.010.

B. Relevance and Admissibility

1. Relevance

Relevance to the subject matter of the action is a broad standard. A matter is relevant if it might aid a party in assessing the case, preparing it for trial, or facilitating a settlement. Stewart v. Colonial Western Agency, Inc., 87 Cal.App.4th 1006, 105 Cal.Rptr.2d 115 (2001). The concept of relevance is flexible, depending on the complexity of the issues in a case.

2. Reasonably Calculated to Lead to Discovery of Admissible Evidence

A matter need not be admissible in evidence in order to be discoverable, as long as its discovery might reasonably lead to the discovery of other evidence that would be admissible at trial. For example, a party may not object to discovery on the ground that the matter constitutes inadmissible hearsay if the hearsay might lead to other admissible evidence.

3. *Compare Federal Procedure*

Federal law also imposes relevance and admissibility limitations on the scope of discovery. FRCP 26(b)(1). The basic federal relevance standard, however, is slightly narrower than that in California: a matter is discoverable if it is relevant to "any party's claim or defense." A party may seek to discover information relevant to the "subject matter involved in the action" only by court order on a showing of good cause. FRCP 26(b)(1).

4. Illustration

Paula worked as a dispatcher in the Blue Lake Police Department. She resigned from her job on the ground of sexual harassment. In her subsequent lawsuit filed in Humboldt County Superior Court against the Department, Paula alleged that several lewd photographs of a female resembling Paula were displayed in the men's locker room. The supervising sergeant ordered the photos to be removed, and they were placed in the sergeant's filing cabinet. Several days later, Paula was handed an envelope containing the photos. The Department served Paula with interrogatories asking how she acquired the photos. Paula refused to answer. The Department

> filed a motion to compel answers to the interrogatories on the ground that the information sought was relevant to the subject matter of the action and was not privileged or otherwise protected. The trial court will order Paula to respond. The information is relevant because it might reasonably assist the Department in evaluating the case, preparing for trial, and facilitating settlement. It is also relevant to assessing Paula's credibility regarding any role she might have played in removing the photos from the sergeant's file, which could affect the type and amount of damages she might recover. Gonzalez v. Superior Court, 33 Cal.App.4th 1539, 39 Cal.Rptr.2d 896 (1995).

C. Privileges

1. Types of Privileges

California law recognizes a number of privileges that, if applicable, limit the scope of discovery. Some information and communications are subject to absolute privileges (e.g., attorney-client, physician-patient, clergy-penitent). Others (such as trade secrets and police personnel files) are subject to qualified privileges, requiring disclosure only if the interests of justice in permitting discovery outweigh the interests in preventing disclosure.

2. Privilege Procedure

A party may claim a privilege either by objecting to a discovery request on that ground (thereby forcing the proponent of the discovery to file a motion to compel further responses), or by filing a motion for a protective order. The court typically requires the party objecting on the ground of privilege to file a "privilege log" that sets out the basic information concerning items as to which the privilege applies and the ground for asserting the privilege.

3. Waiver

The holder of a privilege (e.g., client, patient, penitent, etc.) might waive the privilege by disclosing, or consenting to the disclosure of, a significant part of the communication. Waiver may also occur by failing to claim the privilege. An unintentional disclosure of privileged information by an attorney might constitute a waiver by the client, but California law is not definitive on this point.

4. *Compare Federal Procedure*

Federal law also limits the scope of discovery of privileged matters. FRCP 26(b)(1). The Federal Rules of Evidence govern privilege issues in federal question cases, but in diversity cases, state law determines the availability and scope of a privilege. FRE 501. District courts evaluating claims of privilege often require the objecting party to provide a privilege log. FRCP 26(b)(5)(A).

5. Illustration

Penn, a former member of the Clark Community Church, sued the Church in San Joaquin County Superior Court for sexual abuse committed by a former youth minister when Penn was a child. A year before the suit was filed, when the abuse allegations had come to light, the Church's current head minister, Pastor Garcia, sent a letter to her congregation reaching out to others who might have been affected by the youth minister's abuse. Pastor Garcia assured her congregants that all communications with her would be confidential. Pastor Garcia received a dozen responses to her letter from members of the congregation (none of whom was a party to Penn's lawsuit). In the lawsuit, Penn served interrogatories and document demands on the Church, seeking identifying information about anyone with knowledge about the alleged sexual abuse committed by the youth minister. The Church responded with an objection based on the clergy-penitent privilege. Penn filed a motion to compel responses, arguing that the privilege did not apply because the letters to Pastor Garcia were not confessional in nature and therefore were not penitential communications. The court will likely uphold the privilege. The communications were "penitential" because they were: (1) intended to be confidential; (2) actually made in confidence in the presence of no third persons; (3) made to a clergy member who, in the course of her practice, is accustomed to receiving such communications; and (4) made to a clergy member with a duty, under church tenets, to keep the communications confidential. Doe 2 v. Superior Court, 132 Cal.App.4th 1504, 34 Cal.Rptr.3d 458 (2005).

D. Work Product Protection

An attorney's work product may be withheld from discovery in order to "[p]reserve the rights of attorneys to prepare cases for trial with that degree of privacy necessary to encourage them to prepare their cases thoroughly" and to "[p]revent attorneys from taking undue advantage of their adversary's industry and efforts." CCP § 2018.020. The attorney is the holder of work product protection and thus may waive it.

1. Absolute Protection

Any writing that "reflects an attorney's impressions, conclusions, opinions, or legal research is not discoverable under any circumstances."

CCP § 2018.030(a). "Writing" is defined broadly to include such items as charts, graphs, photographs, recordings, pictures, videos and computer data. CCP § 2016.020(c); Cal. Evid. Code § 250.

2. Qualified Protection

Work product not absolutely protected may be subject to qualified protection. Qualified work product is not discoverable "unless the court determines that denial of discovery will unfairly prejudice the party seeking discovery . . . or will result in an injustice." CCP § 2018.030(b). Qualified protection is afforded only to "derivative materials"—those created or derived from an attorney's work on behalf of a client that reflect the attorney's strategy or interpretation. Examples of protected derivative materials include charts, reports or compilations prepared by consultants. Examples of nonderivative materials that are not protected work product include witness statements that do not reflect counsel's evaluation, and documents identifying the location of physical evidence.

3. *Compare Federal Procedure*

Federal work product protection operates similarly to California's. Under the qualified work product protection under FRCP 26(b)(3), "a party may not discover documents and tangible things that are prepared in anticipation of litigation or for trial." One state/federal distinction is in the language regarding when qualified work product is subject to disclosure. Under the federal rule, disclosure is permitted if the party seeking discovery shows a "substantial need" for the information and cannot, without "undue hardship," find the "substantial equivalent" in another way. FRCP 26(b)(3)(A)(ii). California's statute requires a showing of undue prejudice or injustice. While California law offers absolute work product protection for an attorney's mental impressions, conclusions, opinions and legal theories, federal protection for core work product is slightly more equivocal. FRCP 26(b)(3)(B) provides only that the court "must protect against disclosure" of such material when the court has ordered that qualified work product be disclosed.

4. Illustration

Draxo Pharmaceuticals makes and distributes Tranquility, a prescription anti-anxiety medication. Draxo sent a shipment of Tranquility to Pill Hill Drug Stores, Inc., a pharmacy chain with retail outlets all over Central California. Unfortunately, the bottles were misla-

> beled. Those customers who thought they were receiving Tranquility actually got WakeUp, a stimulant. Some of those customers suffered serious side effects from taking WakeUp, and word of mouth spread that Pill Hill was not committed to quality control. Pill Hill sued Draxo in San Luis Obispo County Superior Court for damages from lost business. In the discovery phase, Pill Hill served a deposition (document) subpoena on Accurate Auditors, Draxo's accounting firm. Pill Hill was seeking Draxo's attorney's written response to an audit inquiry letter Accurate had sent to Draxo months ago. The attorney's response included a description of Pill Hill's lawsuit, an evaluation of Draxo's likelihood of success, and an estimate of the potential damages for which Draxo could be liable. Because Draxo's counsel's response contains counsel's ideas, explanations and conclusions, it is subject to absolute work product protection. Draxo's attorney did not waive the protection by sharing his opinions with Accurate. Disclosure was made to a third party who had an interest in maintaining the confidentiality of the information, and there was no evidence that the auditors would reveal the contents of counsel's response in the audit report or otherwise. Laguna Beach County Water District v. Superior Court, 124 Cal.App.4th 1453, 22 Cal.Rptr.3d 387 (2004).

E. Privacy

The California Constitution expressly provides "an inalienable right of privacy." Cal. Const., art. I, § 1. Even if a matter is relevant, admissible and not privileged, it may still be shielded from discovery because its disclosure would violate the right to privacy.

1. Nature of Protection

Privacy protection is not absolute. When faced with a privacy objection, the court first evaluates whether the party claiming privacy protection:

- possesses a legitimate privacy interest;
- possesses a reasonable expectation of privacy under the particular circumstances; and
- has suffered a serious invasion of privacy.

If these criteria are satisfied, the court then balances the need for the information to fairly resolve the suit against the privacy interest of the party opposing discovery. Discovery will be permitted only if a compelling public interest exists. Pioneer Electronics (USA), Inc. v. Superior Court, 40 Cal.4th 360, 53 Cal.Rptr.3d 513, 150 P.3d 198 (2007). Examples of information protected by privacy include personal financial records, membership in associations or groups, medical and personnel records, and sexual history.

2. ***Compare Federal Procedure***

Although the U.S. Constitution does not contain an explicit privacy clause, as does the California Constitution, federal courts recognize a desire for privacy in the discovery context. The district court may balance the need for discovery against the need to protect a person from "annoyance, embarrassment, [or] oppression." FRCP 26(c)(1).

3. **Illustration**

Phoebe was married to Dave in Weed, California. After they had been married about a year, a blood test revealed that Phoebe was HIV positive. Phoebe believed that Dave had infected her. Phoebe sued Dave in Siskiyou County Superior Court for intentional and negligent infliction of emotional distress and for fraud. Phoebe alleged that Dave knew he was HIV positive, but he did not tell Phoebe and did not engage in protected sex with her. In response, Dave alleged that he is HIV positive because Phoebe infected him. Seeking to discover Dave's sexual history and the timing of his awareness of his HIV status, Phoebe propounded interrogatories and a request for admissions on Dave. Dave objected on the ground that inquiry into his sexual history and behavior violates his right of privacy. The court must balance Dave's right to privacy against Phoebe's right to ascertain the truth and to a fair trial. Dave has a reduced expectation of privacy in this case because he has admitted that he is HIV positive and he has put his HIV status in controversy by arguing that Phoebe infected him. Nevertheless, because of Dave's right to privacy, Phoebe's requests must be restricted to the time period between the earliest date on which Dave could have been infected until the date when Phoebe and Dave ceased sexual relations. John B. v. Superior Court, 38 Cal.4th 1177, 45 Cal.Rptr.3d 316, 137 P.3d 153 (2006).

F. Other Limitations on Discovery

A court may issue a protective order to restrict discovery. (See section IV(C), below.)

III. DISCOVERY METHODS

A. Informal Discovery

During the pendency of a lawsuit, a party typically utilizes one of the statutorily-approved methods of discovery. However, a party is not precluded from conducting its own lawful exploration of the facts using informal methods. For example, if the plaintiff was injured in a public location, she may visit that location to conduct an investigation or make observations. Pullin v. Superior Court, 81 Cal.App.4th 1161, 97 Cal.Rptr.2d 447 (2000). A party may also obtain information available through a public agency, over the Internet, or through a cooperative third party, without the need for a formal discovery request.

B. Statutorily-Authorized Discovery Devices

In unlimited civil cases, there are six distinct methods of discovery authorized under California's discovery laws: interrogatories, inspection demands, requests for admission, depositions, physical and mental examinations, and exchange of expert witness information. CCP § 2019.010. (See section III(C), below, regarding more restricted discovery in limited civil cases.) In deciding which discovery devices to use in a given action, a party must consider such factors as cost, efficiency, timing, the benefit of written versus oral responses, and the value of spontaneous versus prepared responses.

1. Interrogatories

Interrogatories are written questions propounded from one party to another party. Interrogatories are a useful method to obtain basic background information about another party's claims, defenses, contentions or evidence.

a. Propounding Interrogatories

1) Form Interrogatories

The Judicial Council of California has made available a set of form interrogatories applicable to many types of civil lawsuits. CCP § 2033.710; Judicial Council Form DISC–001. A party may ask an unlimited number of form interrogatories of another party. CCP § 2030.030(a)(1).

2) Specially-Drafted Interrogatories

A party may serve specially-prepared (non-form) interrogatories that allow for questions more tailored to the litigation. These interrogatories typically seek factual information as well as a party's contentions. A propounding party may ask up to a total of 35 specially-drafted interrogatories of another party, unless the propounding party also serves a declaration attesting to the need for additional interrogatories. CCP §§ 2030.030–.050. In the absence of a declaration for additional discovery or a stipulation between the parties, specially-drafted interrogatories in excess of 35 need not be answered. Specially-drafted interrogatories are also subject to a number of restrictions—they may not include, for example, subparts, conjunctive or disjunctive questions, a preface or instructions. Each interrogatory must be complete in and of itself, without reference to other interrogatories or outside materials. CCP § 2030.060.

b. Responding to Interrogatories

1) Types of Responses

Three types of responses to interrogatories are permitted:

- Answers: Answers must be complete and straightforward, based on information reasonably available to the responding party.

- Objections: Common objections include that a privilege or work product protection exists, the numerical limit has been exceeded, or the interrogatories are burdensome or oppressive. Objections are waived by the failure to timely raise them, either in response or by motion for protective order.

- Option to produce documents: If the interrogatories seek information contained in files or records, and the response requires compilation or summarization of information, the responding party may elect to allow the propounding party to inspect and copy records (if the burden of searching the records is substantially the same for both parties).

CCP §§ 2030.210–.220.

2) Timing and Verification of Response

The responding party must serve a response within 30 days of service of the interrogatories. CCP § 2030.260. An untimely response waives all objections to the interrogatories, unless the court grants relief from the waiver. CCP § 2030.290. Interrogatory answers must be signed under oath by the responding party; objections must be signed by the attorney, but not under oath. CCP § 2030.250. An unverified response (where a verification is required) is treated as no response at all.

c. *Compare Federal Procedure*

Federal interrogatory practice is largely similar to California's. A key distinction is that a party in federal court may serve no more than a total of 25 interrogatories (including subparts) on another party, unless the court orders or the parties stipulate otherwise. FRCP 33(a)(1). Although form interrogatories are not available in federal court, the automatic initial disclosures made after a federal action has been filed provide some of the information a party may obtain via California's form interrogatories. FRCP 26(a)(1).

d. Illustration

Plaintiff Pilar took the deposition of defendant Delta in an action filed in Sierra County Superior Court. The deposition lasted for eight days and covered hundreds of pages. Following Delta's deposition, Delta propounded the following interrogatory to Pilar: "Do you contend that any of the answers that Delta gave at her deposition is untrue? If so, identify the question asked and the answer given by stating the date of the deposition, the volume number, and the page and line number of the questions you contend that Delta answered untruthfully." Delta's interrogatory to Pilar is not full and complete in and of itself, as required by CCP § 2030.060(d). A response to the interrogatory would require Pilar to refer to and incorporate questions and answers from the hundreds of pages of Delta's deposition. Because the interrogatory essentially asks thousands of individual questions, it violates the "Rule of 35" of CCP § 2030.030(a)(1). If Delta had served a declaration for additional discovery (CCP § 2030.050) with the interrogatory, Pilar's options would be to answer the interrogatory without objection as to the number or form of individual questions, or to move for a protective order. Catanese v. Superior Court, 46 Cal.App.4th 1159, 54 Cal.Rptr.2d 280 (1996).

2. Inspection Demands

A party may make a written demand to inspect any document, tangible thing, or land of another party.

a. Propounding Demand

A demand must contain a description of each item or a reasonably particular categorization of items, and a reasonable place and time for inspection (at least 30 days after service of the demand). CCP § 2031.030. There is no limit to the number of inspection demands a party may serve on another party.

b. Responding to Demand

1) Types of Responses

The three types of permissible responses to an inspection demand are:

- Agreement to comply: an agreement to produce the items requested that are in the possession, custody or control of the responding party.
- Inability to comply: an explanation of the reasons why, after a diligent search and reasonable inquiry, the items demanded cannot be produced.
- Objections: see Interrogatories, section III(B)(1)(b), above.

CCP §§ 2031.210–.240.

2) Timing and Verification of Response

The responding party must serve a written response within 30 days after service of the inspection demand. CCP § 2031.260. An untimely response waives all objections to the inspection demand, unless the court grants relief from the waiver. CCP § 2031.300. A response containing an agreement to comply must be verified by the responding party. Any objections must be signed by the attorney for the responding party. CCP § 2031.250.

c. Obtaining Documents from Nonparty

Several statutes provide methods for obtaining documents from a nonparty. They include: CCP § 2020.010 et seq. (documents and business records from nonparty deponent); § 2034.010 et seq. (writings of expert); § 1985.3 et seq. (subpoena for personal records of consumer); and § 1985.6 (subpoena for employment records).

d. *Compare Federal Procedure*

FRCP 34 sets out a similar procedure for a request to produce documents or tangible things, or to enter onto land. However, a response to a Rule 34 request need not be verified by the responding party; it only must be signed by the attorney. Acceptable responses to a Rule 34 request are an agreement to allow inspection or an objection. There is no express option to state an inability to comply as exists under the California statute. In addition, there is no timing requirement for the date of inspection. A party may obtain documents or electronically stored information from a nonparty via the subpoena procedure in FRCP 45.

e. Illustration

Pasha served a document demand on Deco. Deco served a hybrid response, containing both specific responses to some requests and objections based on privilege to other requests. The response was served on time but was not verified by Deco. On her motion to compel further responses, Pasha argued that the lack of verification made the entire response untimely and thus resulted in a waiver of all objections. CCP § 2031.300(a). However, objections set forth in a discovery response do not have to be verified by the party; they only need to be signed by the attorney. Only the fact-specific responses must be verified by a party. Deco's fact-specific responses were unverified, and thus untimely, and objections as to those requests are waived. However, the unverified objections signed by counsel are not waived. Pasha may move for an order to compel verified fact-specific responses, and she may seek sanctions for the untimely unverified response. Food 4 Less Supermarkets v. Superior Court, 40 Cal.App.4th 651, 46 Cal.Rptr.2d 925 (1995).

3. Requests for Admission

Requests for admission (RFA) allow the propounding party to obtain written responses from another party admitting or denying the truth of facts and other matters, as well as the genuineness of documents.

CCP § 2033.010. Such admissions are binding against the responding party at trial and in any dispositive pretrial motions. CCP § 2033.410.

a. Propounding Requests

1) Number and Format of RFA

A party may use a Judicial Council form or may propound specially-drafted RFA. CCP § 2033.710. In either case, the propounding party may request an unlimited number of RFA as to the genuineness of documents, but she is limited to 35 RFA for requests as to the truth of matters, unless a declaration for additional discovery is served with the RFA or the parties stipulate to an increased number. CCP §§ 2033.030–.050. Similar restrictions as those for interrogatories apply to RFA (e.g., no subparts, no conjunctive or disjunctive questions, etc.). CCP § 2033.060.

2) Types of Requests

In addition to RFA as to the genuineness of documents, a party may ask another party to admit or deny the truth of facts, opinions related to facts, and legal conclusions (i.e., the application of law to fact). CCP § 2033.010.

b. Responding to Requests

1) Types of Responses

A party may respond to RFA in three ways:

- Admission or denial: The responding party admits the portions of the RFA that are true and denies the remainder, based on information readily available to that party.

- Inability to admit or deny: The responding party states that after a reasonable inquiry, she has insufficient information to admit or deny the RFA.

- Objections: see Interrogatories, section III(B)(1)(b), above.

CCP §§ 2033.220–.230.

2) Timing and Verification of Response

The response must be served within 30 days after service of the RFA. CCP § 2033.250. An untimely response waives all objections to the RFA. It also permits the propounding party to file a motion to deem the genuineness of documents and/or truth of matters contained in the RFA admitted (unless the responding party serves a proposed response that substantially complies with the statute before the hearing of the motion). CCP § 2033.280. A response containing admissions and denials must be verified under oath by the responding party. Objections are signed by the attorney. CCP § 2033.240.

c. Amending or Withdrawing Admissions

A responding party may move the court for an order permitting amendment or withdrawal of an admission (including a "deemed" admission). The court will grant the motion if the admission was a result of the responding party's mistake, inadvertence or excusable neglect, and if no substantial prejudice will result to the propounding party. CCP § 2033.300.

d. *Compare Federal Procedure*

FRCP 36 is largely similar to the California RFA statutes. One contrast is that there is no numerical limitation on RFA for any purpose. Another important distinction is that in federal practice, a matter will automatically be deemed admitted if the responding party files an untimely response. The propounding party is not required to file a motion. FRCP 36(a)(3).

e. Illustration

Paolo sued Dr. Dirk in Monterey County Superior Court for medical malpractice. Dr. Dirk served a set of requests for admission asking Paolo to admit that Dr. Dirk was not negligent and that no action of Dr. Dirk had resulted in personal injury to Paolo. Paolo did not respond to these requests. Dr. Dirk filed a motion to deem the requests admitted under CCP § 2033.280(b). Because Paolo did not serve verified responses prior to the hearing on the motion, the court had no discretion but to order that Dr. Dirk's

> requests for admission be deemed admitted. However, Paolo may seek leave of court to withdraw the deemed admissions under CCP § 2033.300(a). The court will require a strong showing that the admissions were the result of mistake, inadvertence or excusable neglect, and that Dr. Dirk will not be substantially prejudiced by the withdrawal. Wilcox v. Birtwhistle, 21 Cal.4th 973, 90 Cal.Rptr.2d 260, 987 P.2d 727 (1999).

4. Depositions

Depositions permit a party to obtain the in-person oral pretrial testimony of an individual under oath. Oral depositions are the discovery device best suited to evaluating witness demeanor and to soliciting spontaneous responses. Depositions may also be taken on written questions.

a. Oral Depositions of Parties

1) Notice

A deposition of a party is initiated by serving a notice on the deponent at least ten days before the date of the deposition. CCP § 2025.270. Service of a proper notice requires the deponent to appear and, if requested, to produce documents, unless the deponent serves timely objections or seeks a protective order. CCP § 2025.280. A notice to a corporation or other entity includes a description of the matters to be addressed at the deposition. The entity is then required to designate the officers, directors, or other persons most qualified to testify on those matters on behalf of the entity. CCP § 2025.220. A deposition notice may also be served directly on an officer, director, managing agent or employee of an entity. CCP § 2025.280.

2) Number of Depositions

Unless the court issues a protective order, a party may take an unlimited number of depositions in an action, and there is no limit to the length of depositions. However, only one deposition may be taken of a natural person unless the court orders successive depositions on a showing of good cause. CCP § 2025.610.

3) Conduct of Deposition

a) Scope of Examination

A deponent is required to answer questions based solely on his personal knowledge. He is not required to guess, or to investigate or inquire of other sources. All parties have the right to attend a deposition and to cross-examine a deponent. The grounds for objection to questions are narrow, and some objections (such as those addressed to the form of the question and those based on privilege) are waived if not properly raised at the deposition. CCP § 2025.460.

b) Control of Questioning

If a deponent is subjected to abusive questioning, his counsel may object or may suspend the deposition and move for an order to limit or terminate questioning. CCP §§ 2025.460–.470. Court intervention may also be necessary if a deponent fails or refuses to answer questions or produce documents. CCP § 2025.480.

b. Oral Depositions of Nonparties

1) Subpoenas

A deposition of a nonparty witness is initiated by serving a subpoena. A deposition notice is not sufficient. The subpoena may require the following:

- oral testimony only;
- production of business records only; or
- both oral testimony and production of business records or other documents.

CCP § 2020.020. A witness may challenge the subpoena by serving written objections, a motion to quash or modify the subpoena, or a motion for protective order.

2) Personal Records of Consumer

Special rules apply to subpoenas for personal records of a consumer (e.g., bank, school, health) or employment records of an employee. See, e.g., CCP §§ 1985.3, 1985.6.

c. Depositions on Written Questions

A party may take a deposition on written questions rather than orally. The deposition notice must attach the written direct examination questions. Other parties in the action may then serve cross questions on the deponent (followed by redirect and recross questions). The party noticing the deposition may forward the direct examination questions to the deponent in advance of the deposition. However, the deponent may not preview the cross, redirect, or recross questions. The deponent may assert objections to questions or may seek a protective order. CCP § 2028.010 et seq.

d. Use of Deposition Transcript

A party may use the deposition of another party or party-affiliated witness at trial for any purpose (i.e., as substantive evidence or for impeachment purposes). A nonparty deposition may be used to impeach that nonparty's testimony at trial. Any deposition may also be offered at trial if certain special circumstances exist, such as where a deponent is unavailable to testify at trial because of death or disability, or the deponent resides more than 150 miles from the place of the trial. CCP § 2025.620.

e. *Compare Federal Procedure*

FRCP 30, 31, 32 and 45 govern depositions of parties and nonparties. Each side in a federal action is limited to ten depositions per side, unless the court orders otherwise. FRCP 30(a)(2)(A)(i). In addition, in the absence of a court order, each deposition is limited to one day consisting of seven hours. FRCP 30(d)(1).

f. Illustration

Puma sued her former employer, Dunne Co., in Yuba County Superior Court for wrongful termination from her job in Olivehurst. Puma's counsel took the deposition of Ace, a manager of Dunne Co. Puma's lawyer asked Ace questions about Puma's supervisor and his working relationship with other female employees. Ace's attorney instructed Ace not to answer on the ground that the information sought was irrelevant. The information was relevant to the subject matter of the action. Moreover, a relevance objection during the discovery phase is generally not a valid ground for instructing a deponent not to answer a question. A relevance objection is not waived even if it is not raised at the deposition. Stewart v. Colonial Western Agency, 87 Cal.App.4th 1006, 105 Cal.Rptr.2d 115 (2001).

5. Physical and Mental Examinations

Any party may take a physical or mental examination of a party or party-affiliate whose physical or mental condition is "in controversy" in the action. CCP § 2032.020. A party's condition is in controversy if that party's pleadings allege physical or emotional injuries, or if discovery reveals that a party's physical or mental condition is relevant.

a. Physical Examination of Plaintiff by Demand

Assuming that the "in controversy" requirement is met, a defendant (or cross-defendant) is entitled to take one physical examination of the plaintiff (or cross-complainant) by serving a demand. No court order is required. CCP § 2032.220.

1) Limitations on Demand

The examination must be performed by a licensed physician or other licensed health care practitioner. CCP § 2032.020(b). It may not involve painful, protracted or intrusive tests. The examination must take place within 75 miles of the examinee's residence. CCP § 2032.220(a).

2) Response to Demand

a) Timing of Response

A written response must be served within 20 days after service of the demand. CCP § 2032.230(b). An untimely response waives all objections to the demand. CCP § 2032.240.

b) Content of Response

The responding party may respond as follows:

- agreement to comply in full;
- agreement to comply upon specified conditions; or
- refusal to comply for reasons stated in response.

CCP § 2032.230. There is no requirement that the response be verified.

b. Physical Examination by Court Order

Any additional physical examinations of a plaintiff beyond the one permitted on demand, and any physical examinations of a person other than the plaintiff, require leave of court on a showing of good cause. CCP § 2032.310. The examination may not take place more than 75 miles from the examinee's residence, unless the court finds good cause and orders the moving party to make advance payment of reasonable travel expenses. CCP § 2032.320(e).

c. Mental Examination

A mental examination requires a court order. CCP § 2032.310. The moving party must show that the potential examinee's mental condition is in controversy and must establish good cause for the mental examination. A party might be able to avoid a mental examination by stipulating that: (1) no claim is being made for mental or emotional injuries beyond those usually associated with the physical injuries claimed; and (2) no expert testimony will be offered at trial to support a claim for damages for this usual mental or emotional distress. CCP § 2032.320.

d. Presence of Attorney

An examinee has the right to have her attorney (and a court reporter) present during any portion of a physical examination. CCP § 2032.510. During a mental examination, attorneys generally do not attend, as their presence might interfere with the rapport between the examiner and examinee. However, the court has discretion to permit the presence of the examinee's attorney. Vinson v. Superior Court, 43 Cal.3d 833, 239 Cal.Rptr. 292, 740 P.2d 404 (1987). In addition, the examinee has the right to audio record the mental examination in its entirety. CCP § 2032.530.

e. *Compare Federal Procedure*

FRCP 35 permits physical and mental examinations of parties whose condition is in controversy in the action. FRCP 35(a) requires leave of court for all examinations (physical and mental), a distinction from California's practice of allowing one physical examination of the plaintiff on demand if her physical condition is in controversy. An examinee in a federal action is not entitled to have an attorney present during any examination; a court may allow the attorney to be present only for good cause. FRCP 26(c)(1)(E).

f. Illustration

Pryce sued her dentist, Dr. Doyle, in Nevada County Superior Court for malpractice arising from brain damage allegedly caused by the anesthesia Dr. Doyle used during a root canal. Pryce suffered serious effects of the anesthesia, requiring hospitalization in Truckee. Pryce alleges that before the dental procedure, she had above-average intelligence, but after the procedure, she has diminished intelligence, memory loss and reduced functioning. Dr. Doyle's position is that these effects have psychological roots and are not the result of organic brain damage from the anesthesia. Dr. Doyle served a demand for a physical examination of Pryce with a neurologist, who concluded that her condition was not a result of brain damage. Dr. Doyle then requested, and the court ordered, that Pryce undergo a mental examination with a neuropsychologist. Although the neuropsychologist expressed a similar opinion to that of the neurologist, the findings were inconclusive. Both the neurologist and the neuropsychologist recommended that Pryce undergo a full psychiatric evaluation. Dr. Doyle then requested that the court order a second mental examination, this time with a psychiatrist. Pryce objected, arguing that the discovery statutes authorize only one mental examination. However, the court may order additional mental examinations if there is a sufficient showing of good cause. CCP § 2032.320(a). There is no statutory limit on the number of mental examinations. Shapira v. Superior Court, 224 Cal.App.3d 1249, 274 Cal.Rptr. 516 (1990).

6. Expert Witness Discovery

Expert witness testimony is a common feature of civil trials. Pretrial exchange of expert witness information allows parties to conduct depositions in order to prepare to present or challenge expert testimony during trial. Parties may obtain discovery regarding those experts who have been retained to provide an expert opinion at trial. The opinions and work product of experts hired solely as consultants who will not testify at trial are not subject to discovery.

a. Exchange of Expert Witness Information

1) Procedure for Demand

Any party may serve on another party a written demand for exchange of expert witness lists. Service of the demand by one party obligates all others to make a simultaneous exchange. CCP § 2034.260(a). The demand must be in writing and must specify the date for the exchange of expert witness lists and any other materials included in the demand (such as expert witness declarations and discoverable writings of experts). CCP § 2034.230.

2) **Timing of Demand and Exchange**

Any party may make a demand on another party for disclosure of expert witnesses any time after the setting of the initial trial date. The deadline for the demand is ten days after the initial trial date has been set, or 70 days before the initial trial date, whichever is later. CCP § 2034.220. Any disclosed expert may be deposed before trial, so that all parties may better learn the nature of the expert's testimony. CCP § 2034.410. The simultaneous exchange of the expert witness information requested in the demand must take place 50 days before the initial date set for trial, or 20 days after service of the demand, whichever is earlier (unless the court orders a different date). CCP § 2034.230.

3) **Contents of Demand**

a) **Information and Documents**

A party may demand that the exchange include the name and address of any person whose expert witness testimony is expected to be offered at trial. The demand may also request the discoverable reports and other writings of an expert for whom an expert witness declaration must be served. CCP § 2034.210.

b) **Expert Witness Declaration**

If a designated expert is a party or an employee of a party, or has been retained for the purpose of forming and stating an opinion at trial, the designation of that witness must include the submission of an expert witness declaration signed by the attorney for the party designating that expert. CCP § 2034.210(b). The declaration must include: (1) a statement of qualifications; (2) a statement of the general substance of the witness's expected testimony; and (3) a representation that the witness is sufficiently familiar with the pending action to submit to a deposition concerning his expected trial testimony. CCP § 2034.260.

b. Supplementing or Augmenting Expert Witness List

If an opponent's expert witness list states that the opponent intends to offer expert testimony at trial on a subject not addressed in other parties' lists, the other parties may supplement their lists with the names of witnesses whose expert opinion will be offered on those previously omitted subjects. CCP § 2034.280. A party may move the court to augment an expert witness list to add a subsequently retained expert, or to amend an expert witness declaration regarding the substance of the testimony a previously designated expert is expected to give. CCP § 2034.610.

c. Failure to Comply with Exchange Requirements

With some exceptions, the trial court will exclude the testimony of an expert witness if the party offering that testimony has unreasonably failed to list that witness as an expert, submit an expert witness declaration when one was required, produce requested discoverable writings of the expert, or make the expert available for deposition. CCP § 2034.300. In addition, if the substance of an expert's testimony is not disclosed in the expert witness declaration, and the expert broaches the previously undisclosed subject at trial, the testimony of that witness may be excluded. Bonds v. Roy, 20 Cal.4th 140, 83 Cal.Rptr.2d 289, 973 P.2d 66 (1999).

d. Conflict of Interest

A conflict of interest may arise when an expert has been consulted (but not retained for trial) by one party, is then dismissed, and is later hired by the opposing party to offer an opinion at trial. The expert may be disqualified if he actually possesses confidential information obtained during the prior consultation. Potential access to confidential information is not sufficient to justify disqualification. Western Digital Corp. v. Superior Court, 60 Cal.App.4th 1471, 71 Cal.Rptr.2d 179 (1998).

e. *Compare Federal Procedure*

In contrast to California, FRCP 26(a)(2) requires a party to automatically disclose, without formal demand, those expert witnesses who may testify at trial. The timing of the disclosure is ordinarily directed by the court. In the absence of court instruction or party stipulation, the federal rules require disclosure at least 90 days before trial. FRCP 26(a)(2)(C). Federal procedure also requires the equivalent of an expert witness declaration from a witness retained to provide expert testimony, in the form of a written report, signed by the witness, which must include: (1) a complete statement of all opinions and the basis for those opinions; (2) the data considered; (3) any exhibits that will be used to support the opinions; (4) the qualifications of the witness; (5) the compensation paid to the witness, and (6) a list of any other cases the witness has testified in over the last four years. FRCP 26(a)(2)(B). A party may depose a "person identified as an expert whose opinions may be presented at trial" but not those experts who are not expected to testify at trial. FRCP 26(b)(4).

f. Illustration

Patricia brought a medical malpractice claim in Contra Costa County Superior Court against Dr. Dingle for injuries. Dr. Dingle allegedly negligently severed a nerve in Patricia's arm during a procedure performed at a hospital in Richmond. Both parties exchanged expert witness declarations. Dr. Dingle designated Dr. Buddy as an expert witness. Dr. Buddy's expert witness declaration stated that he would testify about the extent of Patricia's damages. On the last day of trial, Dr. Dingle's attorney sought to elicit testimony from Dr. Buddy about the applicable standard of care. Any such testimony should not be allowed because it would expand the general substance of the testimony noted in Dr. Buddy's declaration. Although Dr. Buddy's expert witness declaration could have been amended earlier to include the expanded testimony, it was too late at trial to seek an amendment. Bonds v. Roy, 20 Cal.4th 140, 83 Cal.Rptr.2d 289, 973 P.2d 66 (1999).

7. Electronic Discovery

In recognition of the usefulness of technology in conducting discovery, particularly in complex cases, the California Legislature adopted procedures permitting the use of technology to supplement written discovery. CCP §§ 2017.710 et seq.

a. Court Order

Electronic discovery must be authorized by court order and will be permitted only if it does not cause an undue burden or expense to that party's opponent. CCP § 2017.730. In some cases, the court may order the propounding party to pay the cost of production of electronic data compilations. CCP § 2031.280(b); Toshiba America Electronic Components, Inc. v. Superior Court, 124 Cal.App.4th 762, 21 Cal.Rptr.3d 532 (2004).

b. *Compare Federal Procedure*

The FRCP include several provisions governing electronic discovery. For example, parties must include issues related to discovery of electronically stored information in a discovery plan submitted to the court during a scheduling conference. FRCP 26(f)(3)(C). Parties are not required to provide electronic information not reasonably accessible to the responding party because of undue burden or expense, unless ordered otherwise by the court. FRCP 26(b)(2)(B). Although the cost of discovery is ordinarily borne by the responding party, the court may order costs to be shifted to the party propounding requests for electronic data that is not reasonably accessible. Zubulake v. UBS Warburg LLC, 217 F.R.D. 309 (S.D.N.Y. 2003).

c. Illustration

Podtech Co. sued Digitech, Inc. in San Mateo County Superior Court for unfair competition and misappropriation of trade secrets. Podtech demanded hard copies of all the internal e-mails and other electronically stored documents Digitech had sent or produced in the month of July. The e-mails are stored on back-up tapes. Extracting the requested information would be time-consuming and technically challenging. The cost of processing the tapes and producing the information is $2 million. Although the general rule, under both California and federal law, is that the responding party bears the cost of producing discovery, CCP § 2031.280 reflects legislative concern for fairness by shifting the cost of translating data compilations into usable form to the propounding party. In light of this cost-shifting, the court must determine the reasonable expense that Podtech must pay. Toshiba America Electronic Components, Inc. v. Superior Court, 124 Cal.App.4th 762, 21 Cal.Rptr.3d 532 (2004).

8. Supplemental (Continuing) Discovery

a. No Obligation to Automatically Supplement

A California litigant is not required to automatically update any previous discovery responses that were true and correct when served. A party may propound a single supplemental interrogatory to obtain information acquired after the original interrogatory responses were served. The supplemental interrogatory may be served twice before the initial setting of the trial date, and once after the initial setting of the trial date. CCP § 2030.070.

b. *Compare Federal Procedure*

In marked contrast to California procedure, a federal litigant has an affirmative duty to update her disclosures and discovery responses (interrogatories, document requests, or requests for admission) when new information is acquired and is not known to the other party. FRCP 26(e).

c. Illustration

Parker sued his employer Diechem Corp. in Placer County Superior Court, alleging that it knowingly exposed Parker to asbestos in Roseville. Diechem propounded an interrogatory asking Parker to identify any persons who have knowledge of his work with Diechem. Parker responded that he did not know of anyone. Subsequently, Diechem brought a summary judgment motion against Parker. In response, Parker included the declaration of Cal, whom Parker had later recalled had worked with him at Diechem. Diechem objected to the declaration and sought to have it excluded on the ground that Parker should have supplemented his interrogatory answer when Cal's identity became known. However, under CCP §§ 2030.290 and 2030.300, Parker had no duty to supplement his interrogatory answer with the new information. As his initial responses were not willfully false, he was under no obligation to amend his answers in the absence of a supplemental interrogatory from Diechem. Therefore, the declaration may be used in the summary judgment motion. Biles v. Exxon Mobil Corp., 124 Cal.App.4th 1315, 22 Cal.Rptr.3d 282 (2004).

C. Limited Civil Cases

The use of some of the discovery tools discussed in section III(B), above, is curtailed in limited civil cases. Only one oral or written deposition is allowed, and each party is permitted to use a combined total of up to 35 interrogatories, requests for admission and demands for inspection against each adverse party. CCP §§ 94–95. However, a plaintiff in a limited civil case may obtain additional information by serving a case questionnaire on the defendant, requesting basic information such as identity of witnesses, relevant documents, and insurance coverage. If the plaintiff serves the defendant with a completed questionnaire along with the complaint, the defendant must serve a completed questionnaire with the answer. CCP § 93.

D. International Discovery

Document discovery and depositions in international litigation are subject to special procedures.

1. Discovery in Actions Pending in Another Nation or State

A party in a California action may take the deposition of another party or a nonparty in a foreign country. CCP § 2027.010. A deposition may be taken in California for an action pending in another country or state under the procedures set out in CCP § 2029.010.

2. Hague Evidence Convention on Taking Evidence Abroad in Civil or Commercial Matters

In addition to other means of obtaining discovery, a signatory to the Hague Evidence Convention in one country may send letters of request to a signatory in another country requesting a deposition and/or documents of a witness in the second country.

3. *Compare Federal Procedure*

Federal courts may choose to utilize the discovery procedures under the Hague Evidence Convention. If the court does not require these procedures, the FRCP authorizes discovery involving persons outside the United States. For example, FRCP 28(b) governs the taking of depositions in foreign countries in several instances, such as where there is an underlying treaty or convention or a letter of request.

IV. JUDICIAL OVERSIGHT OF DISCOVERY

A. Role of Court in Discovery

Although California discovery is intended to be self-executing, parties may need the assistance or intervention of the court. In some cases, a court order is required to undertake discovery. (See, e.g., Mental Examinations, section III(B)(5), above.) In others, discussed below, the court may be asked by a party to step into a discovery dispute and issue orders to compel compliance with the discovery statutes or to prevent or address misuse of the discovery process.

B. Orders Compelling Discovery

1. Compel Response to Discovery

If a party does not serve a timely written response to a discovery request, or serves a timely but unverified response, the propounding party may move the court for an order compelling a response. All objections to that discovery are deemed waived, unless the responding party requests relief from the waiver by filing a response in substantial compliance with the statutory requirements. See, e.g., CCP §§ 2030.290, 2031.300.

2. Compel Further Response to Discovery

a. Procedure

If the responding party provides incomplete, evasive or otherwise improper written responses to discovery, or responds with unfounded objections, the propounding party may bring a motion to compel a further response. See, e.g., CCP §§ 2030.300, 2031.310. For most motions, the moving party must file a separate statement, which places all of the disputed discovery requests, answers, objections, and basis for the moving party's position in one document. CRC 3.1020. The motion must be brought within 45 days of the challenged discovery response. See, e.g., CCP §§ 2030.300, 2031.310(c). Generally, a motion to compel a further response will be granted if the moving party can show good cause for the discovery sought.

b. Meet and Confer

The parties to a motion to compel a further response must "meet and confer" about each matter in dispute before the moving party files the motion. The moving party must file a declaration showing that the parties made "a reasonable and good faith attempt at an informal resolution of each issue presented by the motion." CCP § 2016.040.

3. Compel Compliance with Discovery Order

If a party fails to obey a court order compelling a response to discovery, the court may impose sanctions for noncompliance. See, e.g., CCP §§ 2030.300(e), 2032.320(c), 2033.290(e).

4. *Compare Federal Procedure*

Federal discovery motions are procedurally similar to those under California law. One distinction is that, unlike the California motions to compel further responses, which must be brought within the statutory time limit, federal motions must be brought only within a reasonable time. FRCP 37(a).

5. Illustration

Piper sued Dr. Devin in Modoc County Superior Court for the wrongful death of Piper's mother, who died while undergoing surgery. Piper served Dr. Devin with interrogatories in an attempt to discover information about the cause of death and the events leading up to the death. Dr. Devin's responses stated that she did not have sufficient information to answer the interrogatories concerning cause of death. After attempting to resolve the issue, Piper filed a motion to compel further responses. However, Dr. Devin's answers are proper, and Piper is not entitled to further responses. Beyond consulting readily available information, Dr. Devin was not required to conduct an investigation in order to obtain information to respond to the interrogatories. Holguin v. Superior Court, 22 Cal.App.3d 812, 99 Cal.Rptr. 653 (1972).

C. Protective Orders

1. When Protective Order Available

The court may enter a protective order under several discovery statutes. One example is where the burden, expense or intrusiveness of the discovery outweighs the likelihood that the discovery sought will lead to admissible evidence. CCP § 2017.020. Another is where the discovery sought is cumulative, duplicative or unduly burdensome or expensive, or is obtainable from another source. CCP § 2019.030. In addition, many of the statutes authorizing the various methods of discovery contain specific provisions for protective orders to protect against annoyance, harassment or oppression. See, e.g., CCP § 2025.420 (depositions); CCP § 2030.090 (interrogatories); CCP § 2031.060 (inspection demands); CCP § 2033.080 (requests for admission). Before moving for a protective order, the moving party must meet and confer with the opposing party.

2. *Compare Federal Procedure*

FRCP 26(c)(1) authorizes a court to issue protective orders to protect "a party or person from annoyance, embarrassment, oppression, or undue burden or expense." The rule lists several forms of protective orders, which may be issued on a showing of good cause.

3. Illustration

Giant Co., a chemical manufacturer, hired contractors to work with local businesses near Visalia to clean up dangerous residue generated by Giant and buried in landfill deposits years before. O, an employee of Giant, reported to a Giant manager that some of the contractors were being paid for services they were not actually providing. Giant filed suit in Tulare County Superior Court against these contractors for breach of contract and fraud. At his deposition, the Giant manager refused to disclose O's identity. One of the defendant contractors moved to compel the manager to reveal O's identity. In response, O filed a sealed declaration stating that his life had been threatened because he had been a whistleblower, and he sought a protective order. The court will prohibit disclosure of O's identity. CCP § 2025.420(b)(9) permits a protective order requiring that "certain matters not be inquired into." The court must balance O's interests against the contractors' need for the information. In the absence of a compelling reason for disclosure, the protective order will be issued because disclosure could jeopardize O's safety. John Z. v. Superior Court, 1 Cal.App.4th 789, 2 Cal.Rptr.2d 556 (1991).

D. Sanctions

1. Availability of Sanctions

The court may sanction a party who misuses the discovery process. Misuse includes: failing to respond; providing evasive responses; raising unmeritorious objections; making or opposing (without substantial justification) a motion to compel discovery; failing to meet and confer to informally resolve a discovery dispute; and disobeying a court order to provide discovery. See CCP § 2023.010, and the individual statutes governing the different methods of discovery. Sanctions may be imposed on a party, its attorney, or both. Notice to all parties is required before any sanctions may be imposed.

2. Purpose of Sanctions

Discovery sanctions in California are meant to compel disclosure and to compensate for enforcement of the discovery statutes. Discovery sanctions are not intended to create a reward or windfall, but rather to place the non-sanctioned party in the same position he otherwise would have occupied but for the misuse of the discovery process.

3. Types of Sanctions

CCP § 2023.030 sets out an escalating series of sanctions, which may be imposed for misuse of the discovery process:

- Monetary: Any misuse of the discovery process "shall" result in a monetary sanction, unless the party subject to sanctions acted with "substantial justification" or monetary sanctions would be "unjust." Monetary sanctions are the most common form of discovery sanctions, typically covering the attorney's fees and costs incurred in compelling further responses.

- Issue: If a monetary sanction is ineffective, or a party has failed to comply with an order compelling further responses, the court may impose an issue sanction. This sanction designates certain facts as established.

- Evidence: If a party has engaged in severe misconduct, the court may order an evidentiary sanction, which precludes the sanctioned party from introducing certain matters into evidence.

- Terminating: Also known as the "doomsday" sanction, a terminating sanction may apply to egregious misconduct and can include striking all or part of the pleadings, staying further proceedings, dismissing the action, or rendering a default judgment.

- Contempt: The court may issue a contempt sanction in which the misuse of the discovery process is treated as a contempt of court.

4. *Compare Federal Procedure*

FRCP 37(b)–(f) sets out numerous federal sanctions available for many types of discovery misconduct. Federal discovery sanctions are largely the same as California's escalating set of sanctions. However, federal discovery sanctions can be more punitive in nature. Federal judges have greater leeway to impose discovery sanctions with the objective of deterring the misuse of discovery.

5. Illustration

Polo filed a personal injury claim against Duffy in Glenn County Superior Court. Polo designated Dr. Cave as an expert witness. Duffy attempted to set up Dr. Cave's deposition, but Dr. Cave would not make himself available. The trial court granted Duffy's motion to compel Dr. Cave's attendance, but Dr. Cave continued to postpone and delay the deposition. He: (1) insisted that the date of the deposition be changed seven times to accommodate his schedule, thus delaying the deposition for six months; (2) required that the deposition be conducted after business hours; and (3) when the parties had finally agreed on a deposition date, walked out in the middle of a deposition session because he had to attend a personal meeting. Duffy moved for an order excluding Dr. Cave's testimony at trial based on his uncooperative behavior. The court is authorized to issue this evidence sanction under CCP §§ 2023.010(d) and 2023.030(c). Waicis v. Superior Court, 226 Cal.App.3d 283, 276 Cal.Rptr. 45 (1990).

E. Special Punitive Damages Discovery

1. Court Order for Financial Condition Discovery

To prevail on a claim for punitive damages, a plaintiff must establish, by clear and convincing evidence, "oppression, fraud, or malice." Cal. Civ. Code § 3294(a). Discovery of a defendant's financial condition is often necessary to make this showing. It aids in the determination of an amount of punitive damages sufficient to punish the defendant and deter future misconduct. Financial condition discovery is permitted only by court order under Cal. Civ. Code § 3295(c). The court will order such discovery only after it weighs the evidence presented by both parties and makes a determination that the plaintiff is "very likely to prevail on his claim for punitive damages." Jabro v. Superior Court, 95 Cal.App.4th 754, 115 Cal.Rptr.2d 843 (2002).

2. *Compare Federal Procedure*

In federal lawsuits seeking punitive damages, discovery of the financial condition of a defendant is normally permitted under the broad scope of discovery articulated in FRCP 26(b)(1). There is no special order or showing required, although the defendant may seek a protective order under FRCP 26(c)(1).

3. Illustration

Pax was an investor in a limited partnership that owned several movie theaters near Fresno. Pax filed suit in Fresno County Superior Court against the general partner, Dov, for mismanagement of funds. Pax included a claim for punitive damages in his complaint. Pax served a document request on Dov seeking detailed financial information about Dov and the partnership. When Dov refused to provide it, Pax moved to compel production. Dov opposed the motion on the ground that the information was protected under Cal. Civ. Code § 3295. Section 3295 significantly limits a plaintiff's access to financial information for the purpose of a punitive damages claim. However, if the financial discovery is fundamentally related to the cause of action, and the plaintiff is likely to prevail on the merits, financial condition discovery will be permitted. Pax's claims against Dov arise out of Dov's alleged misappropriation of funds, and his financial records are key to Pax's proof. Rawnsley v. Superior Court, 183 Cal.App.3d 86, 227 Cal.Rptr. 806 (1986).

F. Completion of Discovery

1. Discovery Cut-Off

Discovery must be completed on or before 30 days before the initial trial date set in an action. Motions regarding discovery must be heard on or before 15 days before the initial trial date. CCP § 2024.020(a). A continuance or postponement of the trial date does not extend the time for completing discovery, unless the court makes an order reopening discovery. CCP § 2024.020(b). In cases involving discovery following a mistrial, an order granting a new trial, or a remand for a retrial following a reversal on appeal, discovery is reopened and a new completion date is set based on the initial date of the new trial. Fairmont Insurance Co. v. Superior Court, 22 Cal.4th 245, 92 Cal.Rptr.2d 70, 991 P.2d 156 (2000).

2. *Compare Federal Procedure*

The district court sets the time for the completion of discovery as part of its scheduling order under FRCP 16(b)(3)(A). The rule does not define "completion of discovery," but district court local rules or the court's case management order may provide more specific guidance. On a showing of good cause, a party may seek an order from the court to extend the discovery cut-off date. FRCP 16(b).

3. Illustration

Petula sued Duke for damages from a fire that Duke allegedly set on Petula's property in San Bernardino. Petula served Duke with a document demand. Duke assured Petula that he would serve a timely response, but he did not do so. Duke cancelled his deposition twice, and when he finally appeared, he did not bring the requested documents. He promised to send them, but he never did. One day before the discovery cut-off date for bringing discovery motions, Petula filed a motion to compel production and for sanctions. Duke objected to the motion on the ground that it was untimely. The court will grant the motion. Duke gave Petula several false assurances that he would produce the requested documents. He is thus equitably estopped from relying on the discovery cut-off date. Sears, Roebuck & Co. v. National Union Fire Insurance Co., 131 Cal.App.4th 1342, 32 Cal.Rptr.3d 717 (2005).

CHAPTER 4

SAMPLE EXAM QUESTIONS

OBJECTIVE QUESTIONS

The questions in this section are based on the following hypothetical:

While shopping at a mall in Hollister, Adam slipped on the floor, fell, and broke his ankle. He realized that someone had spilled a drink in the spot where he slipped. After consulting with an attorney, Adam filed suit in San Benito County Superior Court against the shopping mall's owner, Super Shop, Inc.

---

(1) Adam's attorney hired an expert who went to the mall during ordinary business hours and conducted some experiments on the slipperiness of the floor. Super Shop's attorney contends that the experiments do not constitute permissible discovery. What result?

a. The discovery is improper because the attorney was required to serve a statutorily-authorized discovery request on Super Shop;

b. The discovery is improper unless the expert obtained the permission of Super Shop before he arrived at the mall to conduct his experiment;

c. The discovery is proper as long as the expert who conducted the experiment does not testify at the trial;

d. The discovery is proper because parties are permitted to conduct lawful, informal discovery without the necessity of a discovery request.

(2) True or False: The notes Adam's attorney took reflecting his thoughts about the expert's conclusions about the floor experiment are discoverable by Super Shop if the court determines that denial of discovery will unfairly prejudice Super Shop in the preparation of its defense.

(3) Adam wishes to take the deposition of Super Shop, and of a witness (not a party to the lawsuit) who observed Adam's fall. Which of the following is true about these depositions:

a. Each deposition that Adam wishes to take may not be lengthier than seven hours;

b. Adam may notice the deposition of Super Shop, but he must serve a deposition subpoena on the person who witnessed the fall;

c. Adam may use the deposition transcripts of both deponents at trial for impeachment purposes only;

d. All objections to questions Adam's attorney asks at the two depositions are waived at trial unless raised on the record at the deposition.

(4) True or False: If the trial court orders a new trial in Adam's action, no further discovery is permitted because discovery must have been completed at least 30 days before the date initially set for trial.

(5) Super Shop has served Adam with a set of 40 inspection demands for documents. Adam served a timely response signed by Adam's attorney containing only objections to all of the document demands. Super Shop responded by immediately filing a motion to compel further responses to the inspection demands, and for sanctions. What result?

a. The motion should be denied because Super Shop's motion does not show that Super Shop met and conferred with Adam to attempt to resolve the discovery dispute before filing the motion;

b. The motion should be granted because Adam did not verify the response;

c. Even if the motion to compel is granted, the motion for sanctions should be denied because sanctions are proper only if Adam fails to comply with the order compelling further responses;

d. The motion should be denied because Super Shop propounded a number of inspection demands in excess of the statutory limit and did not include a declaration for additional discovery.

(6) True or False: If Adam seeks electronic discovery from Super Shop, the court may exercise its discretion to shift to Adam the cost of providing the electronic discovery.

(7) True or False: As in federal practice, Adam may propound no more than 35 requests for admission on Super Shop.

(8) If Adam fails to respond to Super Shop's interrogatories in a timely manner:

a. Adam waives any objections to the interrogatories;

b. Adam waives any right to exercise the option to produce writings;

c. Adam is subject to an evidence sanction unless he can show good cause for the failure to respond on time;

d. Both a and b.

(9) True or False: In California, it is not a valid objection to Super Shop's interrogatories for Adam to respond that the matter to be discovered is not admissible evidence.

(10) After Adam has responded to Super Shop's interrogatories, Super Shop may later obtain supplemental/updated information from Adam in the following way:

a. Adam is obligated to update the information in his original responses without a formal request from Super Shop;

b. Super Shop may propound a supplemental interrogatory to Adam as of right twice before the setting of the initial trial date, and once after the trial date is set;

c. Super Shop may propound a supplemental interrogatory to Adam only if the court grants leave to do so on a showing of good cause;

d. The discovery statutes do not give Super Shop the right to request that Adam update his original responses, and they do not obligate Adam to automatically update his responses.

(11) True or False: Any witness who will provide expert testimony for Adam at trial must submit an expert witness declaration to Super Shop.

(12) Super Shop wishes to obtain an initial physical examination of Adam. Super Shop:

a. Must obtain an order from the court after establishing good cause for the examination;

b. Must ensure that only a licensed physician conducts the examination;

c. May demand that Adam submit to the examination without leave of court provided the examination is not painful, protracted or intrusive and occurs within 75 miles of Adam's home;

d. Must agree to let a medical professional of Adam's choosing participate in conducting the examination.

(13) Assume that Super Shop contends that Adam's mental condition is in controversy in the action. Adam has moved for a protective order to prevent Super Shop from inquiring into his mental condition in any deposition, based on Adam's right to privacy. The objection:

a. Will require the court to balance Adam's privacy interest against Super Shop's interest in disclosure;

b. Will be upheld for even a minimal invasion of privacy as long as Adam has a legitimate privacy interest and a reasonable expectation of privacy;

c. Will not be upheld because privacy is not a proper ground to limit discovery in California;

d. Serves as an absolute protection against disclosure.

(14) True or False: The court may permit Adam's attorney to be present during any mental examination conducted on Adam.

Answers to Objective Questions

(1) **d.** Parties are permitted to conduct lawful informal discovery. The mall is open to the public, and the expert was not required to seek permission or make a formal discovery request before conducting his investigation.

(2) **False**. The notes of Adam's attorney are subject to absolute work product protection. The court would examine the prejudice to Super Shop only for materials subject to qualified protection. CCP § 2018.030.

(3) **b.** A deposition notice is used for a deposition of a party (corporate or individual), but a subpoena is issued to compel a nonparty to attend a deposition.

(4) **False**. The general discovery cut-off rule is 30 days before the initial trial date. CCP § 2024.020. However, the court may set a new cut-off date if a new trial is ordered. CCP § 2024.050(a).

(5) **a.** A motion to compel a further response to an inspection demand must be accompanied by a "meet and confer" declaration. CCP §§ 2031.310(b)(2); 2016.040. Adam need not verify a response containing only objections; it is sufficient that the response is signed by the attorney. Monetary sanctions are mandatory under CCP § 2031.310(d) if Super Shop's motion is granted, unless the court finds that Adam acted with substantial justification in opposing the motion or if the imposition of a sanction is unjust. There is no limit on the number of inspection demands that may be served.

(6) **True**. Although the expense of providing electronic discovery is usually borne by the responding party, the court has discretion to shift the cost to the propounding party. CCP § 2031.280(b).

(7) **False**. There is no numerical limit for requests for admission in the federal system. California permits 35 requests for admission concerning the truth of matters, but an unlimited number of requests concerning the genuineness of documents. CCP § 2033.030(a).

(8) **d.** Both a and b are correct. An untimely response waives all objections to the interrogatories (including privilege and work product protection) and the right to produce writings as permitted under CCP § 2030.230. See CCP § 2030.290.

(9) **True**. A matter need not be admissible evidence in order to be discoverable. It is sufficient that the discovery request be reasonably calculated to lead to the discovery of admissible evidence. CCP § 2017.010.

(10) **b.** Adam must update his interrogatory responses only if Super Shop serves one or more proper and timely supplemental interrogatories on him. CCP § 2030.070.

(11) **False**. An expert witness declaration is required only for a designated expert who is a party or employee of a party, or has been retained by a party for the purpose of expressing an expert opinion. CCP §§ 2034.210(b), 2034.260. Adam's treating physician, for example, would not require an expert witness declaration because, although he might provide an expert opinion at trial, he was retained to treat Adam's injuries and not as an expert witness.

(12) **c.** Because Adam is seeking recovery for personal injuries, Super Shop may demand one physical examination of him by a licensed health care practitioner or physician without leave of court as long as the two requirements are met. CCP § 2032.220.

(13) **a.** An objection to discovery based on privacy requires the court to balance the rights and interests of the parties.

(14) **True**. The court has discretion to permit or prohibit Adam's attorney from attending the mental examination. Even if the court does not permit the attorney's attendance, Adam still has the right to audio-record the examination. CCP § 2032.530.

ESSAY QUESTION

James hired XYZ Construction, Inc. (XYZ) to remodel his cabin in Big Bear Lake, California. James, who lived 180 miles away in Bakersfield, did not supervise the construction on a day-to-day basis. He did, however, go to Big Bear Lake every other weekend to check on XYZ's progress. During one of his trips, James began to suspect XYZ of shoddy construction.

Six months later, XYZ completed the construction job. Shortly after moving his belongings into the house, James discovered that his suspicions were correct—XYZ had significantly cut corners during the construction. James consulted Lars, a construction defect lawyer, who recommended that James sue XYZ. James filed a negligence and breach of contract lawsuit against XYZ in Kern County Superior Court.

Lars has utilized a variety of discovery tools to obtain information from XYZ. First, he sent a set of 22 form interrogatories and 31 special interrogatories (several of which had subparts and compound questions) to XYZ. Second, he propounded 15 inspection demands for production of documents, including several documents Lars believed were in the possession of XYZ's attorneys regarding their investigation of the Big Bear Lake job site. Finally, Lars noticed 21 depositions, including the depositions of XYZ and numerous independent subcontractors. In the notice to XYZ, Lars specifically requested that the owner/CEO of XYZ and the supervisor of the Big Bear Lake construction job appear for depositions on behalf of the company.

Lars heard "through the grapevine" that the supervisor had recently sustained a serious back injury, was in the middle of an ugly divorce, and had recently started taking medication for depression. As a result, Lars served a demand for physical and mental examinations of the XYZ supervisor. Lars requested that the examinations take place in Bakersfield where suitable examiners are available, even though the supervisor lives in Big Bear Lake.

XYZ has failed to respond to any of the interrogatories, document demands, deposition notices, and examination demands.

Lars has hired two construction defect experts to testify at trial about the construction plans, the feasibility of those plans, and the ways in which XYZ failed to comply with the plans.

You are an associate in Lars' office. Lars has asked to you to analyze the following issues:

(1) any objections XYZ might have to James' discovery requests;

(2) how to compel XYZ to respond to James' requests, and the possibility of obtaining sanctions against XYZ for its failure to respond; and

(3) James' obligation to provide information to XYZ about his expert witnesses.

<u>ESSAY ANSWER</u>

(1) <u>XYZ's Objections</u>

- Interrogatories:
  - 31 special interrogatories: may violate limit of 35 because subparts and compound questions count as additional interrogatories. If there are more than 35, XYZ is required to answer only the first 35.

    - If the special interrogatories number more than 35, James should have served a Declaration for Additional Discovery with the interrogatories.

    - James may serve an unlimited number of form interrogatories.

- Document demands:

    - There is no limit to the number of document demands James may serve, so the 15 demands are not objectionable for that reason. If the requests are unduly burdensome or expensive, XYZ may move for a protective order.

    - Documents in the possession of XYZ's attorneys regarding their investigation may be protected by the work product doctrine or the attorney-client privilege.

- Depositions:

    - XYZ might object to the notice of the deposition of XYZ. James must identify the topics of the deposition of XYZ, and the company then designates the person(s) most knowledgeable to testify on the areas described in the notice. James may also directly notice the depositions of XYZ's officers and managers.

    - There is no limit on the number of depositions James may take (as compared to the limit of ten under the FRCP), unless XYZ files a motion for protective order to limit the number.

- Physical and mental examinations:

    - James may not demand examinations of the supervisor. A defendant is entitled to one physical examination of a plaintiff whose physical condition is "in controversy" in the action. Here, James is not entitled to demand a physical examination of an employee of the defendant. Also, the supervisor has not put his physical condition in controversy, so the court will not grant such a request.

    - The court will not order a mental examination of the supervisor because his mental condition is not in controversy.

    - If the examinations are ordered, they must take place within 75 miles of the supervisor's residence, or the court must find good cause for the travel and order James to pay the supervisor in advance for reasonable travel expenses. CCP § 2032.320(e).

(2) Motion to Compel Response and for Sanctions

- There is no meet and confer requirement for a motion to compel a response to discovery. (A motion to compel a further response requires the moving party to submit a meet and confer declaration with the motion.)

- An untimely response to James' discovery requests waives any objections XYZ has to the discovery, unless the court relieves XYZ of its waiver.

- The court must award monetary sanctions against the party who unsuccessfully made or opposed the motion to compel, unless that party acted with substantial justification or the sanction is otherwise unjust.

(3) Expert Witness Discovery

- James has no obligation to provide information about James' expert witnesses unless XYZ or James demands that all parties simultaneously exchange expert trial witness information.

  - If an exchange demand is made, all parties must provide the names and addresses of the testifying experts.

  - For each expert who is a party or employee of a party or who has been retained for the purpose of expressing an expert opinion at trial, the designation of that witness must include an expert witness declaration with:

    - a brief narrative of the expert's qualifications and general substance of the expected testimony;

    - a representation that the expert will testify at trial; and

    - a representation that the expert is sufficiently familiar with the action that he will be able to give a meaningful deposition.

    - a demand for mutual production of reports and writings of the expert may be included for any expert for whom an expert witness declaration is required.

*

CHAPTER 5

DISPOSITION WITHOUT TRIAL

I. ALTERNATIVE DISPUTE RESOLUTION

"Alternative dispute resolution" refers to "a process, other than formal litigation, in which a neutral person or persons resolve a dispute or assist parties in resolving their dispute." CRC 3.800. Either through agreement or by order of court, parties may utilize dispute resolution devices that bypass or minimally involve the court system. Principal examples of these devices (discussed below) include contractual arbitration, judicial arbitration, and mediation.

A. Contractual Arbitration

1. California Arbitration Policy

The California Legislature has enacted a detailed statutory scheme to implement a system of private dispute resolution by way of contractual arbitration. CCP §§ 1280–1296. The statutes reflect a strong policy in favor of contractual arbitration because it is perceived as a prompt and relatively inexpensive dispute resolution tool.

2. Arbitration Agreements

a. Arbitrability and Enforceability

A written agreement to arbitrate a current or future dispute is valid and enforceable unless a ground exists for revocation of the agreement. CCP § 1281. The parties' agreement defines the scope of private arbitration and the powers of the arbitrator. If a question arises as to the arbitrability of an issue, the court, not the arbitrator, decides.

1) Grounds for Revocation

Grounds for revocation of the arbitration agreement include lack of agreement, fraud in the inducement of the arbitration clause, illegality, or unconscionability.

2) Unconscionability

A court may refuse to enforce an arbitration agreement it finds to be unconscionable. Cal. Civ. Code § 1670.5. Unconscionability may be *procedural* (focusing on whether the contract was obtained through oppression, surprise or the like), or *substantive* (focusing on whether the terms of the agreement are overly harsh or one-sided). Depending on the degree and type of unconscionability, the court may void the entire contract or sever the unconscionable portion. Armendariz v. Foundation Health Psychcare Services, Inc., 24 Cal.4th 83, 99 Cal.Rptr.2d 745, 6 P.3d 669 (2000).

b. Arbitration of Statutory Rights

Statutory rights (such as those under the California Fair Employment and Housing Act) may be subject to arbitration only if the arbitration agreement meets certain requirements: (1) the agreement must provide for neutral arbitrators; (2) the agreement may not limit the type of relief available or the scope or amount of any remedies; (3) the parties must be afforded an adequate opportunity for discovery; (4) the agreement must provide for a written award that, under the appropriate circumstances, may be subject to judicial review; and (5) when an employer requires its employees to submit to arbitration, the agreement must not require the employee to pay costs and arbitration fees beyond what the party would have to pay in a court proceeding. Id.

3. Obtaining Arbitration

a. Demand for Arbitration

A party to the agreement typically sets the arbitration in motion by making a demand for arbitration on the other party. If there is no question as to the arbitrability of the dispute or the enforceability of the agreement, the arbitration proceeds without court intervention.

b. Court Intervention

1) Petition to Compel Arbitration

If a party has made an arbitration demand and the demand is refused—but no lawsuit has yet been initiated—the demanding party may invoke court assistance by filing a petition to compel arbitration. The court will examine the parties' arbitration agreement and decide whether the issues in dispute are arbitrable. If so, the court will order the parties to arbitrate unless it finds that the demanding party has waived the right to arbitration or that the agreement is unenforceable. CCP § 1281.2.

2) Motion to Compel Arbitration and to Stay Proceedings

If a party to an arbitration agreement has already filed suit instead of pursuing arbitration, the party who wishes to proceed with the arbitration may file a motion to compel arbitration as well as to stay the court proceedings. CCP § 1281.4. The court conducts the same inquiry as it does on a petition to compel arbitration.

3) Waiver of Right to Compel Arbitration

The court may find that a party has waived the right to compel or demand arbitration if that party has performed acts inconsistent with the right to arbitration. Such acts may include active participation in litigation, unreasonable delay in seeking arbitration, or bad faith conduct. Because California law favors arbitration, a strong showing of waiver must be made.

4. Arbitration Proceedings

Arbitration agreements often specify that the arbitration proceedings will be conducted according to the rules of a particular alternative dispute resolution organization such as the American Arbitration Association or JAMS (Judicial Arbitration and Mediation Services).

a. Selection of Arbitrator

Arbitrators are required to be neutral (impartial).

1) Parties' Agreement

The parties' agreement may specify the method by which the arbitrator (or arbitrators) will be selected. If the agreement calls for a single arbitrator, each party must agree on the selection. If the arbitration agreement calls for a panel of three arbitrators, each side typically selects one arbitrator, and those arbitrators agree on the selection of the third arbitrator.

2) Compare: "Rent-a-Judge" System

Parties may agree to submit their dispute to a retired judge (sometimes referred to as a referee), who resolves the matter outside of the court system. CCP § 638. The referee may render a final and binding decision that may be entered as a judgment, similar to the arbitrator's award in contractual arbitration proceedings. (In addition, a court may send a matter to a private referee, similar to the reference to judicial arbitration. CCP § 639.)

b. Discovery and Evidence

The right to discovery in contractual arbitration proceedings is restricted by statute. CCP §§ 1283.05, 1283.1. The arbitrator is not required to follow the rules of evidence and procedure. CCP § 1282.2(d).

5. Arbitration Award

a. Requirements for Award

At the conclusion of the arbitration, the arbitrator renders a written signed award, which includes the arbitrator's determination of the issues presented. CCP § 1283.4. The arbitrator serves a signed copy of the award on all of the parties. CCP § 1283.6.

b. Confirmation of Award

A party to arbitration may petition the court to confirm the arbitration award. Upon confirmation, the court enters judgment on the award, which may be enforced like any other court judgment. CCP § 1287.4.

c. Judicial Review of Award

An arbitration award is subject to judicial review on only very narrow statutory grounds. Generally, an award may not be reviewed for errors of law or fact, even if those errors appear on the face of the award and cause substantial injustice. Moncharsh v. Heily & Blase, 3 Cal.4th 1, 10 Cal.Rptr.2d 183, 832 P.2d 899 (1992). Parties to contractual arbitration assume the risk of arbitrator error in exchange for a speedy and inexpensive resolution of their dispute. Upon petition or response, an award must be vacated, corrected or modified under the limited circumstances set out in the arbitration statutes.

1) Vacating Arbitration Award

A court must vacate an arbitration award if it determines that:

- The award was obtained by corruption or fraud;
- There was corruption of any of the arbitrators;
- The rights of a party were substantially prejudiced by misconduct of a neutral arbitrator;
- The arbitrator exceeded her powers and the award cannot be corrected without affecting the merits of the decision;
- The arbitrator substantially prejudiced a party by refusal to postpone a hearing on sufficient cause, refusal to hear material evidence, or other conduct contrary to the arbitration statutes; or
- The arbitrator failed to disclose disqualifying information or failed to disqualify herself upon receipt of a timely demand.

CCP § 1286.2.

2) Correcting or Modifying Arbitration Award

A court must modify or correct an arbitration award if it determines that:

- The arbitration award evidences a miscalculation of figures or a mistaken description of a person or thing;
- The arbitrator exceeded her powers but the award may be corrected without affecting the merits of the decision; or
- The award was imperfect in a matter of form not affecting the merits of the controversy.

CCP § 1286.6.

d. Appeal

A party may appeal from: (1) an order dismissing a petition to confirm, correct or vacate and award; (2) an order vacating an award; or (3) a judgment entered on the award. CCP § 1294. In an appeal from a judgment following confirmation of the award, review is limited to the grounds set forth in CCP § 1286.2 for vacating the award. The appellate court does not review the merits of the dispute or the arbitrator's reasoning.

6. International Arbitration

California has enacted the California International Arbitration and Conciliation Act (CCP §§ 1297.11 et seq.) to encourage and facilitate dispute resolution within the state involving foreign parties. The Act applies to commercial arbitrations in which any one of the following conditions is present:

- The parties' places of business are in countries other than where the arbitration agreement was executed;

- The dispute has close connections with a third country, or a substantial portion of the parties' agreement is supposed to be performed in that third country;

- The agreement expressly states that the subject matter of the arbitration agreement relates to commercial interests in more than one country; or

- The subject matter of the arbitration agreement is otherwise connected to commercial interests in more than one country.

CCP § 1297.13.

7. *Compare Federal Procedure*

The Federal Arbitration Act (FAA) governs written arbitration agreements involving interstate or international commerce. 9 USC §§ 1 et seq. Like the California arbitration statutes, the FAA manifests a strong federal policy favoring contractual arbitration. The FAA applies in both California and federal courts and preempts conflicting state law. "[W]hen parties agree to arbitrate all questions arising under a contract, state laws lodging primary jurisdiction in another forum, whether judicial or administrative, are superseded by the FAA." Preston v. Ferrer, 552 U.S. ___, ___, 128 S.Ct. 978, 981, 169 L.Ed.2d 917 (2008).

8. Illustration

Phyllis went to work for Danby Corp. in Red Bluff. Phyllis signed an employment agreement that included a mandatory arbitration clause. The clause required all disputes and causes of action of any kind arising out of the employment relationship to be arbitrated, and it required the parties to split the costs of arbitration. When Danby Corp. fired Phyllis after only a year, she filed a suit for wrongful termination in the Tehama County Superior Court. Danby Corp. moved the court to compel arbitration. Phyllis opposed the motion on the ground that the agreement was unenforceable in several respects. The court will likely agree with Phyllis. First, the requirement that Phyllis pay half the costs of arbitration violated public policy. An employer may not categorically compel an employee to pay forum costs that are unique to arbitration. Second, the arbitration agreement was procedurally unconscionable. Given the unequal bargaining positions of the parties, Phyllis had no meaningful opportunity to negotiate the arbitration clause when she signed her employment agreement. It was offered on a "take it or leave it" basis. Third, the arbitration agreement was substantively unconscionable. It contained one-sided provisions that gave Danby Corp. more favorable terms than those given to Phyllis. Abramson v. Juniper Networks, Inc., 115 Cal.App.4th 638, 9 Cal.Rptr.3d 422 (2004).

B. Judicial Arbitration

1. Characteristics of Judicial Arbitration

Judicial arbitration is a dispute-resolution process conducted under the auspices of and managed by the Superior Court to attempt to resolve smaller civil actions without trial. CCP §§ 1141 et seq.; CRC 3.811 et seq. The term "judicial arbitration" is somewhat of a misnomer, since it is not true binding arbitration to which the parties have agreed, and it is not conducted by a judge.

2. Obtaining Judicial Arbitration

a. Actions Subject to Judicial Arbitration

Any Superior Court with at least 18 judges may mandate judicial arbitration for unlimited civil cases in which the amount in controversy is $50,000 or less for each plaintiff. Limited civil cases may also be required to submit to judicial arbitration if a court's local rule so provides. CCP § 1141.11. In addition, parties may stipulate to judicial arbitration, or the plaintiff may elect to participate in judicial arbitration and agree that the award will not exceed $50,000. CCP § 1141.12.

b. Cases Exempt from Judicial Arbitration

Actions exempt from the requirement of judicial arbitration include class actions, family law matters, probate cases, small claims appeals, unlawful detainer proceedings, and those actions involving a nonfrivolous or substantial request for equitable relief. CRC 3.811; CCP § 1141.13.

3. Arbitration Proceedings

a. Selection of Arbitrator

The parties to judicial arbitration may stipulate to the selection of an arbitrator. In the absence of a stipulation or a local rule governing the selection of arbitrators, the court provides names of potential arbitrators to the parties and appoints an arbitrator who has not been rejected by the parties. CRC 3.815.

b. Conduct of Arbitration

Unlike contractual arbitration, parties to judicial arbitration possess full discovery rights. CRC 3.822. With certain limited exceptions, judicial arbitration is conducted according to the rules of evidence and procedure. CRC 3.823.

c. Arbitration Award and Judgment

The arbitrator must render a written and signed award determining the issues presented. Within ten days after the arbitration has concluded, the arbitrator must file the award with the clerk and provide proof of service upon all parties. CRC 3.825. The clerk enters the award as a judgment if no party has requested a new trial (trial de novo) within 30 days after the arbitrator has filed the award. CRC 3.827. The judgment has the same effect as any court judgment, except that it may not be appealed. The judgment may be vacated by the trial court only on limited grounds, including those provided in CCP § 1286.2 (a)(1)–(3) for vacation of contractual arbitration awards (see section I(A)(5)(c), above), or on a ground provided in CCP § 473 for vacation of judgments and orders. CRC 3.828.

4. Trial De Novo

a. Request for Trial De Novo

Within 30 days after the arbitrator has filed the award with the clerk, a party may request a trial de novo as to both law and facts. CRC 3.826; CCP § 1141.20(b). The case must proceed to trial under the court's case management order. CRC 3.826. Neither the parties nor the court may refer to the arbitration at the trial de novo. CRC 3.826; CCP § 1141.25. Discovery is not allowed after an arbitration award and before the trial de novo except by stipulation of the parties or by court permission on a showing of good cause. CCP § 1141.24.

b. Outcome of Trial De Novo

If the judgment entered following the trial de novo is less favorable than the arbitration award for the party who requested the trial, the court must order that party to pay certain costs and fees, unless the order would create substantial economic hardship. CCP § 1141.21(a).

c. Effect of Failure to Request Trial De Novo

If a party does not make a timely request for a trial de novo or to vacate the award, the court enters judgment on the award. The judgment has the same effect as any other Superior Court judgment, except that it may not be appealed. CCP § 1141.23.

5. *Compare Federal Procedure*

Each district court must authorize the use of at least one type of alternative dispute resolution process. 28 USC § 651. The district court may make a referral to court-annexed arbitration only where the parties consent. 28 USC § 654(a). Court-annexed arbitration is prohibited when the action is based on a constitutional or civil rights violation, or when the amount in controversy exceeds $150,000.

6. Illustration

Ped filed a breach of contract complaint against Dinah in Madera County Superior Court. After numerous pretrial proceedings and a settlement conference, Ped and Dinah stipulated to submit the case to "binding" arbitration. The stipulation referred to the Judicial Arbitration Act and included a waiver of the right to a trial de novo. The court will employ the ordinary rules of contract interpretation to determine whether the parties agreed to contractual or judicial arbitration. Despite the agreement to pursue "binding arbitration," the parties appear to have intended to seek judicial arbitration with an advance waiver of the trial de novo right (a right that arises only in the judicial arbitration context). Porreco v. Red Top RV Center, 216 Cal.App.3d 113, 264 Cal.Rptr. 609 (1989).

C. Mediation

Mediation is "a process in which a neutral person or persons facilitate communication between the disputants to assist them in reaching a mutually acceptable agreement." CCP § 1775.1. The California Legislature has recognized the importance of mediation in the timely, informal and cost-efficient resolution of disputes. CCP § 1775.

1. Mediation Programs

a. Court-Annexed Mediation

California has enacted the Civil Action Mediation Program. CCP §§ 1775–1775.15. Currently, only the Los Angeles County Superior Court is required to participate in this program, but the superior courts of other counties may elect to participate as well (and several have). CCP § 1775.2.

1) Actions Submitted to Mediation

The court determines the amenability of a matter to mediation on a case-by-case basis, not categorically. CRC 3.871(b). The court may order cases into mediation on largely the same basis as those ordered into judicial arbitration, including those in which the amount in controversy does not exceed $50,000 for each plaintiff. CCP § 1775.5. Unlike judicial arbitration, however, an action may be submitted to mediation even if it requests equitable relief. In addition, parties may stipulate to submit their matter to mediation, regardless of the amount in controversy. CRC 3.871(a)(2). Cases referred to judicial arbitration may not also be ordered submitted to mediation. CCP § 1775.4.

2) Selection and Role of Mediator

The mediator is selected from a panel maintained by the court, unless the parties stipulate to the selection of a mediator. CCP § 1775.6. The mediator does not have decision-making power; the role is to facilitate the process by which the parties reach their own voluntary agreement. Jeld-Wen, Inc. v. Superior Court, 146 Cal.App.4th 536, 53 Cal.Rptr.3d 115 (2007); CRC 3.853.

3) Conclusion of Mediation

The mediation must be completed within 60 days of the reference to mediation, unless the court extends the deadline for good cause. CRC 3.876(c). Within ten days of the conclusion of the mediation, the mediator must file with the court a Statement of Agreement or Nonagreement, informing the court whether a settlement has been reached. CCP § 1775.9. In order to preserve confidentiality, no other information may be included in the Statement. If no agreement has been reached, the case is returned to the trial calendar.

b. Voluntary Mediation

Some courts that have not elected to establish a court-annexed mediation program have adopted voluntary mediation programs. Courts cannot require participation, and there are no sanctions for failing to participate.

2. Confidentiality of Mediation Proceedings

a. Written or Oral Communications

Unless an express statutory exception exists, parties and mediators are prohibited from disclosing any written or oral communications made during mediation. Such communications are not discoverable or admissible. Cal. Evid. Code § 1119. The confidentiality continues after the mediation ends. Cal. Evid. Code § 1126. Under certain limited conditions, however, a written or oral settlement agreement reached during mediation may be disclosed. See Cal. Evid. Code §§ 1123–1124.

b. Reports or Findings

A mediator may not submit to the court any reports or findings related to the conduct of the mediation, unless the parties agree otherwise. Cal. Evid. Code § 1121. However, a party may advise the court about bad faith conduct by other parties during the mediation. Foxgate Homeowners' Association, Inc. v. Bramalea California, Inc., 26 Cal.4th 1, 108 Cal.Rptr.2d 642, 25 P.3d 1117 (2001).

3. *Compare Federal Procedure*

The district court may utilize "special procedures to assist in resolving the dispute when authorized by statute or local rule." FRCP 16(c)(2)(I). All district courts, by local rule, must require civil litigants to consider using at least one alternative dispute resolution process (including mediation) during the litigation. 28 USC § 652(a).

Courts must adopt local rules to provide for appropriate confidentiality of ADR proceedings. 28 USC § 652(d).

4. Illustration

Paki was injured in an airplane crash. He filed a personal injury lawsuit in Solano County Superior Court against Dusty Air Co. In an attempt to resolve the dispute, the parties held a mediation session. When the case did not settle, a second mediation session was scheduled, and each side submitted mediation briefs to the mediator. Dusty Air's attorney stated in his brief that Paki's attorney had communicated a settlement demand for $1 million, an amount far lower than Paki's earlier demand. On the day before the second mediation, an e-mail exchange occurred between counsel for Paki and Dusty Air discussing the discrepancy in the settlement demands and the authority of Paki's counsel to lower the demand. The e-mails referred to and quoted from the mediation brief. The second mediation session settled the case, but Paki brought a malpractice action against his attorneys based on the less favorable settlement Paki received. The contents of the mediation briefs and e-mails were protected by confidentiality and may not be used as evidence in the malpractice action. Wimsatt v. Superior Court, 152 Cal.App.4th 137, 61 Cal.Rptr.3d 200 (2007).

II. CASE MANAGEMENT

A. Court's Obligation

Superior Court judges are responsible for "active management and supervision of the pace of litigation from the date of filing to disposition." CRC 3.713(c); see also Cal. Gov't Code § 68607. Within 180 days after the filing of a civil complaint, the court must hold an initial case management conference to review the case and make initial determinations about alternative dispute resolution or trial setting. CRC 3.721, 3.722. In addition to the initial conference, the court may set, either on its own motion or pursuant to request by a party, additional case management conferences. CRC 3.723. The court must render a case management order setting forth a schedule for future events in the litigation and addressing other issues of case management. CRC 3.728.

B. Case Disposition ("Fast Track")

The Legislature, in enacting the Trial Court Delay Reduction Act (otherwise known as "Fast Track"), authorized the Judicial Council to adopt statewide rules of court, and the superior courts to adopt local rules, to achieve the goal of expeditious disposition of Superior Court actions.

1. Case Disposition Time Goals

a. Unlimited and Limited Civil Cases

Under the case disposition rules applicable to Fast Track, the court should attempt to dispose of 75 percent of unlimited civil cases within 12 months, 85 percent within 18 months, and 100 percent within 24 months. For limited civil cases, the disposition goals are 90 percent within 12 months, 98 percent within 18 months, and 100 percent within 24 months. CRC 3.714.

b. Exempt Cases

Uninsured motorist cases and cases included in a petition for coordination are exempt from the Fast Track case disposition rules. CRC 3.712(b)–(c). In addition, the court may exempt cases from the disposition time goals if it determines that they involve exceptional circumstances, in which case the court should attempt to dispose of the action within three years. CRC 3.714(c). Juvenile, probate and domestic relations cases, as well as cases assigned to a single judge for all purposes, may not be assigned to a delay reduction program. Cal. Gov't Code § 68608(a).

c. Factors in Determining Disposition Goal

The court must consider each case on its own merits in setting case disposition goals. CRC 3.714. The court evaluates several factors in determining the appropriate disposition time goal, including: (1) the number of parties, causes of action and cross-complaints; (2) the complexity of the issues; (3) the nature and extent of discovery; and (4) the estimated length of trial. CRC 3.715.

2. Pretrial Time Goals

With exceptions, Fast Track rules require service of the complaint within 60 days of filing, and service of a responsive pleading within 30 days of service of the complaint. The parties may also stipulate to one continuance within 30 days of service of the responsive pleading. A Superior Court may generally impose its own time periods for other litigation activities, such as service of a cross-complaint, but the court cannot impose shorter time periods for these specific events than are permitted under statute. Cal. Gov't Code § 68616.

3. **Sanctions**

The Fast Track statutes give judges the broad power to "impose sanctions authorized by law" in order to achieve the purpose of the statutes. Cal. Gov't Code § 68608(b). Permissible sanctions may range from monetary sanctions to termination of the litigation. A judge may dismiss a plaintiff's action or strike a defendant's pleading if less severe sanctions would not be effective. Id. However, the judge may not dismiss or strike a party's pleadings when counsel, and not the party, was responsible for failing to comply with Fast Track rules. CCP § 575.2(b). See Garcia v. McCutchen, 16 Cal.4th 469, 66 Cal.Rptr.2d 319, 940 P.2d 906 (1997).

4. ***Compare Federal Procedure***

FRCP 1 states aspirationally that the rules "shall be construed . . . to secure the just, speedy, and inexpensive determination of every action." The federal rules do not require judges to dispose of a certain percentage of cases within a given time period. However, the rules do provide time frames for certain litigation events. For example, service of summons and complaint must be completed within 120 days of filing, and the defendant ordinarily must serve the response to the complaint within 20 days of service of summons and complaint. See FRCP 4(m), 12(a)(1)(A). Moreover, the district court must promptly issue a scheduling order. FRCP 16(b)(2).

5. **Illustration**

Restaurant owner Pierre filed suit in Stanislaus County Superior Court against his landlord, Della Corp., for failure to comply with the terms of his lease for a restaurant property located in Modesto. Pierre's attorney, Busy Bob, attempted to serve the complaint on the president of Della Corp. nine times over the course of 70 days, but he was unsuccessful. Local fast track rules required plaintiffs to complete service within 60 days. The court issued an Order to Show Cause for the failure to timely serve Della Corp. Busy Bob did not appear at the Order to Show Cause hearing, and the judge dismissed the case in its entirety. The dismissal is inappropriate for two reasons: (a) the judge did not consider whether less severe sanctions might be effective; and (b) Pierre's lawsuit cannot be terminated as a sanction for Busy Bob's failure to comply with the Fast Track rules. Service of process is ordinarily within the power of counsel, not of the client. Therefore, monetary sanctions should be imposed on Busy Bob for failure to timely serve the complaint. Tliche v. Van Quathem, 66 Cal.App.4th 1054, 78 Cal.Rptr.2d 458 (1998).

III. DISMISSALS

A. Involuntary Dismissal Under Diligent Prosecution Statutes

For cases not part of the court's Fast Track system, the court is authorized to involuntarily dismiss a plaintiff's action under what are known as "diligent prosecution" statutes. CCP §§ 583.110 et seq. These statutes obligate plaintiffs (and cross-complainants) to diligently manage their lawsuits and move them forward. CCP § 583.130. Involuntary dismissal may occur if the plaintiff fails to complete service of the complaint or to bring the action to trial within the applicable deadlines. The court may dismiss on motion of a party or on its own motion. Involuntary dismissals are without prejudice and may be either mandatory or discretionary.

1. Failure to Serve Complaint

a. Mandatory Dismissal

In non-Fast Track actions, the plaintiff must serve the defendants (both named and Doe) with the summons and complaint within three years of the filing of the action. CCP § 583.210(a). In addition, the plaintiff has 60 days beyond the three-year deadline to file the return (proof) of service with the court. CCP § 583.210(b). If the plaintiff fails to meet either of these deadlines, dismissal is mandatory. CCP § 583.250(b).

1) Tolling

The court will not dismiss the plaintiff's action for failing to timely serve process if a statutory tolling provision applies. The time during which any of the following statutory excuses lasts is excluded from the calculation of the three-year deadline:

- The defendant was not amenable to the process of the court.
- The prosecution of the action or proceedings in the action was stayed and the stay affected service.
- The validity of service was the subject of litigation by the parties.

- Service, for any other reason, was impossible, impracticable, or futile due to causes beyond the plaintiff's control.

CCP § 583.240. The plaintiff has the burden to show that a valid excuse exists and that the plaintiff exercised reasonable diligence in attempting to serve process.

2) Other Extensions

In addition to the above tolling provisions, the three-year deadline may be extended by the parties by written stipulation or oral agreement in open court. CCP §§ 583.220, 583.230.

b. Discretionary Dismissal

The court has discretion to involuntarily dismiss an action that has not been served within two years from the filing of the complaint. CCP § 583.420(a)(1). In exercising its discretion, the court must consider several factors found in CRC 3.1342, including: (1) the nature and complexity of the case; (2) the extent of any settlement negotiations; (3) the plaintiff's diligence in attempting to achieve service of process; and (4) the nature of any delays attributable to the parties. The court may toll the two-year period on any of the grounds applicable under the provisions for tolling the three-year mandatory dismissal deadline for failure to serve process, discussed in section III(A)(1)(a), above. See CCP § 583.240.

2. Failure to Bring Case to Trial

a. Mandatory Dismissal

The court must involuntarily dismiss an action if the plaintiff has failed to bring it to trial within five years of its filing. CCP §§ 583.310, 583.360.

1) "Brought to Trial"

"Trial," in the context of the diligent prosecution statutes, commences when the jury panel is sworn (jury trial) or when the first witness is sworn (bench trial). Other pretrial proceedings that result in a final disposition of an action may constitute "trial" for this purpose (such as an order granting summary judgment or an order sustaining a demurrer without leave to amend). In re Marriage of Dunmore, 45 Cal.App.4th 1372, 53 Cal.Rptr.2d 450 (1996).

2) **Tolling**

In calculating the five-year period in which the action must be brought to trial, the court will not include in the calculation the time during which any of the following occurred:

- The jurisdiction of the court to try the action was suspended.
- Prosecution or trial of the action was stayed or enjoined.
- Bringing the action to trial, for any other reason, was impossible, impracticable, or futile.

CCP § 583.340. The plaintiff has the burden to show the existence of one of the statutory excuses and to establish reasonable diligence at all stages of the litigation in attempting to bring the case to trial. Tamburina v. Combined Insurance Co. of America, 147 Cal.App.4th 323, 54 Cal.Rptr.3d 175 (2007). If, after a period of tolling, fewer than six months remain in which to bring the action to trial, the action may not be dismissed as long as trial commences within six months after the conclusion of the period of tolling. CCP § 583.350.

3) **Other Extensions**

The five-year deadline may be extended by written or oral stipulation. CCP § 583.330.

b. **Discretionary Dismissal**

The court has discretion to dismiss an action that has not been brought to trial within two years of its filing. CCP § 583.420(a)(2)(B); CRC 3.1340. The court must apply the factors found in CRC 3.1342 in exercising its discretion to dismiss. The same tolling provisions as apply in the mandatory dismissal context also apply to discretionary dismissals for failure to bring the case to trial. CCP §§ 583.420(b), 583.340. See section III(A)(2)(a), above.

3. Diligent Prosecution Statutes and "Fast Track"

The diligent prosecution statutes are not the only means by which a court may involuntarily dismiss an action. A case that is subject to the Trial Court Delay Reduction Act (aka "Fast Track"; see section II(B), above), may be involuntarily dismissed under different (usually shorter) time limits than those imposed by the diligent prosecution statutes. For example, under Cal. Gov't Code § 68616 and the local rules of many superior courts, a court may involuntarily dismiss an action if plaintiff has failed to serve process on defendant within 60 days of the filing of the complaint. The diligent prosecution statutes do not limit the court's authority to dismiss an action under another applicable statute or court rule or under the court's inherent authority. CCP § 583.150.

4. *Compare Federal Procedure*

A defendant may move the court for an involuntary dismissal of an action under FRCP 41(b) if the plaintiff has failed to prosecute, to comply with the Federal Rules, or to comply with an order of the court. The district court also possesses inherent power to dismiss on its own motion. With limited exceptions, such an involuntary dismissal is with prejudice. Rule 41(b), unlike the California diligent prosecution statutes, does not state the types of conduct that constitute a failure to prosecute, and does not include specific time limits and tolling provisions. Federal courts are reluctant to impose a drastic measure such as dismissal unless the conduct of the plaintiff has demonstrated willful or repeated delay or noncompliance, and prejudice to defendant.

5. Illustration

Pedro filed a sexual orientation discrimination action in Kings County Superior Court against his employer, Dall Co. The parties entered into five stipulations, which resulted in the continuance of the trial setting conference date and the trial date for 424 days. All of the stipulations were based on Pedro's poor health and multiple surgeries. At the expiration of five years since the complaint was filed, Dall Co. moved to dismiss the action for failure to bring it to trial within five years. The five-year period will be tolled by the impracticability exception of CCP § 583.340(c) if Pedro can meet three requirements: (a) Pedro's lengthy illness and repeated surgeries must constitute a circumstance of impracticability; (b) there must be a causal connection between the length of the illness and the inability to move the case to trial; and (c) Pedro must have exercised diligence at all stages of the proceedings to bring the matter to trial. Tamburina v. Combined Insurance Co. of America, 147 Cal.App.4th 323, 54 Cal.Rptr.3d 175 (2007).

B. Other Involuntary Dismissals

Additional statutory bases for involuntary dismissal include the following:

- The court sustains a demurrer or grants a motion to strike the complaint without leave to amend (CCP § 581(f));
- The plaintiff fails to timely amend the complaint when leave to amend has been granted (CCP § 581(f));
- The court orders a terminating sanction for misuse of the discovery process or for a party's violation of Fast Track rules (CCP § 2023.030(d); Cal. Gov't Code § 68608(b)); or
- The plaintiff or the defendant fails to appear for trial (CCP § 581(b)).

C. Voluntary Dismissals

A plaintiff may voluntarily dismiss her action, or may request the court to dismiss the action, at any time before "the actual commencement of trial." CCP § 581(b)(1), (c). A dismissal may be either with or without prejudice.

1. Commencement of Trial

The actual commencement of trial precludes a plaintiff from dismissing her action without prejudice. Under CCP § 581(a)(6), "trial" commences at any of the following points:

- the beginning of opening statement or argument;
- if there is no opening statement, the time of the administration of an oath or affirmation to the first witness; or
- the introduction of any evidence.

Courts have expanded the definition of "trial" to include various dispositive pretrial proceedings in which the court makes a final determination of an issue of law or fact. Franklin Capital Corp. v.

Wilson, 148 Cal.App.4th 187, 55 Cal.Rptr.3d 424 (2007). Examples include the filing of a motion for terminating sanctions in a discovery dispute, a tentative ruling sustaining a demurrer without leave to amend, and an order sustaining a demurrer with leave to amend where the time for amendment has expired.

2. With or Without Prejudice

Dismissal with prejudice precludes a plaintiff from bringing a new action based on the same causes of action as in the dismissed action. Dismissal without prejudice permits the plaintiff to bring a new lawsuit on the same causes of action, assuming those causes of action are not barred by the applicable statutes of limitation. Once trial has actually commenced, a voluntary dismissal may be entered only with prejudice, unless the court orders otherwise for good cause or the affected parties consent to a dismissal without prejudice. CCP § 581(e).

3. *Compare Federal Procedure*

In contrast to the unlimited number of voluntary pretrial dismissals without prejudice permitted under the California statute, FRCP 41(a)(1) permits a plaintiff to voluntarily dismiss the action without prejudice only once without leave of court. Moreover, if the plaintiff has already voluntarily dismissed a previous action on the same claim, the voluntary dismissal is with prejudice. FRCP 41(a)(1)(B). The right of voluntary dismissal without leave of court is available only if the defendant has not answered or filed a summary judgment motion, or if all parties who have appeared in the action stipulate to the dismissal. In all other circumstances, plaintiff must obtain court permission to voluntarily dismiss her case. FRCP 41(a)(2).

4. Illustration

Patient had surgery performed at Death Valley Hospital, from which she had a long and difficult recovery because of infection. Patient brought a medical malpractice suit in Inyo County Superior Court against Hospital. Hospital filed a motion for summary judgment. One day before Patient's opposition to the summary judgment motion was due, she moved to dismiss her action without prejudice. Patient may dismiss her case without prejudice any time before the actual commencement of trial. Patient moved to dismiss prior to the deadline for filing opposition to the summary judgment motion, a hearing on the motion, and a tentative ruling. As the case was dismissed before a stage where a final ruling on the summary judgment motion was a "mere formality," Patient's voluntary dismissal was timely and appropriate. Zapanta v. Universal Care, Inc., 107 Cal.App.4th 1167, 132 Cal.Rptr.2d 842 (2003).

IV. DEFAULT AND DEFAULT JUDGMENT

Entry of default and default judgment are two distinct procedures.

A. Entry of Default

If a defendant fails to file a timely answer, demurrer, or other acceptable response to the complaint, the plaintiff may seek the entry of the defendant's default. The plaintiff must request the court clerk to enter the default—it is not automatic. After the clerk enters the default, the defendant has no right to appear or participate in the proceedings or to receive notice. The court has no jurisdiction over the defendant except to consider a motion to set aside the default.

B. Entry of Default Judgment

After the entry of default, the plaintiff may seek a default judgment against the defendant.

1. Entry of Default Judgment by Clerk

In limited circumstances (actions arising from a contract or a judgment for a fixed amount of damages where service of process was achieved other than by publication), the court clerk may enter a default judgment. CCP § 585(a).

2. Entry of Default Judgment by Court

In all other cases, the court must enter the default judgment after the plaintiff provides the court with evidence to "prove up" her right to relief. CCP § 585(b).

a. Prove-Up Hearing

The court must conduct a "prove-up hearing," at which the plaintiff appears either in person or through submission of affidavits. The defendant has no right to receive notice of, or to appear at, the prove-up hearing—even to contest the amount of damages.

b. Amount of Recovery

The amount awarded to the plaintiff must not exceed the amount pleaded in the prayer of the complaint (or the body of the complaint if the prayer is defective). CCP § 580(a). In personal injury or wrongful death cases, in which the amount of damages must not be stated in the complaint (see Chapter 3(III)(B)), the amount awarded to the plaintiff must not exceed that set out in the plaintiff's statement of damages under CCP § 425.11. Punitive damages may not exceed the amount stated in the plaintiff's statement of punitive damages under CCP § 425.115. The plaintiff must have served the defendant with the statement of damages and/or punitive damages before the court will enter default judgment. Due process considerations require that the defendant must have adequate notice of the specific relief that the plaintiff seeks against him.

C. Setting Aside Default and Default Judgment

1. Discretionary and Mandatory Relief from Default and/or Default Judgment

The defendant may move the court to vacate the entry of default and/or default judgment under CCP § 473(b). The statute contains both discretionary and mandatory relief provisions, as well as time limits for filing the motion. See Chapter 6(V)(E)(1), regarding relief from judgment.

2. Vacating Default and Default Judgment Based on Lack of Actual Notice

If service of process did not result in actual notice to the defendant in time to respond to the complaint, the defendant may move to set aside any resulting default and/or default judgment. CCP § 473.5. The defendant must seek relief within a reasonable time, in no case later than two years after entry of default judgment or 180 days after service of written notice that a default or default judgment has been entered (whichever is earlier). The court has discretion to set aside the default and/or default judgment so long as the defendant's lack of actual notice was not caused by his avoidance of service or by inexcusable neglect.

D. *Compare Federal Procedure*

FRCP 55(b) permits entry of a default judgment by either the clerk or the court. In contrast to California procedure, a defendant who has made a previous appearance in federal proceedings has a right to be notified of a prove-up hearing and appear to contest the plaintiff's showing. FRCP 55(b)(2). A federal court may set aside an entry of default on a showing of good cause. A default judgment may be vacated as provided in FRCP 60(b). FRCP 55(c).

E. Illustration

Palti sued Decker Co. in Riverside County Superior Court for damages arising from an identity theft scheme. Palti timely served the complaint on Decker Co., but Decker Co. did not respond within 30 days. Palti requested the entry of Decker Co.'s default. A copy of the request for entry of default was served on Decker Co. The clerk entered Decker Co.'s default. The court conducted a prove-up hearing, awarding Palti $900,000. Seven months later, Decker Co. filed a motion to set aside the default and default judgment. Decker Co. argued that it was entitled to receive notice of a case management conference and the prove-up hearing. The court will deny the motion. The default and default judgment were properly entered, and Decker Co. had no legitimate excuse for its failure to act in a timely fashion to move to vacate the default and default judgment. Upon the entry of its default, Decker Co. ceased to be an active party entitled to notice. Sporn v. Home Depot USA, Inc., 126 Cal.App.4th 1294, 24 Cal.Rptr.3d 780 (2005).

V. SETTLEMENT

The vast majority of California civil lawsuits settle before trial. California has a strong policy in favor of settlement, which furthers judicial efficiency by disposing of cases prior to trial. The court may, either on its own motion or on a party's motion, set a mandatory settlement conference. CRC 3.1380. However, parties have no obligation to settle.

A. Settlement Agreement

1. Dismissal of Action

When the parties agree on the terms of a settlement, the plaintiff must file a request for dismissal with the court within 45 days of the settlement. CRC 3.1385. Dismissal of all claims against a party terminates that party's involvement in the lawsuit, and the court ceases to have jurisdiction over that party.

2. Enforcement of Agreement

The court does not automatically oversee the enforcement of the settlement. However, the parties to the settlement may request in writing, prior to dismissal, that the court retain jurisdiction to enforce the terms of the settlement until performed. CCP § 664.6.

B. Terms of Settlement

1. Settlement Allocation

Where there are multiple defendants, and one defendant settles with the plaintiff, the other defendants are entitled to have any amount of economic damages they owe in a judgment offset by the amount the settling defendant paid. CCP § 877(a). However, no defendant is entitled to any offset for the noneconomic (pain and suffering) damages paid by the settling defendant, because liability for noneconomic damages is several and can never be shared. Espinoza v. Machonga, 9 Cal.App.4th 268, 11 Cal.Rptr.2d 498 (1992). Each defendant may be liable for noneconomic damages only in proportion with its percentage of overall fault. Cal. Civ. Code § 1431.2.

2. Good Faith Settlement

a. Good Faith Settlement Determination

Where there are multiple defendants and one of the defendants settles with the plaintiff, any party to the action is entitled to a hearing to determine whether the settlement was entered in good faith. CCP § 877.6. Otherwise, the possibility exists of a defendant settling for an extremely low amount, leaving the remaining defendants exposed to disproportionate liability.

b. Factors

In order for a settlement to be considered in good faith, it must be reasonably within the range of the share for which the settling defendant could have been liable. Tech–Bilt, Inc. v. Woodward–Clyde & Associates, 38 Cal.3d 488, 213 Cal.Rptr. 256, 698 P.2d 159 (1985). Determining whether a settlement was entered in good faith requires a rough approximation based on the facts known at the time of the settlement, and includes consideration of such factors as the solvency and insurance limits of the settling defendant, any appearance of fraud or collusion in the settlement, and the recognition that a party typically pays less in settlement than at trial.

3. *Compare Federal Procedure*

While settlement is encouraged in federal practice, the federal rules provide only general authority to the trial judge to facilitate settlement, leaving the particulars to local rules or specific statutes. See FRCP 16. Federal practice does not inquire into the good faith of the settlement by one of multiple defendants. Instead, if the settling defendant settles for an amount that turns out to be less than its proportionate liability as determined at trial, the remaining defendants are entitled to a dollar-for-dollar set-off credit from the settling defendant. McDermott, Inc. v. AmClyde, 511 U.S. 202, 114 S.Ct. 1461, 128 L.Ed.2d 148 (1994).

4. Illustration

Pello was injured due to prolonged exposure to asbestos throughout his career. He subsequently sued 46 different asbestos manufacturers for his injuries. Before trial, Pello settled with 45 of the asbestos manufacturers for $1,500,000 and released them from all claims arising from his asbestos exposure. At trial, the jury found the one remaining defendant, Dalton Industries, liable for Pello's injuries. The jury found Pello's economic damages to be $1,000,000 and his noneconomic damages for pain and suffering to be $3,500,000. The jury apportioned 2% of the fault for Pello's injuries to Dalton Industries. To determine how much Dalton Industries owed Pello, the trial court first divided Pello's economic damages ($1,000,000) by his total damages ($4,500,000) to determine what percentage of his total damages were economic damages (22%). The trial court then multiplied the total pretrial settlement amount ($1,500,000) by 22% to determine what amount of the pretrial settlement was for economic damages ($333,333). Because economic damages are joint and several, Dalton Industries, as the sole remaining defendant, was liable for $666,667 in economic damages ($1,000,000 as assigned by the jury, minus the $333,333 already paid in settlement). Because noneconomic damages are several and not shared, Dalton Industries was liable for $70,000 in noneconomic damages ($4,500,000 as assigned by the jury, multiplied by 2% fault assigned to Dalton Industries). Pello may not recover the remainder of his noneconomic damages. Jones v. John Crane, Inc., 132 Cal.App.4th 990, 35 Cal.Rptr.3d 144 (2005).

VI. OFFER OF JUDGMENT

A. Statutory Basis

California's offer of judgment procedure, as set forth in CCP § 998, reflects the state's policy of encouraging settlements. Section 998 sets out a statutory exception to the general rule under CCP § 1033.5(b)(1) that a prevailing party is entitled to recover costs as a matter of right. Under CCP § 998, a party, even if not the prevailing party, may recover her costs and possibly expert witness fees, if: (1) she submits a timely written section 998 offer; (2) the offer is not accepted; and (3) the party who failed to accept the offer does not obtain a more favorable judgment at trial or contractual arbitration.

B. Offer

1. Form and Timing

As late as ten days before trial, any party may serve on any other party a written section 998 offer of judgment. CCP § 998(a). The offer must state the terms and conditions of the proposed judgment, and must contain a provision allowing the offeree to accept the offer by signing a statement of acceptance. CCP § 998(b).

2. Revocation

The offeror may revoke an offer any time prior to acceptance. T.M. Cobb Co. v. Superior Court, 36 Cal.3d 273, 204 Cal.Rptr. 143, 682 P.2d 338 (1984). A simple letter by the offeror sent prior to notification of the offeree's acceptance is sufficient. Also, death of the offeror or offeree, or a subsequent offer by the offeror, will serve as a revocation of any standing section 998 offer.

3. Token Offer Limitation

CCP § 998 carries with it an implied requirement that the offer be in good faith. A token or nominal offer does not meet this requirement. For an offer to meet the good faith requirement, "[t]he offer must carry with it some reasonable prospect of acceptance. One having no expectation that his or her offer will be accepted will not be allowed to benefit from a no-risk offer made for the sole purpose of later recovering large expert witness fees." People ex rel. Lockyer v. Fremont General Corp., 89 Cal.App.4th 1260, 1271, 108 Cal.Rptr.2d 127, 135 (2001). Even a very modest offer can fulfill the good faith requirement if a defendant reasonably believes there is no liability. When a rejected offer turns out to be more favorable than the judgment received, it is prima facie evidence that the offer was made in good faith and was reasonable.

C. Response to Offer

1. Acceptance

For an acceptance to be effective, it must be in writing, signed by the accepting party's counsel (or by the accepting party if he or she does not have representation), and filed with the court. Upon its filing, the judge or clerk must enter judgment in accordance with the offer. CCP § 998(b)(1). The acceptance must be unequivocal and must be communicated to the offeror before the time for acceptance expires.

2. Offer Not Accepted

If the offer lapses without acceptance 30 days after the offer or before trial, whichever comes first, the offer is deemed withdrawn. It cannot be presented at trial as evidence. CCP § 998(b)(2). A rejection of a section 998 offer must be unequivocal. Mere criticism, requests for a better offer, or making a counteroffer do not serve as rejections for section 998 purposes.

D. Effect of Failing to Accept Section 998 Offer

1. Plaintiff's Failure to Accept Defendant's Offer

If the defendant submits a section 998 offer to the plaintiff, the offer is not accepted, and the plaintiff fails to obtain a more favorable judgment at trial or arbitration, the plaintiff may not recover her postoffer costs and must pay the defendant's postoffer costs. Furthermore, the court may, in its discretion, award expert witness fees and costs to the defendant from the time the complaint was filed. CCP § 998(c). The defendant's costs are deducted from the plaintiff's award, and if the defendant's costs exceed the plaintiff's award, judgment for the defendant will be entered in the net amount. CCP § 998(e).

2. Defendant's Failure to Accept Plaintiff's Offer

If the plaintiff submits a section 998 offer to the defendant, the offer is not accepted, and the defendant fails to obtain a more favorable judgment at trial or arbitration, the defendant must pay the plaintiff's costs of suit. In addition, the court may, in its discretion, order the defendant to pay the plaintiff's postoffer expert witness fees. CCP § 998(d).

E. *Compare Federal Procedure*

In contrast to California practice authorizing any party to make a section 998 offer, FRCP 68 permits only the defendant to make an offer of judgment. FRCP 68 offers are normally irrevocable for ten days after the offer is made, while section 998 offers may be revoked at any time. The federal rule does not apply to judgments in favor of defendants. For a defendant to recover costs under Rule 68, the plaintiff must obtain a judgment less favorable than the offer. Delta Air Lines, Inc. v. August, 450 U.S. 346, 101 S.Ct. 1146, 67 L.Ed.2d 287 (1981). The postoffer costs awarded under FRCP 68 are those authorized by the relevant underlying substantive statute. If that statute defines costs as including attorney's fees, those fees are awardable under FRCP 68. Marek v. Chesny, 473 U.S. 1, 105 S.Ct. 3012, 87 L.Ed.2d 1 (1985). Finally, 28 USC § 1821(b) sets a maximum of $40 per day per witness (lay or expert) unless there is specific statutory or contractual authorization that would allow for a greater amount.

F. Illustration

Shoddy Construction, Inc. was the general contractor for the construction of a new library at a law school in Irvine. Shoddy entered into a subcontracting agreement with Over–Budget Builders to perform mechanical work. When that work cost more than anticipated, Over–Budget sued Shoddy in Orange County Superior Court for $200,000, alleging that Shoddy's poor management caused Over–Budget to incur huge cost overruns. In an effort to settle the case, Shoddy presented a written timely section 998 offer in the amount of $100,000, which Over–Budget summarily rejected. Shoddy then prepared for trial in earnest, retaining experts to serve as consultants and trial witnesses. At trial, the jury rendered a verdict for Over–Budget of $80,000. Since this outcome was less favorable than the amount of the section 998 offer, the court ordered Over–Budget to pay Shoddy's postoffer costs of suit, which amounted to $90,000. In addition, the court exercised its discretion to award Shoddy $40,000 toward the costs of the services of its expert witnesses. Hence, despite the fact that Over–Budget was the "prevailing" party, it owed Shoddy $50,000. Scott Co. of California v. Blount, Inc., 20 Cal.4th 1103, 86 Cal.Rptr.2d 614, 979 P.2d 974 (1999).

VII. SUMMARY JUDGMENT AND SUMMARY ADJUDICATION

A. Summary Judgment

A party may move for summary judgment on the ground that the entire action has no merit or that there is no defense to the action. CCP § 437c(a). A trial court may grant a motion for summary judgment if the parties' papers show that "there is no triable issue as to any material fact and that the moving party is entitled to a judgment as a matter of law." CCP § 437c(c). If granted, summary judgment disposes of all causes of action in a complaint or all defenses in an answer, leaving nothing for further adjudication. California's summary judgment law conforms "largely but not completely" to the federal procedures. Aguilar v. Atlantic Richfield Co., 25 Cal.4th 826, 849, 107 Cal.Rptr.2d 841, 860, 24 P.3d 493 (2001).

1. Papers Filed on Motion

a. Moving Party

The moving party must support the motion with evidence in the form of "affidavits, declarations, admissions, answers to interrogatories, depositions, and matters of which judicial notice shall or may be taken." CCP § 437c(b)(1). Additionally, the moving party must file a "separate statement," which sets out the material facts contended to be undisputed and references to the evidence that supports those material facts. CCP § 437c(b)(1); CRC 3.1350(d), (h). A notice of the motion and a memorandum of points and authorities are also required. CRC 3.1350(c).

b. Opposing Party

In addition to presenting evidence and a memorandum of points and authorities in opposition to the motion, the opposing party must file a separate statement stating whether each of the moving party's facts is disputed or undisputed, and noting supporting evidence for each allegedly disputed fact. The opponent may also present additional material facts in dispute. CCP § 437c(b)(3); CRC 3.1350(c), (d).

c. Evidentiary Objections

A party may make objections to the evidence presented in the other party's papers. Evidentiary objections must be made no later than the time of the hearing or they are waived. CCP § 473c(b)(5). In the absence of objections that the trial court sustains, the court considers all evidence presented by the parties and all inferences reasonably deducible from the evidence. CCP § 473c(c).

2. Parties' Respective Burdens

a. Moving Party

1) Burdens of Persuasion, Production and Proof

At all stages of the summary judgment process, the moving party bears the burden of persuasion that there is no triable issue of material fact. The moving party also initially possesses the burden of production of evidence to establish a prima facie showing that there are no material facts in dispute. See CCP § 473c(p). The standard of proof which would apply at trial is relevant on summary judgment. If the plaintiff is the moving party, she must produce evidence establishing the underlying facts by a preponderance of evidence or clear and convincing evidence, depending on the appropriate trial standard of proof. If the defendant is the moving party, he must present evidence that would permit the trier of fact to *not* find any underlying material fact according to the relevant standard of proof at trial. *Aguilar.*

2) **Satisfying Moving Party's Burden**

To meet its burden of production, the moving party must present evidence, not merely argument. A moving defendant must show that one or more elements of the plaintiff's cause of action cannot be established, or that there is a complete defense to the cause of action. CCP § 473c(p)(2). The moving defendant may either affirmatively negate an element of the plaintiff's cause of action, demonstrate that the process of discovery has yielded no evidence to support an element of a cause of action, or show that a complete defense to the cause of action exists. A moving plaintiff may show that there is no defense to a cause of action by providing evidence to support each element of the cause of action. CCP § 473c(p)(1). The moving plaintiff need not affirmatively disprove defenses.

b. **Opposing Party**

If the moving party satisfies the burden of production by establishing a prima facie case showing no material facts in dispute, the burden of production shifts to thc opposing party to present evidence that at least one triable issue of material fact exists. CCP § 473c(p).

3. **Timing of Notice and Hearing**

Summary judgment motions are subject to the lengthiest notice period of any California motion. The moving party must serve the papers on all other parties at least 75 days prior to the date of the hearing. CCP § 437c(a). The notice period may be longer if the papers are served other than by personal delivery. The opposing party must file and serve any opposition to the motion at least 14 days before the hearing. CCP § 437c(b)(2). The moving party must file any reply papers at least five days before the hearing. CCP § 473c(b)(4). The motion must be heard at least 30 days before the scheduled trial date. CCP § 437c(a).

4. Entry of Judgment and Appellate Review

In granting or denying summary judgment, the trial court must render a detailed order setting out the reasons for its ruling and referring specifically to the supporting and opposing evidence on the motion. CCP § 437c(g). The Court of Appeal may review the entry of summary judgment as a final appealable judgment. It may also review the entry of a nonfinal order denying summary judgment upon petition for extraordinary writ. CCP § 437c(m)(1). (See Chapter 8(III)(B)(1).)

5. *Compare Federal Procedure*

FRCP 56, governing summary judgment, is far less detailed than its California statutory equivalent. In a series of cases, the U.S. Supreme Court liberalized the federal summary judgment standards, encouraging courts to utilize such motions to dispose of cases. See Matsushita Electric Industrial Co. v. Zenith Radio Corp., 475 U.S. 574, 106 S.Ct. 1348, 89 L.Ed.2d 538 (1986); Anderson v. Liberty Lobby, Inc., 477 U.S. 242, 106 S.Ct. 2505, 91 L.Ed.2d 202 (1986); Celotex Corp. v. Catrett, 477 U.S. 317, 106 S.Ct. 2548, 91 L.Ed.2d 265 (1986). California's summary judgment law and procedures are largely identical to those under the federal rule and cases. Some notable differences are: (a) FRCP 56 allows a defendant to move for summary judgment without presenting any supporting affidavits, but by merely arguing that the plaintiff does not have and cannot obtain sufficient proof to bear her burden. In California, the moving defendant may not merely rely on argument but must present evidence. (b) Rule 56 does not contain an analogous provision to California's separate statement requirement. (c) The federal notice period for summary judgment motions is much shorter than in California. FRCP 56(c) permits a party to file and serve a summary judgment motion up to ten days before the hearing, and the non-moving party may file her response on the day before the hearing.

6. Illustration

Perth was making a daytime delivery in Sonora to an apartment building owned by Dunne Properties. While walking through an outdoor courtyard, Perth was assaulted by three unknown persons and seriously injured. Perth filed suit in Tuolumne County Superior Court against Dunne Properties for negligence. Perth's complaint alleged that Dunne Properties failed to provide adequate security guards and gates around the premises. Dunne Properties filed a summary judgment motion against Perth on the ground that Perth could not establish the element of causation. In meeting its initial burden of production, Dunne Properties pointed to Perth's discovery responses that did not establish the fact that his injuries were actually caused by a breach of duty on the part of Dunne Properties to provide more adequate security. Dunne Properties was not required to affirmatively negate the causation element of Perth's negligence cause of action. Because Perth had ample time to obtain discovery supporting his contention that Dunne Properties' omissions were a substantial factor in causing his injuries, Perth's factually devoid discovery responses led to the inference that Perth could not prove causation. Based on Dunne Properties' showing, the burden of production shifted to Perth to show a triable issue of fact regarding causation. Perth's evidence was insufficient to meet his burden. Therefore, the court correctly granted Dunne Properties' motion for summary judgment. Saelzler v. Advanced Group 400, 25 Cal.4th 763, 107 Cal.Rptr.2d 617, 23 P.3d 1143 (2001).

B. Summary Adjudication

1. Grounds for Motion

A motion for summary adjudication may be filed as a separate motion or as an alternative to a motion for summary judgment. CCP § 437c(f)(2). Summary adjudication motions may be brought only on four limited grounds:

- A cause of action has no merit;
- There is no defense to a cause of action;
- A claim for punitive damages under Cal. Civ. Code § 3294 has no merit; or
- A defendant did or did not owe a duty to the plaintiff.

CCP § 437c(f)(1).

2. Effect of Granting of Motion

If the trial court grants summary adjudication on one or more of the above matters, the prevailing party no longer needs to present evidence on that matter at trial. The motion must completely dispose of the matter to which it is addressed. In all other respects, a summary adjudication motion proceeds in the same manner as a motion for summary judgment. CCP § 437c(f)(2).

3. *Compare Federal Procedure*

"Partial summary judgment" under FRCP 56(a) is the equivalent of California's summary adjudication. A party may move for summary judgment on "any part" of her case. Unlike the California statute, FRCP 56(a) does not limit the specific issues on which a party is authorized to move for partial summary judgment.

4. Illustration

Phyre filed suit in Lake County Superior Court against her former attorney Daryl for legal malpractice. Daryl had represented Phyre in a lawsuit she filed against her former business partners. In the subsequent malpractice complaint, Phyre sought two items of compensatory damages based on Daryl's negligence: recovery of the unreasonably high settlement amount Daryl negotiated for her to pay to her former partners, and "lost opportunities" that she did not pursue based on Daryl's faulty legal advice. Daryl subsequently filed a motion for summary adjudication to dispose of the claim for lost opportunity damages. Summary adjudication is not appropriate, and the court should deny the motion. Summary adjudication of a claim for damages is permitted only on the issue of punitive damages, not compensatory damages. Moreover, adjudication of Phyre's lost opportunity damages claim would not completely dispose of the cause of action for legal malpractice. DeCastro West Chodorow & Burns, Inc. v. Superior Court, 47 Cal.App.4th 410, 54 Cal.Rptr.2d 792 (1996).

CHAPTER 5

SAMPLE EXAM QUESTIONS

OBJECTIVE QUESTIONS

The question in this section are based on the following hypothetical:

Rita was fired from her job as an technician in the bottling department of Swill Beverage Co. Rita sued Swill in Colusa County Superior Court for wrongful termination based on age discrimination, under California's Fair Employment and Housing Act (FEHA). She seeks compensatory damages of $40,000.

---

(1) Rita's lawsuit is placed within the court's "Fast Track" system. This system is:

a. A means of guaranteeing litigants access to speedy appeals;

b. Inapplicable in domestic relations, juvenile, probate and wrongful termination cases;

c. A method of ensuring that civil cases are disposed of within two years after filing;

d. Intended to weed out unmeritorious cases during the early stages of the lawsuit.

(2) True or False: Assume that after receiving notice, Rita's attorney repeatedly failed to appear for three case management conferences after being ordered by the court to attend. Despite the attorney's misconduct, the trial court may not dismiss Rita's action as a sanction.

(3) Rita wishes to voluntarily dismiss her lawsuit. The dismissal:

a. May be filed without seeking leave of court after the court's tentative ruling granting Swill's motion for summary judgment;

b. May be entered upon oral or written request to the court at anytime before commencement of the trial;

c. Is always without prejudice;

d. Both b and c.

(4) Assume that Rita's action is governed by California's diligent prosecution statutes. Those statutes:

a. Provide that the judge has discretion to dismiss the case if Rita has not brought it to trial within two years of the filing of the complaint;

b. Provide that the judge must dismiss the case if Rita has not brought it to trial within five years of the filing of the complaint;

c. Set out absolute time limits that are not subject to expansion or tolling;

d. Both a and b.

(5) Assume that Swill has not filed a response to the complaint and the court has entered its default. Before obtaining a default judgment against Swill, Rita must:

a. Give Swill notice of the court's prove-up hearing;

b. Re-serve Swill with the complaint;

c. Serve Swill with a statement noting the amount of compensatory damages sought;

d. None of the above.

(6) True or False: Summary adjudication is an appropriate motion for Swill to bring against Rita if one of Swill's defenses is that Rita owed Swill a duty as an employee to use her best efforts to complete her work tasks.

(7) If Swill brings a motion for summary judgment against Rita, Swill must:

a. Serve the notice of motion and supporting papers on Rita at least 75 days before the hearing;

b. Serve the notice of motion and supporting papers on Rita at least ten days before the hearing;

c. Satisfy its burden of persuasion before the burden shifts to Rita to show a triable issue of material fact;

d. Serve a separate statement of disputed material facts and the evidence supporting those facts.

(8) Rita wishes to make a CCP § 998 offer of judgment to Swill. Which of the following is NOT true about a section 998 offer of judgment:

a. Rita's section 998 offer must be submitted in writing;

b. Rita may expressly revoke her section 998 offer at any time prior to Swill's acceptance;

c. Rita may not make a section 998 offer because only defendants may make such offers;

d. If Rita's section 998 offer is not accepted before trial or within 30 days of the offer, whichever is earliest, it is deemed withdrawn.

(9) True or False: Assume that Rita's employment agreement requires her to arbitrate any dispute she might have with Swill. The court will not enforce the arbitration agreement between Rita and Swill because statutory FEHA claims must be adjudicated only by a court, not in arbitration.

(10) True or False: If the dispute between Rita and Swill is arbitrated, Rita may request the Superior Court to vacate the resulting arbitration award if the face of the award contains a material error that causes substantial injustice to Rita.

(11) True or False: If the court submits Rita's action to judicial arbitration, the court may not also require that Rita and Swill participate in court-annexed mediation.

Answers to Objective Questions

(1) **c.** California's "Fast Track" case management system sets the goal that 100% of nonexempt limited and unlimited civil cases should be resolved within two years of filing. CRC 3.714(b). Juvenile, probate, and domestic relations (but not wrongful termination) cases are statutorily excluded from Fast Track requirements. Cal. Gov't Code § 68608(a).

(2) **True**. If the failure to comply with the court orders to appear at the conferences is the fault of Rita's attorney and not of Rita, the court may not dismiss Rita's case as a sanction. CCP § 575.2(b). Additionally, the court may order dismissal only if it appears that less severe sanctions would not be effective. Cal.Gov't Code § 68608(b).

(3) **b.** Voluntary dismissals may be entered at any time prior to commencement of trial upon written or oral request to the court. CCP § 581(b)(1).

(4) **d.** Both a and b are correct. Subject to statutory tolling provisions, if Rita fails to bring her case to trial two years after the action was filed, the court has discretion

to dismiss it. CCP § 583.420(a)(2)(B); CRC 3.1340. The court must dismiss the action if it is not brought to trial within five years. CCP §§ 583.310, 583.360.

(5) **d.** None of these requirements applies to Rita's action. Rita is not required to serve a statement of damages on Swill, under CCP § 425.11, because her action is not one for personal injury or wrongful death.

(6) **False**. Summary adjudication may be used to adjudicate whether Swill (the defendant) owes Rita (the plaintiff) a duty, but not to adjudicate whether Rita owes Swill a duty. CCP § 437c(f)(1).

(7) **a.** Swill must file its motion at least 75 days before date of the hearing. CCP § 437c(a). The burden of persuasion always remains with the moving party. It is the burden of production that may shift to Rita. Swill must submit with its motion a separate statement of *undisputed* facts. CCP § 437c(b)(1).

(8) **c.** Either party may make a written section 998 offer in California. CCP § 998(b). In contrast, FRCP 68 permits only a defendant to make an offer of judgment.

(9) **False**. FEHA and other statutory claims may be subject to contractual arbitration as long as: (1) the agreement provides for neutral arbitrators; (2) the agreement does not limit the type of relief available or the scope or amount of any remedies; (3) Rita and Swill are afforded adequate opportunity for discovery; (4) the agreement provides for a written award that, under the appropriate circumstances, may be subject to judicial review; and (5) in requiring Rita and other employees to submit to arbitration, the agreement must not require Rita to pay costs and arbitration fees beyond what she would have to pay in a court proceeding.

(10) **False**. The arbitration award may be vacated on only limited grounds. CCP § 1286.2. Error by the arbitrator is not one of those grounds, even if the error is material and substantially prejudices Rita.

(11) **True**. The court may not order cases that it has referred to judicial arbitration into mediation. CCP § 1775.4.

<u>ESSAY QUESTION</u>

Jay was employed as a mechanical engineer for 30 years. During that time, he worked for several employers on numerous job sites, including eight years on naval vessels in San Diego. Shortly after his retirement, Jay discovered he had mesothelioma, a type of cancer caused by exposure to asbestos. Jay filed a product liability action in San Diego County Superior Court against LAC, Inc., a manufacturer and supplier of asbestos to the U.S. Navy during the time Jay was working on naval ships. Jay is seeking $500,000 in general damages, $250,000 in special damages, including medical costs, and an additional $1,000,000 in punitive damages.

LAC immediately noticed Jay's deposition. During the deposition, Jay admitted that while he had heard of LAC, he did not know whether LAC had manufactured the asbestos he was exposed to on the naval vessels and could not remember ever receiving any shipments of LAC products.

Immediately following Jay's deposition, LAC sent Jay an e-mail offering to settle the case for $10,000 pursuant to CCP § 998. The offer was kept open for 30 days. Further, LAC immediately filed and served a summary judgment motion based on Jay's testimony at the deposition.

You are an associate working at the law firm representing Jay. The partner in charge of the case has asked you to research and analyze the following issues:

(1) Has LAC made a proper section 998 offer of judgment? If so, what is required of Jay to accept the section 998 offer?

(2) What are the consequences to Jay if he rejects or fails to respond to the section 998 offer of judgment and then recovers nothing at trial?

(3) What is the likelihood that the court will grant LAC's summary judgment motion?

<u>Answer to Essay Question</u>

(1) <u>Section 998 Offer of Judgment</u>

- Requirements for offer: must be in writing, must specify that the offer is made pursuant to CCP § 998, and must be made at least ten days before the start of trial. It must contain the offer itself and the terms of the judgment, and it must allow Jay to indicate his acceptance by signing a statement of acceptance. CCP § 998(b).

    - Here, LAC has made a written offer expressly under section 998 offer. An e-mail constitutes a writing. The statute does not require a signed offer.

    - It is not known from the facts whether the offer includes provisions regarding Jay's acceptance of the offer.

    - The offer appears to be timely.

- Is the offer token or nominal? Given the doubt about whether LAC manufactured the asbestos in question, LAC's offer probably reflects its good faith belief in its lack of liability because Jay may not be able to prove causation.

- Acceptance of offer:

  - Jay must make an unequivocal acceptance of the offer in writing, signed by his attorney. The acceptance must be filed with the court and must be communicated to LAC before the time for acceptance expires.

(2) Failure to Accept Section 998 Offer

- If Jay does not respond to the offer within 30 days, the offer is deemed withdrawn. If Jay intends to reject the offer, he must do so in an unequivocal writing within 30 days.

  - If Jay rejects or does not respond to the offer, and he then fails to obtain a more favorable judgment at the trial, Jay may not recover his postoffer costs, and he must pay LAC's postoffer costs. The court also has discretion to award expert witness fees and costs to LAC. CCP § 998(c)(1).

  - LAC's costs are deducted from Jay's judgment. If LAC's costs exceed Jay's judgment, the court will enter judgment for LAC in the net amount. CCP § 998(e).

  - More favorable judgment at trial: Jay must actually obtain more than the amount of the 998 offer. Here, Jay would have to recover more than $10,000.

  - The postoffer costs Jay might be required to pay include:

    - Filing costs

    - Service of process costs

    - Cost of making motions

    - Cost of deposition transcripts

    - Fees for appearances and travel of lay witnesses

- Expert witness fees:
    - CCP § 998(c)(1) makes an award of expert witness fees to LAC discretionary.

(3) <u>Summary Judgment Motion</u>

- Standard: LAC must show that the action has no merit by establishing that there is no triable issue of material fact and that LAC is entitled to judgment as a matter of law.
    - Burden: LAC has the burden of persuasion throughout the process. LAC also has the initial burden of production to make a prima facie showing that the sole cause of action for product liability has no merit.
        - A cause of action has no merit when one or more elements cannot be established. Here, LAC will likely focus on the element of causation.
        - LAC may meet its burden of production by showing that despite an adequate opportunity for discovery, Jay's discovery responses are factually devoid. Alternatively, LAC may affirmatively negate the causation element with evidence of its own.
        - LAC's motion must be supported by evidence and must include a separate statement of undisputed facts.
        - If LAC satisfies its burden of production, the burden shifts to Jay to produce evidence establishing a triable issue of material fact. Jay must submit a separate statement in response to LAC's separate statement.
- Application:
    - Jay admitted during his deposition that he does not know whether LAC manufactured the asbestos to which he was exposed. Moreover, Jay had many jobs where he could have been exposed to asbestos.
    - LAC will likely offer Jay's factually devoid deposition testimony as evidence that there is no triable issue with regard to the element of causation. The burden of production will then shift to Jay to provide evidence to show LAC's products actually caused his injuries.
    - Unless Jay can provide such evidence, LAC will likely prevail on summary judgment.

CHAPTER 6

TRIAL

I. SETTING TRIAL DATE

A. Trial Setting Conference

The court must conduct an initial case management conference within 180 days of the filing of the complaint. CRC 3.721, 3.722. The case may be set for trial at the initial conference, but it is more likely that trial setting will occur at a later conference scheduled at the court's discretion. CRC 3.723. In setting a case for trial, the court must consider a variety of factors listed in CRC 3.729, including the complexity of the issues, the amount of discovery yet to be conducted, and the number of parties in the action.

B. Trial Setting Preference

Some parties are entitled to preference in trial setting, such as those over the age of 70, those with a terminal illness, and those under the age of 14 claiming wrongful death or personal injury damages. CCP § 36.

II. CHALLENGES TO TRIAL JUDGE

Once an action is assigned to a Superior Court trial department, the trial judge may be disqualified, either through a challenge for cause or a peremptory challenge. These challenges may also be used to disqualify a Superior Court judicial officer other than the trial judge, such as a law and motion judge, settlement judge, commissioner, or referee. The disqualification statutes do not apply to appellate judges.

A. Challenges for Cause

1. Grounds for Disqualification

Disqualification is required if a statutory ground exists under CCP § 170.1. These include circumstances where the judge:

- has personal knowledge of disputed evidentiary facts;
- has a physical impairment that would render her unable to properly conduct the proceeding;
- has a financial interest in the subject matter of or a party to the proceeding; or
- believes there is a substantial doubt as to her capacity to be impartial.

In addition, disqualification is mandatory under an objective standard if a "person aware of the facts might reasonably entertain a doubt that the judge would be able to be impartial." CCP § 170.1(a)(6)(A)(iii).

2. Procedure

The judge herself initially determines whether grounds for disqualification exist. As soon as the judge is aware of any ground for disqualification for cause, she must cease participation in the proceedings (except for very limited power to act pending assignment to a new judge), unless the parties and attorneys waive the disqualification. CCP § 170.3. If a judge ought to disqualify herself but refuses or fails to do so, a party may file with the court clerk a statement of the grounds for disqualification.

B. Peremptory Challenges

A party or attorney may challenge a trial judge on the ground that the judge is prejudiced against the party or attorney, without providing any further reasons for the challenge. CCP § 170.6. Each side may exercise this peremptory challenge once as a matter of right. A formal written motion is not required—the challenge may be made orally with no prior notice. As long as the challenge is timely and properly brought, the trial judge must promptly recuse herself. If she fails to do so, any subsequent orders or judgments are void as being in excess of jurisdiction. In re Needles Cases, 148 Cal.App.4th 489, 55 Cal.Rptr.3d 708 (2007).

C. *Compare Federal Procedure*

A district court judge must disqualify himself for cause "in any proceeding in which his impartiality might reasonably be questioned," as well as under several grounds similar to those listed in the corresponding California statute. 28 USC § 455. In addition, a party may file an affidavit setting forth specific facts and reasons that the assigned judge has a personal bias or prejudice against him or in favor of an opposing party. 28 USC § 144. There is no federal equivalent to California's peremptory challenge.

D. Illustration

Judge Jesse is married to Kara. Judge Jesse was about to begin a bench trial in a lawsuit filed in Yolo County Superior Court by Union for damages arising out of a labor strike against Veggie, Inc. four years earlier. While in informal conversation with the attorneys for Union and Veggie, Inc. about halfway into the lengthy trial, Judge Jesse mentioned that he had just remembered that his wife had worked for two days as a temporary worker for the defendant company Veggie, Inc. Union made a motion under CCP § 170.1(a)(6)(A)(iii) to disqualify Judge Jesse for cause on the ground that Kara's employment with Veggie, Inc. would raise a reasonable doubt as to whether he would be an impartial trial judge and finder of fact. Under the objective "average person on the street" standard, the judge will not be disqualified. A reasonable person would not doubt Judge Jesse's impartiality based on his wife's brief employment years before. United Farm Workers of America v. Superior Court, 170 Cal.App.3d 97, 216 Cal.Rptr. 4 (1985).

III. OBTAINING A JURY TRIAL

A. Right to Trial By Jury

The right to a jury trial is one of the fundamental rights afforded litigants in a court action. As guaranteed by the California Constitution, "[t]rial by jury is an inviolate right and shall be secured to all." Cal. Const., art. I, § 16.

1. When Right Attaches

In deciding whether the right to a jury trial attaches, California courts have adhered to the historical approach of assessing whether a jury right existed at common law at the time of the adoption of the California Constitution in 1850. Thus, if there was a right to a jury trial at common law (including English common law) in 1850, then there is a constitutional right to a jury trial today in California's courts. In recognition of the fact that the law has evolved and new causes of action have come into being since 1850, the right to a jury has been "extended to cases of like nature as may afterwards arise." People v. One 1941 Chevrolet Coupe, 37 Cal.2d 283, 231 P.2d 832 (1951).

a. Law Versus Equity

Generally, a litigant is entitled to a jury in civil actions at law but not in actions in equity. Actions that are considered *legal* and thus within the domain of the jury include those for:

- recovery of specific real or personal property;
- money due under a contract;
- damages for breach of contract;
- damages for fraud;
- damages for negligence;
- damages for injury to real or personal property; and
- damages for violation of a statute.

CCP § 592.

Matters that are considered *equitable* and thus within the domain of the court include those for:

- injunctive relief;
- specific performance of a contract;
- petitions or motions to compel arbitration;
- rescission of a contract;
- damages or relief under the doctrine of promissory estoppel;
- paternity actions; and
- defenses such as res judicata and equitable estoppel.

1) "Gist of the Action"

In many actions, there is a mix of legal and equitable issues and causes of action. If these issues are intertwined to such a degree that they cannot be reasonably separated, the court will employ the "gist of the action" test. When the action deals mainly with ordinary common law rights, it is an action at law and a jury right exists. Conversely, if the action depends primarily on the application of equitable doctrines, no jury right attaches. C & K Engineering Contractors v. Amber Steel Co., 23 Cal.3d 1, 151 Cal.Rptr. 323, 587 P.2d 1136 (1978).

2) "Equity First" Rule

If the issues are severable, the court can hold separate jury and non-jury phases. California ordinarily follows the "equity first" rule—equitable causes of action are tried first by the court, followed by legal causes of action tried by the jury. But this rule is not rigid. A court has discretion to decide whether to try the equitable or legal issues first. Cal. Evid. Code § 320. This choice can impact the case in at least two ways: (a) the decision rendered in the first phase may render the second phase moot; and (b) findings of fact made during the first phase are binding on the trier of fact during the second phase.

3) Equitable "Clean-Up" Doctrine

California observes the equitable clean-up doctrine, which precludes the right to a jury trial in actions in which the legal issues are "incidental" to the equitable issues.

b. *Compare Federal Procedure*

One of the most salient differences between the California and the federal systems is the derivation of the right to a jury trial. The Seventh Amendment to the U.S. Constitution provides: "In Suits at common law, where the value in controversy shall exceed twenty dollars, the right of trial by jury shall be preserved. . . . " However, since this amendment has not been applied to the states, the California right to a jury in civil trials derives from the state Constitution only. There is no need to follow U.S. Supreme Court precedent interpreting the Seventh Amendment. When the U.S. Supreme Court revised the historical test starting in the late 1950's, and expanded the right to trial by jury, the California Supreme Court adhered to the historical test. For example, when an action in federal court involves both equitable and legal issues, the jury will almost always hear the legal issues first. As a result of the expansion of the jury right, the federal system has also rejected the equitable clean-up doctrine; no legal issues are considered "incidental." While there are many differences between the federal and California systems, there is one important similarity: the U.S. Congress and the California Legislature each have the power to create the right to a jury trial by statute for additional causes of action.

c. Illustration

While driving on the Golden Gate Bridge, careless driver Denise was talking on her cellular phone and trying to add sweetener to her half-caf, no foam, double shot, extra hot, ultra-super grande, vanilla-hazelnut latte with extra whip cream and chocolate shavings. Amidst her multitude of tasks, she forgot to keep an eye on the road and ran into the back of Paddy's car. Both Paddy and Denise were uninjured, but Paddy's car sustained $3,000 in damage. Paddy sued Denise in the Small Claims Division of the Marin County Superior Court to recover the cost of repairs. Judgment was entered for Paddy. At the appeal (de novo trial) in the Superior Court initiated by Denise, Paddy demanded a jury trial, even though the small claims statutes do not provide for one. The court must deny his demand. While damages for negligence are considered legal in nature, and thus triable by jury, a jury trial was not available for small monetary claims such as Paddy's at the time of the adoption of the California Constitution. Because in 1850, cases involving small sums of money were usually adjudicated by juryless tribunals, Paddy has no constitutional right to a jury in either small claims court or at the trial de novo in Superior Court. Crouchman v. Superior Court, 45 Cal.3d 1167, 248 Cal.Rptr. 626, 755 P.2d 1075 (1988).

2. Securing a Jury

a. Jury Demand

A party must make a timely and proper demand for a trial by jury. A demand is considered timely if it is made at the time the cause is first set for trial, or within five days after notice of setting if the trial date is set without notice or stipulation. CCP § 631(d)(4). This demand requires only that the party announce, either in writing or orally, that a jury is wanted. Once this demand has been properly made, it applies to the original trial and any subsequent retrials that may occur. In addition to making a timely demand, a party must post jury fees in advance of the trial. CCP § 631(b). Starting on the second day of trial, and every day thereafter, the party must provide another deposit equal to that day's jury fees. CCP § 631(c).

b. Waiver of Jury Trial Right

The California Constitution provides that a party may waive the right to a jury. Cal. Const., art. I, § 16. Waiver may occur in several ways, including failing to appear at trial, filing written consent to a bench trial with the court clerk, orally consenting to waiver in open court, failing to make a timely demand for a jury, and failing to deposit jury fees on time. CCP § 631(d). The means of waiver can be created only by the Legislature. Non-statutory forms of waiver are unenforceable. Grafton Partners L.P. v. Superior Court, 36 Cal.4th 944, 32 Cal.Rptr.3d 5, 116 P.3d 479 (2005).

c. Relief from Waiver

Even if a party waives the right to a jury, deliberately or inadvertently, the court may grant relief from this waiver. CCP § 631(e). Though left to the discretion of the court, California has a policy favoring relief from waiver of the jury right. In general, such a motion will be granted unless it would create substantial hardship to the opposing party. Boal v. Price Waterhouse & Co., 165 Cal.App.3d 806, 212 Cal.Rptr. 42 (1985).

d. *Compare Federal Procedure*

FRPC 38(b) requires a party to serve a timely written demand for a jury trial or else the right is waived. A party may waive the right to a jury by stipulation of the parties (FRCP 39(a)(1)), or consent (FRCP 38(d)). The court may reinstate a jury trial after a waiver (FRCP 39(b)), but federal courts are less generous than California courts in restoring a jury trial after an inadvertent waiver.

e. Illustration

Philo sued Darlene for breach of contract damages in Alpine County Superior Court. The contract contained a pre-dispute waiver of the right to jury trial. When Philo insisted on a bench trial, Darlene objected to the contractual jury trial waiver. The court will not enforce the pre-dispute jury trial

> waiver. CCP § 631 provides the only valid grounds for waiver or forfeiture of the right to jury trial. A contractual waiver that does not fit into one of the statutory grounds is unenforceable. A pretrial jury waiver is not statutorily permitted. The waiver of the right to a jury trial must occur during the pendency of the action. Grafton Partners L.P. v. Superior Court, 36 Cal.4th 944, 32 Cal.Rptr.3d 5, 116 P.3d 479 (2005).

B. Stages of Jury Selection

1. Jury Pool

Each year, the jury commissioner of every county Superior Court must compile a master list of names from which the court may summon potential jurors for jury duty. CCP § 198(b). Prospective jurors for the master list may be chosen from any sources that will provide a "representative cross-section of the population." CCP § 197(a). Common sources for names of potential jurors include voter registration lists, Department of Motor Vehicles lists, telephone directories, and utility company customer lists. The master list is then narrowed down to eliminate persons not qualified for jury service. CCP § 198(c). Those disqualified from jury service include noncitizens, minors, convicted felons, and conservatees. CCP § 203. Those persons on the qualified juror list may be summoned at random to appear for jury service.

2. Jury Venire

When prospective jurors are summoned from the jury pool to the court for possible jury service, they may request postponement of jury service or may seek an excuse from service based on an "undue hardship." CCP § 204(b). Acceptable hardship excuses include lack of reasonably available transportation, extreme financial burden, and risk of mental or physical harm. CRC 2.1008(d). The summoned jurors who remain after postponements and hardship excuses are granted constitute the jury venire.

3. Jury Panel

When a particular department of the Superior Court has a need for jurors, a group of prospective jurors is randomly assigned from the venire and sent to the courtroom to undergo voir dire. CCP § 194(q). Before voir dire commences, the entire panel is sworn. It is from the jury panel that the actual jurors who will hear the case will be selected.

4. Petit Jury

Those members of the jury panel who are not excused during voir dire become the members of the petit jury before whom the action is tried. The petit jury may also include alternate jurors.

C. Composition of Jury Venire

1. Representative Cross-Section of Community

The California Supreme Court has interpreted the constitutional right to a jury trial under article I, section 16 to mean that a party is entitled to a jury drawn from a representative cross-section of the community. Williams v. Superior Court, 49 Cal.3d 736, 263 Cal.Rptr. 503, 781 P.2d 537 (1989). This requirement is also statutory. CCP § 204(a). At each stage of the jury selection process, persons from distinctive groups within the community may not be systematically excluded. People v. Anderson, 25 Cal.4th 543, 106 Cal.Rptr.2d 575, 22 P.3d 347 (2001). California courts apply the standards developed in criminal cases under the Sixth Amendment to civil cases, too, because the entire jury trial right is guaranteed in one provision of the state Constitution. California law is sometimes more strict than federal law, but it cannot be less strict.

2. Test for Violation of Representative Cross-Section Requirement

To establish a prima facie showing that the representative cross-section requirement has been violated, a party must satisfy a three-pronged test:

- The excluded group is a distinctive or cognizable group in the community;
- The representation of this group in the jury venire is not "fair and reasonable" when compared to the number of such persons in the community; and
- The underrepresentation is due to systematic exclusion of that group in the process of jury selection.

Duren v. Missouri, 439 U.S. 357, 99 S.Ct. 664, 58 L.Ed.2d 579 (1979). If the objecting party establishes a prima facie case under this test, the burden shifts to the opposing party to provide a more precise statistical showing that no significant disparity exists, or a compelling justification for the procedure that has resulted in the disparity. People v. Burgener, 29 Cal.4th 833, 129 Cal.Rptr.2d 747, 62 P.3d 1 (2003).

a. Prong 1: Cognizable Group Requirement

There are two requirements for a group to be considered cognizable or distinctive: (1) the members of the group "share a common perspective arising from their life experience in the group"; and (2) "no other members of the community are capable of adequately representing the perspective of the group." People v. Garcia, 77 Cal.App.4th 1269, 1276–1279, 92 Cal.Rptr.2d 339, 343–345 (2000). In general, groups based on race, gender, and religion have been considered cognizable groups. California also recognizes groups based on sexual orientation as distinctive. Id.; CCP § 231.5. In contrast, age and socioeconomic status are insufficient to establish a cognizable group.

b. Prong 2: Fair and Reasonable Representation Requirement

1) Tests for Measuring Disparity

There are two tests currently used by the California courts for measuring underrepresentation. The "absolute disparity" test calculates the difference between the group's percentage in the jury-eligible population and the group's percentage in the jury venire. For example, if African Americans comprise 5 percent of the eligible population but only 3 percent of the jury venire, the absolute disparity would be 2 percent (5%–3% = 2%). The "comparative disparity" test calculates the percentage by which the number in the jury venire is below the number in the jury-eligible population. This figure is calculated by taking the absolute disparity and dividing it by the jury-eligible population. Returning to the above example, the comparative disparity would be 40 percent (2% / 5% = 40%).

2) Problems with Disparity Tests

The courts have failed to establish a clear threshold for when a disparity becomes impermissible. The California Supreme Court has ruled that absolute disparities between 2.7 percent and 4.3 percent and comparative disparities between 23.5 percent and 37.4 percent are allowable. People v. Ramos, 15 Cal.4th 1133, 1156, 64 Cal.Rptr. 892, 938 (1997). Both the absolute and comparative disparity tests have been criticized for statistically distorting the underrepresentation of the excluded group.

3) **Definition of Community**

For the purpose of the fair and reasonable representation requirement, the term "community" refers to the judicial district in which the case is tried. "Community" does not necessarily refer to the entire county in which the court sits or the location of the incident that gave rise to the suit. Williams v. Superior Court, 49 Cal.3d 736, 263 Cal.Rptr. 503, 781 P.2d 537 (1989). For example, each of the 11 judicial districts within the Los Angeles County Superior Court is considered a "community" for purposes of this test.

c. **Prong 3: Systematic Exclusion Requirement**

Statistical proof of a disparity in prong 2 does not, in and of itself, satisfy the objecting party's burden of proof. To establish a violation of the representative cross-section requirement, the objecting party must also prove that the disparity is the product of an improper feature of the jury selection process. The party may show that the criteria for selection are not random or neutral. If the criteria are neutral, the challenging party may attempt to establish that they are applied in a constitutionally impermissible way that accounts for the disparity. People v. Burgener, 29 Cal.4th 833, 129 Cal.Rptr.2d 747, 62 P.3d 1 (2003).

3. ***Compare Federal Procedure***

Like California's requirement, a federal jury must be "selected at random from a fair cross section of the community." 28 USC § 1861. A potential juror cannot be excluded because of race, color, religion, sex, national origin, or economic status. 28 USC § 1862. One notable difference between California and federal law is the definition of "community." Under federal law, each district court may decide to adopt either a district-wide or a division-wide jury pool. 28 USC §§ 1861, 1863. California's four U.S. district courts draw upon far larger communities than the state superior courts, which rely on county-based jury pools.

4. **Illustration**

After several months of living next to his new neighbors, the Whipper–Snappers, plaintiff Carl Curmudgeon filed a nuisance suit against them in Mono County Superior Court. In the complaint,

Curmudgeon alleged that the Whipper–Snappers would often play music after 6 p.m. and could be heard talking in their backyard as late as 7:45 p.m. When the suit reached the jury selection stage, Curmudgeon was appalled to find an absence of senior citizens in the jury venire. He moved to quash the venire on the ground that the venire did not constitute a representative cross-section of the community. Curmudgeon provided statistical evidence that senior citizens make up five percent of Mono County, but only four percent of the jury venire. The court will deny the motion to quash on three independently sufficient grounds. First, distinctions based on age are not sufficient to establish a cognizable group. Second, the absolute disparity of one percent and comparative disparity of 20 percent are well within the acceptable range. Third, Curmudgeon failed to provide proof that this disparity was a product of an impermissible feature of the jury selection process that resulted in systematic exclusion of senior citizens. As such, Curmudgeon failed to establish a violation of the fair cross-section requirement. People v. Burgener, 29 Cal.4th 833, 129 Cal.Rptr.2d 747, 62 P.3d 1 (2003).

D. Composition of Petit Jury

1. Voir Dire

a. Purpose of Voir Dire

The petit jury is selected via the process known as voir dire. In ancient Norman French, the term "voir dire" translates as "to speak the truth." In modern French, it is translated as "see and speak." Voir dire consists of a series ofquestions from the judge and counsel to the prospective jurors on the jury panel. Voir dire serves two main purposes: (1) it assures that the jury is fair and impartial; and (2) it helps counsel in the intelligent exercise of challenges. CCP § 222.5.

b. Conduct of Voir Dire

Before any party questions the prospective jurors, the judge usually conducts an examination. This questioning largely consists of questions regarding the person ability to serve as an impartial juror. Once the judge completes this examination, the parties have the opportunity to question the prospective jurors. CCP § 222.5; CRC 3.1540.

2. Challenges to Prospective Jurors

Challenges to prospective jurors during voir dire fall into two categories: challenges for cause and peremptory challenges. Challenges for cause are exercised first, followed by peremptory challenges. CCP § 226(c).

a. Challenges for Cause

1) Number of Challenges for Cause

There is no limit to the number of challenges for cause. Similarly, there is no limit as to the number of grounds that can be raised against a given prospective juror. These challenges can be lodged either in writing or orally. CCP § 226(b).

2) Grounds for Challenges for Cause

There are three distinct grounds on which an attorney may exercise a challenge for cause, in the following order:

a) Challenge for General Disqualification

A prospective juror may be challenged for general disqualification if the prospective juror: (1) lacks the qualifications required by law to be a competent juror; or (2) has a disability or incapacity that renders the juror unable to perform the duties of a juror. CCP § 228.

b) Challenge for Implied Bias

In some situations, the law presumes that a juror is biased, and thus not fit to serve as a juror. Such situations include the following:

- The prospective juror is related by blood or marriage to any party, to an officer of a corporate party, or to any witness or victim in the case within the fourth degree;

- The relationship between the prospective juror and a party is of a kind listed in CCP § 229(b) (such as landlord-tenant, employer-employee, principal-agent, or debtor-creditor);

- The prospective juror has served as a witness or juror in a trial with the same parties or involving the same offense or cause of action;
- The prospective juror has an interest in the litigation;
- The prospective juror has an unqualified belief or opinion based on knowledge of material facts; or
- The prospective juror has enmity against, or bias toward, either party.

CCP § 229.

c) Challenge for Actual Bias

A prospective juror may be challenged for actual bias when he or she has shown "a state of mind . . . in reference to the case, or to any of the parties, which will prevent the juror from acting with entire impartiality, and without prejudice to the substantial rights of any party." CCP § 225(b)(1)(C).

b. Peremptory Challenges

Peremptory challenges permit a party to remove prospective jurors for any reason that does not violate constitutional limitations. These challenges are often exercised to remove jurors thought to be unsympathetic or overly opinionated.

1) Number of Peremptory Challenges

Unlike challenges for cause, each party gets a limited number of peremptory challenges. In most situations, each party may exercise up to six peremptory challenges. If there are more than two parties, the court will divide the parties into two or more sides and give each side eight peremptory challenges. If there are more than two sides, the court will grant additional peremptory challenges as "the interests of justice may require." CCP § 231(c). The exercise of peremptory challenges alternates between the sides until all challenges have been used or until both sides consecutively choose not to exercise a challenge. CCP § 231(d).

2) Constitutional Limitations on Peremptory Challenges

While peremptory challenges may be exercised without giving a reason, they cannot be used to deliberately and systematically exclude cognizable groups from the jury. This sort of exclusion violates both the Equal Protection Clause of the Fourteenth Amendment, and the California Constitution's representative cross-section requirement.

a) Test Under Equal Protection Clause

The test for a violation of the Equal Protection Clause often arises in the context of a *Batson* challenge. Batson v. Kentucky, 476 U.S. 79, 106 S.Ct. 1712, 90 L.Ed.2d 69 (1986). The objecting party has the initial burden to establish a prima facie case of discrimination by showing that the circumstances surrounding the challenge raise an inference of discrimination. Johnson v. California, 545 U.S. 162, 125 S.Ct. 2410, 162 L.Ed.2d 129 (2005). If the objecting party is successful, the burden shifts to the opponent to provide a neutral explanation for the challenge. The objecting party then has the opportunity to show that the explanation for the challenge is a pretext and that there was purposeful discrimination. Id. The court decides whether the objecting party has proven purposeful discrimination. If the appellate court finds a *Batson* violation or finds that the trial court applied an incorrect standard, it orders limited remand of the case to the trial court rather than automatic reversal of the trial court judgment. People v. Johnson, 38 Cal.4th 1096, 45 Cal.Rptr.3d 1, 136 P.3d 804 (2006). While race and gender discrimination dominate the case law in this area, California also forbids peremptory challenges based on sexual orientation. CCP § 231.5.

b) Test Under California Constitution

Under California law, peremptory challenges are presumed to be properly exercised. To overcome this presumption, the objecting party must: (1) create as complete a record of the circumstances surrounding the challenge as possible; (2) establish that the challenged prospective jurors were part of a cognizable group; and (3) establish a reasonable inference that the excluded jurors were challenged because they were members of the cognizable group. If the objecting party is successful is making this showing, the burden shifts to the opposing party to establish that the challenges were not the product of group bias alone. People v. Wheeler, 22 Cal.3d 258, 148 Cal.Rptr. 890, 583 P.2d 748 (1978). In contrast to a federal *Batson* challenge—where the court typically orders a limited remand—a successful *Wheeler* challenge on California constitutional grounds results in automatic reversal of the trial court judgment. People v. Johnson, 38 Cal.4th 1096, 1105, 45 Cal.Rptr.3d 1, 7, 136 P.3d 804 (2006) (Werdegar, J., concurring).

3. Jury Size

Historically, the petit jury has been composed of 12 jurors. However, California law permits smaller juries in civil cases. "[T]he Legislature may provide that the jury shall consist of eight persons or a lesser number agreed on by the parties in open court." Cal. Const., art. I, § 16. See also CCP § 220.

4. *Compare Federal Procedure*

Federal voir dire, in contrast to California, is largely conducted by the judge. FRCP 47. Though federal judges may allow the attorneys to ask questions of prospective jurors, this practice is more prevalent in state court. Another notable difference is in the number of peremptory challenges each litigant has. Parties in federal civil cases have only three. 28 USC § 1870. Finally, FRCP 48 sets the number of jurors at between six and 12. Six jurors is the bare minimum for federal constitutional purposes. Colgrove v. Battin, 413 U.S. 149, 93 S.Ct. 2448, 37 L.Ed.2d 522 (1973).

5. Illustration

Ponce, owner of an apartment building in Fort Bragg, brought an unlawful detainer action in Mendocino County Superior Courta-gainst Dimitri, a tenant in the building. Dimitri had refused to pay rent over a six month period because he believed that the landlord-tenant system "kept the masses down" and concentrated power in the hands of a few wealthy land owners. During voir dire,

> Dimitri tried to procure a sympathetic jury by using his peremptory challenges to remove affluent prospective jurors. In doing this, Dimitri's attorney exercised peremptory challenges against three company CEOs, two law firm partners, and one state lottery winner. Ponce objected that this tactic violated the California Constitution's representative cross-section requirement. Dimitri's counsel admitted that he was trying to excuse wealthy jurors but contended that this was permissible under California law. The court should agree. While there was a reasonable inference that prospective jurors were being challenged because of their membership in a specific group, this group is not a cognizable one. That is, distinctions based on wealth are not cognizable like distinctions based on race, gender, religion, or sexual orientation. Economic groups do not share a common perspective arising out of their life experience, and other members of the community are capable of adequately representing their perspective on the jury. Accordingly, Ponce's objection will be overruled. People v. Garcia, 77 Cal.App.4th 1269, 92 Cal.Rptr.2d 339 (2000).

IV. CONDUCT OF JURY TRIAL

A. Order of Proceedings

A jury trial proceeds in a statutorily determined order unless the trial judge rules otherwise. CCP § 607. The trial generally proceeds as follows:

- The plaintiff makes her opening statement;
- The defendant makes his opening statement after the plaintiff's statement, or waits until after the plaintiff has presented her evidence;
- The plaintiff presents her evidence;
- The defendant makes his opening statement if he has not already done so;
- The defendant presents his evidence;
- The parties offer rebuttal evidence;
- The plaintiff presents her closing argument;

- The defendant presents his closing argument;
- The court instructs the jury;
- The jury deliberates; and
- The jury renders a verdict.

B. Opening Statements and Closing Arguments

1. Opening Statements

The opening statement is an opportunity for both parties to set out the nature of the action and the facts that will be presented to the jury during the trial proceedings. It is considered a key component of the trial because it often influences the jurors' perception of the case. Argument is not permitted during the opening statement.

2. Closing Arguments

Closing argument is counsel's final opportunity to communicate with the jurors and attempt to shape their interpretation of the evidence before the jury begins its deliberations. The court may admonish the jury and/or strike counsel's remarks if the argument contains irrelevant or inflammatory matter, or if it appeals to the jurors' prejudices or emotionalism. Du Jardin v. City of Oxnard, 38 Cal.App.4th 174, 45 Cal.Rptr.2d 48 (1995). For example, reciting the Golden Rule to the jury constitutes improper argument.

C. Commenting on the Evidence

1. Power to Comment

Judges have the power to "make any comment on the evidence and the testimony and credibility of any witness as in [their] opinion is necessary for the proper determination of the cause." Cal. Const., art. VI, § 10.

a. What Judges May Say

Judges have great leeway in commenting on evidence while charging the jury. Orient Handel v. United States Fidelity and Guaranty Co., 192 Cal.App.3d 684, 237 Cal.Rptr. 667 (1987). If a judge's statement is "accurate, temperate, and 'scrupulously fair' " and does not state an opinion "on the ultimate issue," then the comment will be permissible. People v. Melton, 44 Cal.3d 713, 735, 244 Cal.Rptr. 867, 878, 750 P.2d 741 (1988).

b. Limits on Judge's Power to Comment

While the judge's power is rather sweeping, it is not unlimited. In commenting, the judge may not, for example, withdraw material evidence from the jury's consideration, distort the record, or usurp the jury's ultimate fact-finding authority.

2. *Compare Federal Procedure*

The Federal Rules are silent on the power of federal judges to comment on evidence. The general tenor of federal case law is that, like their California counterparts, federal judges have the power to comment on the evidence (though they often choose not to exercise it). The U.S. Supreme Court has referred to the ability to comment on the evidence as one of the "essential prerogatives of the trial judge." Quercia v. United States, 289 U.S. 466, 469, 53 S.Ct. 698, 699, 77 L.Ed. 1321 (1933). Generally, comments are unacceptable if they are prejudicial or affect the jury's ability to pass upon the evidence in a fair and dispassionate way.

3. Illustration

Presley played a tennis match at his extremely exclusive Newport Beach country club, Diamond Hills. At the end of the match, Presley approached the net to shake his opponent's hand. In an effort to further display his athletic prowess, Presley attempted to jump over the net, only to catch his foot, fall forward, and break both of his wrists. Presley brought a negligence suit in Orange County Superior Court against Diamond Hills, claiming that the net was too high and that this "defect" was the cause of his injuries. At the end of the trial and after the jury instructions had been read, a clearly exasperated trial judge launched into the following monologue:

> Ladies and gentlemen of the jury, I will be honest with you. I was not supposed to be here this week. I was supposed to be on vacation. I had a tee time at Pebble Beach! Do you know how hard those are to get? But instead, I am stuck here just like you, dealing with some knucklehead who injured himself being an idiot. Here's the deal. There is no evidence that there was a defect or that a defect caused Mr. Presley's injuries. The verdict you render should be for the defendant, and if it is not, I will direct a verdict for it.

The jury returned a verdict for Diamond Hills. Presley made a timely motion for a new trial, but the court denied it. On appeal,

> Presley argued that he was entitled to a new trial because the judge's statements were beyond the scope of permissible comment on the evidence. The appellate court will likely agree with Presley's position, noting that the trial judge made two main mistakes: (a) his comments were addressed not only to the evidence, but also to the ultimate question of liability; and (b) he expressly directed a verdict with his comments. As such, Presley was entitled to a new trial. Lewis v. Bill Robertson & Sons, Inc., 162 Cal.App.3d 650, 208 Cal.Rptr. 699 (1984).

D. Instructions on the Law

During a jury trial, the court has the responsibility of instructing (or "charging") the jury on relevant matters of law. CCP § 607a. Ultimately, courts strive to craft instructions that are correct and neutral statements of law that are easily understandable by the jurors. See CRC 2.1050; 1 CACI Preface.

1. Sources of Proper Jury Instructions

a. Form Instructions

Form instructions arc thc sourcc of the vast majority of jury instructions. They are pre-drafted—easy to use and generally accepted as accurate (and thus, not very susceptible to reversal on appeal). While form instructions are commonly used, they may be successfully challenged as inaccurate, irrelevant, or otherwise flawed. Mitchell v. Gonzales, 54 Cal.3d 1041, 1 Cal.Rptr.2d 913, 819 P.2d 872 (1991).

1) CACI Instructions

The Judicial Council of California approved the use of the California Civil Jury Instructions (CACI) in 2003. CACI constitute the official jury instructions in California. CRC 2.1050(a). The use of these instructions is strongly encouraged (CRC 2.1050(e)) and even mandatory in some counties. See, e.g., Orange Superior Court Rule 362 (requiring CACI to be used "insofar as practicable"). CACI include introductory, evidentiary, and concluding instructions as well as a variety of substantive instructions. CACI have supplanted other form instructions as the official instructions in California courts because they provide legally accurate instructions that are written at a high school level of comprehension.

2) BAJI Instructions

The widely-used predecessor to CACI was the California Jury Instructions, Civil (commonly referred to as the "Book of Approved Jury Instructions" or "BAJI"). Much like CACI, BAJI contain introductory, evidentiary, concluding, and substantive instructions. While CACI have superseded BAJI as the approved instructions, courts still occasionally use BAJI. See Fields v. Yusuf, 144 Cal.App.4th 1381, 51 Cal.Rptr.3d 277 (2006) (trial court's refusal to use BAJI instruction instead of CACI instruction was prejudicial because CACI did not provide a complete recital of the relevant law).

b. Other Sources of Instructions

Instructions may be crafted from relevant statutory language or appellate opinions. Other sources of jury instructions include form books, practice guides, legal treatises, restatements of law, and legal and common dictionaries.

2. Submission of Proposed Jury Instructions

a. Timing of Submissions

Prior to the swearing of the first witness, the parties are expected to submit proposed jury instructions "covering the law as disclosed by the pleadings." CCP § 607a. Prior to closing arguments, additional proposed instructions may be submitted regarding questions of law developed by the evidence during the trial that were not disclosed by the pleadings. After closing arguments, the court may give instructions on issues raised during the arguments but not addressed by previous instructions that were given or rejected. If an instruction is proposed late, the court has the discretion to refuse to use it.

b. Court's Responsibilities after Submission

Once counsel have submitted proposed jury instructions, the court must decide whether the each proposed instruction should be accepted, rejected, or modified, determine whether any additional instructions should be given, and apprise counsel of the instructions the court intends to give. CCP § 607a.

3. Charging the Jury

a. Timing of Instructions

Traditionally, the court charges the jury directly before or just after closing arguments. The court retains the power to instruct the jury at other times during the trial. CCP § 607. In some instances, rereading or giving additional instructions may be necessary after deliberations have begun.

b. Juror Comprehension of Instructions

Usually instructions are presented both orally and in writing. In most cases, judges will read the instructions to the jurors first and then allow them to take a complete copy of the instructions into the jury room during deliberations. If the jurors "desire to be informed of any point of law arising in the cause," they may be brought into court and provided with the information they want "in the presence of, or after notice to, the parties or counsel." CCP § 614. California has instituted additional rules intended to increase juror comprehension of jury instructions, including requiring that jurors be permitted to take written notes during trial and instructions, and allowing trial judges to preinstruct juries immediately after being sworn. CRC 2.1031–2.1035.

4. Deliberations

After the court submits the case to the jury and the jury retires to begin its deliberations, the jurors must be kept together under the supervision of a baliff or other court officer until they reach a verdict or the court discharges them. The officer must ensure that no improper communications are made to the jury during their deliberations, which must take place in secret. CCP § 613. The only items ordinarily permitted in the jury room are papers that were entered into evidence, exhibits that the court may deem proper, jury instructions, and notes taken by individual jurors. CCP §§ 612, 612.5. Jurors may request the officer to bring them back into court for testimony to be reread or jury instructions to be clarified. Counsel for all parties must be notified and present in court when the court provides the jury with additional information. CCP § 614.

5. *Compare Federal Procedure*

Unlike California, which requires instructions to be proposed early in the trial process, federal parties must submit instructions "at the close of evidence or at any earlier time the court orders." FRCP 51. Another difference between the two systems is the use of form instructions. While California has an "approved" set of official form instructions (CACI), the federal system does not. Unofficial form instructions (Federal Jury Practice and Instructions) exist but use of these instructions is less prevalent than the use of CACI in California.

6. Illustration

Paris Co. hired the accounting firm of Dulloite, Inc. to perform an independent audit and provide an opinion of its financial condition. Paris Co. and Dulloite disagreed over the financial statements. Contending that the management of Paris Co. was uncooperative, Dulloite resigned before issuing its opinion. Paris Co. sued Dulloite in San Bernardino County Superior Court for breach of contract and professional negligence. At trial, the judge gave a jury instruction requested by Paris Co., which stated that an auditor may resign if doing so does not unreasonably jeopardize the client's interest, as long as the auditor gives notice to the client and provides a reasonable opportunity to hire another accountant. Dulloite objected, arguing that the professional standards governing auditors should be the basis for the instruction. Under those standards, a professional auditor is permitted to resign for good cause, regardless whether the interests of the client are jeopardized. Dulloite's theory was that since the professional standards allowed it to resign for good cause, regardless of the effect on Paris Co.'s interests, Dulloite was entitled to an instruction on that theory. The trial court should have instructed the jury as to the professional standard of auditors. It gave an incorrect statement of the law, which constituted prejudicial error. National Medical Transportation Network v. Deloitte & Touche, 62 Cal.App.4th 412, 72 Cal.Rptr.2d 720 (1998).

E. Verdicts

1. Nonunanimous Verdicts

Unanimity is not required of a civil jury in California. Three-fourths of the jurors are sufficient to reach a verdict. Cal. Const., art. I, § 16; CCP § 618.

2. General, Special and Hybrid Verdicts

a. General Verdicts

A general verdict finds in favor of either the plaintiff or the defendant. CCP § 624. The jury does not specify the reasons for its decision. This is the most commonly used form of verdict in civil cases.

b. Special Verdicts

1) When Used

A special verdict sets out the jury's factual findings on all of the issues presented at trial. The judge then applies the appropriate law to those findings to reach a judgment in the case. CCP § 624. The use of special verdicts is normally within the discretion of the trial judge. Their use is not required except in a handful of situations, such as where the jury renders a verdict for punitive damages. CCP § 625.

2) Agreement on Each Finding Not Required

Under the three-fourths rule, any nine jurors in a jury of 12 may render a valid verdict on each question within the special verdict form. It is not required that the same nine jurors agree on each component of the special verdict. Resch v. Volkswagen of America, Inc., 36 Cal.3d 676, 205 Cal.Rptr. 827, 685 P.2d 1178 (1984).

c. Hybrid Verdicts

In some cases, the jury may render a "hybrid" verdict, which is a general verdict accompanied by responses to specified questions that disclose the basis for the jury's decision. CCP § 625.

3. *Compare Federal Procedure*

A federal jury may render a general verdict, special verdict, or general verdict accompanied by answers to interrogatories. FRCP 49. A federal jury verdict must be unanimous unless the parties stipulate otherwise. FRCP 48.

4. Illustration

After eating dinner at Delicious, one of his favorite restaurants on the Santa Cruz Beach Pier, Pascal slipped while walking down a wet ramp leading from the restaurant to the pier, sustaining severe injuries. Pascal sued Delicious in Santa Cruz County Superior Court for premises liability. The case went to trial, and the jury was directed to render a special verdict on Delicious' liability. The jury's special verdict found that Delicious' negligence and the dangerous condition of the ramp were causes of Pascal's injuries. In response to another question on the special verdict, however, the jury found that the dangerous condition of the ramp did *not* create a foreseeable risk of the type of injury Pascal suffered. Finding these responses to be inconsistent, the trial court sent the jury back for further deliberations to clear up the inconsistency. When the jury returned, question #5 was answered "yes." The judge did not err in requesting the jury to conduct further deliberations. The court did not guide the jury toward a particular outcome. It merely pointed out the unclear set of responses and "provided the jury with an opportunity to render a verdict in accordance with its deliberations." Mizel v. City of Santa Monica, 93 Cal.App.4th 1059, 113 Cal.Rptr.2d 649 (2001).

F. Impeachment of Verdict

1. Jury Misconduct

Cal. Evid. Code § 1150 provides the basis for the impeachment of a jury verdict: "Upon an inquiry as to the validity of a verdict, any otherwise admissible evidence may be received as to statements made, or conduct, conditions, or events occurring, either within or without the jury room, of such a character as is likely to have influenced the verdict improperly." The statute requires objective evidence of misconduct. Evidence of a juror's subjective "mental processes" is not admissible. Examples of impeachable jury misconduct are:

- refusal to follow the court's jury instructions;
- reliance on outside evidence;
- juror inattentiveness and distraction at trial; and
- performance of experiments.

2. *Compare Federal Procedure*

To impeach a federal verdict, a juror may testify regarding "(1) whether extraneous prejudicial information was improperly brought to the jury's attention, (2) whether any outside influence was improperly brought to bear upon any juror, or (3) whether there was a mistake in entering the verdict onto the verdict form." FRE 606(b). Evidence of a juror's mental processes or emotions during the deliberations is not permitted.

> **3. Illustration**
>
> Percy sued Dragster Motor Co. in San Luis Obispo County Superior Court for injuries he sustained when the brakes failed in his Dragster 5000 sports car and Percy collided with a tree in Morro Bay. At the conclusion of the trial, the jury rendered a verdict for Percy. Dragster Motor Co. challenged the verdict on the grounds of juror misconduct. Dragster obtained a declaration from one juror stating that two other jurors were sending text messages to each other and one other juror was working on a crossword puzzle during the presentation of evidence. These activities constitute juror misconduct because the jurors did not satisfy their obligation of attentiveness. However, Dragster Motor Co. is not entitled to a new trial because it did not suffer actual prejudice from the misconduct. Hasson v. Ford Motor Co., 32 Cal.3d 388, 185 Cal.Rptr. 654, 650 P.2d 1171 (1982).

V. JUDICIAL CONTROL OVER JURY VERDICT

California law provides several devices that permit a judge to take a case away from the jury at various stages of the trial, both before and after the jury has rendered a verdict.

A. Nonsuit

1. Nature of Device

Nonsuit allows the trial court to partially or fully resolve the case at an early stage of a trial. The defendant may challenge the legal sufficiency of the plaintiff's causes of action without losing the right to present a defense. CCP § 581c(a). Only a defendant may bring a motion for nonsuit.

a. Timing

The defendant may move for nonsuit at one of two times: (1) at the completion of a plaintiff's opening statement; or (2) after the plaintiff has presented her evidence. CCP § 581c(a).

b. Standard for Granting Nonsuit

A defendant's motion for nonsuit will be granted if the plaintiff's opening statement or presentation of evidence is insufficient to support a prima facie showing of each element of the plaintiff's causes of action.

1) After Plaintiff's Opening Statement

A motion for nonsuit will be granted after a plaintiff's opening statement if, after the plaintiff has summarized all the facts that are expected to be proven at trial, the court finds that those facts would be legally insufficient to establish one or more of the essential elements of the plaintiff's case. Jensen v. Hewlett–Packard Co., 14 Cal.App.4th 958, 18 Cal.Rptr.2d 83 (1993). Nonsuit after a plaintiff's opening statement, however, is highly disfavored and will not be granted unless it is clear that the plaintiff will be unable to make out a prima facie case. The court normally grants the plaintiff a chance to amend the opening statement. Panico v. Truck Insurance Exchange, 90 Cal.App.4th 1294, 109 Cal.Rptr.2d 638 (2001).

2) After Plaintiff's Presentation of Evidence

Similarly, a nonsuit will be granted at the close of the plaintiffs' evidence when, "disregarding conflicting evidence, giving to the plaintiffs' evidence all the value to which it is legally entitled, and indulging every legitimate inference that may be drawn from the evidence in the plaintiffs' favor," no evidence supports the verdict for the plaintiffs. Elmore v. American Motors Corp., 70 Cal.2d 578, 583, 75 Cal.Rptr. 652, 655, 451 P.2d 84 (1969). The court does not weigh the evidence on a nonsuit motion.

2. Complete and Partial Nonsuit

If a complete nonsuit is not appropriate, the court may grant a nonsuit as to certain causes of action brought by a plaintiff, certain defendants, certain plaintiffs, or one of several cases that have been consolidated for trial. CCP § 581c(b).

3. *Compare Federal Procedure*

Federal procedure does not have a precise equivalent of California's nonsuit. The motion for judgment as a matter of law under FRCP 50(a) is the federal counterpart to California's directed verdict motion; it can serve a function similar to a motion for nonsuit. (See section (V)(B)(3), below.)

4. Illustration

After watching the film "Dave's Crazy Robbery Spree," Robbie Robber decided to attempt to rob a jewelry store around the corner from his home in Torrance. During his robbery attempt, Robber damaged several glass display cases, broke two cash registers, and drilled holes into the store's safe. Robber was quickly arrested, but he lacked the funds necessary to reimburse the jewelry store for the damage. The store sued Really Big Movies Studio, the distributor of the movie "Robbery Spree," for the damage. At the commencement of the trial in Los Angeles County Superior Court, the attorney for the jewelry store gave his opening statement. He failed to mention that he would present evidence at trial tending to show that in distributing "Robbery Spree," Really Big recklessly or deliberately encouraged people to commit robbery, an essential element to the store's claim. At the close of the jewelry store's opening statement, Really Big moved for nonsuit. Although nonsuit following opening statement is disfavored, the court will grant the nonsuit motion if the store cannot make out a prima facie case against the studio on all elements of its cause of action. Olivia N. v. National Broadcasting Co., 126 Cal.App.3d 488, 178 Cal.Rptr. 888 (1981).

B. Directed Verdict

1. Nature of Device

A directed verdict motion permits the moving party (either the plaintiff or the defendant) to test the legal sufficiency of the opponent's causes of action or defenses. CCP § 630(a).

a. Timing

An important difference between a motion for directed verdict and a motion for nonsuit is the timing. Any party may move for a directed verdict only after all parties have presented their evidence. CCP § 630(a).

b. Standard for Granting a Directed Verdict

The standard for granting a directed verdict is the same as for a nonsuit motion. If a party brings a motion for a directed verdict at the close of all of the evidence, that motion is properly granted if, "disregarding conflicting evidence, and indulging every legitimate inference which may be drawn from the evidence in favor of the party against whom the verdict is directed . . . there is no evidence of sufficient substantiality to support a verdict in favor of such party." Newing v. Cheatham, 15 Cal.3d 351, 358–359, 124 Cal.Rptr. 193, 198, 540 P.2d 33 (1975). As in a nonsuit motion, the trial court in a directed verdict motion does not weigh the evidence.

2. Partial Directed Verdict

The court is empowered to grant a partial directed verdict when appropriate. CCP § 630(b). The court may direct a verdict on some of many claims or defenses, as to one of many co-parties, or on the issue of liability (leaving the issue of amount of compensatory and/or punitive damages up to the jury).

3. *Compare Federal Procedure*

Judgment as a matter of law is the federal counterpart to California's directed verdict. A judgment as a matter of law is properly granted "[i]f a party has been fully heard on an issue during a jury trial and the court finds that a reasonable jury would not have a legally sufficient evidentiary basis to find for the party on that issue." FRCP 50(a). A motion for judgment as a matter of law may be made at any time before the case is submitted to the jury, including after the opening statement. FRCP 50(a)(2).

4. Illustration

Police Officer sued the Eureka Police Department in Humboldt County Superior Court for wrongful discharge. Police Officer alleged that his employment was improperly terminated during his probationary period because of a hearing disability. After Police Officer's presentation of evidence, the Department brought a directed verdict motion, arguing that in presenting his case at trial, Police Officer had failed to make a prima facie showing that he was initially qualified to be hired for his position. The court should grant the motion because the evidence presented by Police Officer is insufficient to permit the jury to render a verdict in his favor. Police Officer cannot establish that he satisfied the qualifications for the position for which he applied because he did not successfully complete the hearing examination. Quinn v. City of Los Angeles, 84 Cal.App.4th 472, 100 Cal.Rptr.2d 914 (2000).

C. Judgment Notwithstanding the Verdict

1. Nature of Device

A motion for judgment notwithstanding the verdict (JNOV) allows a trial court to resolve an issue in favor of the moving party after the jury has returned a verdict to the contrary. The motion is similar to the common law motion for judgment *non obstante veredicto*. As such, judgment notwithstanding the verdict is often referred to by the acronym, JNOV. Much like motions for nonsuit and directed verdict, a motion for JNOV challenges the legal sufficiency of the opposing side's evidence. A JNOV motion may be brought by either party (provided the jury has returned a verdict against that party) or, occasionally, by the court on its own motion. CCP § 629.

a. Timing

A JNOV motion is made after the jury has rendered its verdict. The moving party must make the motion within the time to serve and file a notice of intent to move for new trial. CCP §§ 629, 659. (See section (V)(D)(1)(c), below.) A trial court is without jurisdiction to consider an untimely JNOV motion. When the trial court makes a motion for JNOV sua sponte, the law is unclear whether the court must adhere to the time limits applicable to party motions. Compare Espinoza v. Rossini, 247 Cal.App.2d 40, 55 Cal.Rptr. 205 (1966) (stating that the strict time limits for a JNOV apply to litigants and courts alike) with Sturgeon v. Leavitt, 94 Cal.App.3d 957, 156 Cal.Rptr. 687(1979) (disregarding the time limits for a JNOV that the trial court initiated on its own motion).

b. Standard for Granting Motion for JNOV

The court is authorized to grant a motion for JNOV whenever a motion for directed verdict would have been granted had it previously been brought. CCP § 629. In other words, JNOV should be granted when the evidence is insufficient to support a verdict in favor of the nonmoving party. Kephart v. Genuity, Inc., 136 Cal.App.4th 280, 38 Cal.Rptr.3d 845 (2006). Essentially, the standards for granting a nonsuit, directed verdict, and JNOV are the same. A trial judge may grant a JNOV even if a previous directed verdict motion was denied. A party is not required to bring a directed verdict motion before moving for JNOV.

2. Partial JNOV

There is no clear statutory authority for the partial granting of a JNOV. At least one court has reasoned that JNOV motions should be treated the same as nonsuits and directed verdicts, both of which may be partially granted. Beavers v. Allstate Insurance Co., 225 Cal.App.3d 310, 274 Cal.Rptr. 766 (1990).

3. Motions for JNOV and New Trial

JNOV motions and motions for new trial are frequently filed simultaneously and in the alternative. CCP § 629. The court then has the option of granting one motion and denying the other. See section (V)(D), below.

4. *Compare Federal Procedure*

In the federal system, what used to be called JNOV is now referred to as a "renewed motion for judgment as matter of law." FRCP 50(b). The standard is identical as the one for a pre-verdict motion for judgment as a matter of law (directed verdict): whether "the evidence, construed in the light most favorable to the nonmoving party, permits only one reasonable conclusion, and that conclusion is contrary to that of the jury." White v. Ford Motor Co., 312 F.3d 998, 1010 (9th Cir. 2002). In order to bring a renewed motion for judgment after the jury has rendered a verdict, a federal court litigant must first have made a motion for judgment as a matter of law after the opposing side has been fully heard on an issue. FRCP 50(b). The rationale for this extra step is that the Seventh Amendment states that "no fact tried by a jury shall be otherwise re-examined by any Court of the United States. . . . " A "renewed" motion for judgment as a matter of law is allowed because the motion is not viewed as a "reexamination." Rather, "the court is considered to have submitted the action to the jury subject to the court's later deciding the legal questions raised" by the previously submitted motion for judgment. FRCP 50(b); see also Weisgram v. Marley Co., 528 U.S. 440, 120 S.Ct. 1011, 145 L.Ed.2d 958 (2000). California, not being bound by the Seventh Amendment, does not require this formality.

5. Illustration

Play Toys, Inc. sued Darn Fun Co. in Ventura County Superior Court for allegedly copying a product idea. Both companies, within a month of each other, put on the market a stuffed animal that "giggles" when tickled. There was evidence that a manager of Play Toys had shown a prototype to a fellow manager at Darn Fun. However, there was also a significant amount of uncontradicted testimony establishing that Darn Fun actually got the idea from other sources. The jury returned a verdict in favor of Play Toys. Darn Fun immediately moved for JNOV. The court will grant the JNOV motion because the evidence is insufficient to support the

> verdict. While the meeting between the managers produced an inference that the idea was stolen, the inference could not hold up against the substantial uncontradicted evidence in favor of Darn Fun, which was of such a nature that it could not rationally be disbelieved by the jury. Teich v. General Mills, Inc., 170 Cal.App.2d 791, 339 P.2d 627 (1959).

D. Motion for New Trial

1. Nature of Motion

Often coupled with a motion for JNOV, a motion for new trial asks the court to reexamine one or more issues after a trial has taken place and a verdict has been rendered. A party, however, also may bring a motion for new trial where an issue of fact or law has been decided without a trial judgment, such as summary judgment, directed verdict, nonsuit, judgment on the pleadings, or an excessive or inadequate default judgment. The trial court shall grant a new trial motion when it is "of the opinion that the error complained of has resulted in a miscarriage of justice." Cal. Const., art VI, § 13.

a. Grounds for New Trial Motion

The court has no inherent power to order a new trial. A motion for new trial must be based on one of the grounds enumerated in CCP § 657:

- Irregularity in the proceedings of the court, jury or adverse counsel (§ 657(1)). Example: erroneous exclusion of evidence, if the court's ruling prejudiced the moving party's right to a fair trial.

- Misconduct of the jury (§ 657(2)). Example: improper communications during jury deliberations.

- Accident or surprise during trial, which ordinary prudence could not have guarded against despite the diligence of the moving party (§ 657(3)). Example: the adverse party calls an expert witness who was not previously disclosed. This ground does not include a simple mistake or negligence or counsel; the accident or surprise must have a prejudicial effect on the moving party.

- Newly-discovered material evidence, which the moving party could not have discovered and produced at trial, despite reasonable diligence (§ 657(4)). Example: willful suppression of material evidence during discovery and trial.

- Excessive or inadequate damages (§ 657(5)). Example: the jury applied an incorrect standard in calculating damages. This statutory ground typically results in a limited new trial on the issue of damages only.

- Insufficient evidence to justify the verdict (§ 657(6)). Example: the court reweighs the evidence and assesses the credibility of witnesses to determine if the weight is against the verdict. This ground is the most common basis for a new trial motion.

- The verdict or other decision is against law (§ 657(6)). Example: the jury has rendered a verdict contrary to the jury instructions.

- An error in law during the trial (§ 657(7)). Example: the court has given an erroneous jury instruction. The error must have been prejudicial, and the moving party must have objected to the error during the trial.

b. Judge's Consideration of New Trial Motion

1) Reweighing the Evidence

In contrast to motions for nonsuit, directed verdict, and JNOV, certain grounds for a new trial permit the judge to reweigh the evidence. This ability is most often exercised when the motion is based on the ground that the evidence was insufficient to justify the verdict (CCP § 657(6)) or that damages awarded were excessive or inadequate (CCP § 657(5)). Because of this power to reweigh the evidence, the judge is often characterized as a "thirteenth juror." In this role, the judge is entitled to disbelieve witnesses and draw reasonable inferences counter to those of the jury. Fountain Valley Chateau Blanc Homeowner's Association v. Department of Veterans Affairs, 67 Cal.App.4th 743, 79 Cal.Rptr.2d 248 (1998).

2) Written Specifications for Court's Ruling

The court is obligated to provide specific written reasons for its ruling granting or denying the new trial motion. The requirement of written reasons forces the court to deliberate when exercising its broad discretion. In addition, written reasons make the appeal more meaningful by focusing the reviewing court's attention on the part of the record that served as the basis for the trial court's order. If the trial court grants the motion but fails to provide specific reasons for its order, the burden of persuasion on appeal is on the respondent (the party seeking to uphold the order). Oakland Raiders v. National Football League, 41 Cal.4th 624, 61 Cal.Rptr.3d 634, 161 P.3d 151 (2007).

3) Conditional New Trial

An order for a new trial may be made conditional on the plaintiff's agreement to instead accept what the court deems to be a fair and reasonable lower amount of damages (remittitur), or the defendant's agreement to pay a higher amount of damages (additur). CCP § 662.5.

c. Timing

Litigants intending to move for a new trial must do so: (1) before the entry of judgment; (2) within 15 days of the clerk's mailing the notice of entry of judgment, or 15 days after service by a party of written notice of entry of judgment, or 180 days after entry of judgment, whichever is earliest; or (3) within 15 days after another party has moved for a new trial. CCP § 659. These deadlines are jurisdictional. They cannot be extended by stipulation of the parties or order of the court. In re Marriage of Beilock, 81 Cal.App.3d 713, 146 Cal.Rptr. 675 (1978). Under CCP § 660, the court has 60 days within which it must render an order granting a new trial. Thereafter, the court has no jurisdiction to grant the motion, and it is deemed denied by operation of law.

2. *Compare Federal Procedure*

The federal version of a motion for new trial under FRCP 59 is very similar to a motion for new trial under the California system. Federal trial judges are given broad discretion when ruling on such a motion. A new trial may be granted "for any reason for which a new trial has heretofore been granted in an action at law in federal court." FRCP 59(a)(1)(A). One major distinction between California and federal new trial motions is that the Seventh Amendment has been interpreted to not permit additur (although remittitur is allowed). The timing requirement for bringing a new trial motion is less complicated in federal court. The motion must be filed no later than ten days after the entry of judgment. FRCP 59(b).

3. Illustration

Pearl sued canine clothing manufacturer Round of A–Paws, whose marketing slogan was "Round of A–Paws: Where your puppy's clothing will always get a standing ovation." Pearl hired Ian Incompetent to represent her in this action in Calaveras County Superior Court, in which she claimed that a bejeweled, argyle doggie sweater-vest produced by the defendant caused her Teacup Poodle/Chihuahua mix to break out in a rash and lose all of its hair. During the jury trial, Incompetent did a very poor job of representing Pearl. To make matters worse, during jury deliberations Pearl found out that Incompetent was not licensed to practice law. Once the jury returned an adverse verdict, Pearl moved for a new trial on the ground that her attorney's incompetence and lack of licensure constituted an "irregularity in the proceedings." CCP § 657(1). The court will grant the new trial motion because Incompetent's actions constituted fraud on the court and denied Pearl a fair trial. Russell v. Dopp, 36 Cal.App.4th 765, 42 Cal.Rptr.2d 768 (1995).

E. Relief from Judgment

A trial court may relieve a party from a judgment or order under limited circumstances.

1. Discretionary Versus Mandatory Relief

a. Discretionary Relief: Party Fault

Under CCP § 473(b), a defendant may move the court to set aside or vacate a judgment, dismissal, order, or other proceeding (e.g., entry of default) "taken against him or her through his or her mistake, inadvertence, surprise, or excusable neglect." The rationale behind this provision is "to alleviate the hardship on parties who lose their day in court due to an inexcusable failure to act on the part of their attorneys." Zamora v. Clayborn Contracting Group, Inc., 28 Cal.4th 249, 257, 121 Cal.Rptr.2d 187, 193, 47 P.3d 1056 (2002). Relief under this provision is discretionary. The motion must be brought "within a reasonable time, in no case exceeding six months" after the judgment was entered. CCP § 473(b). Hence, an application for relief may be well within the six-month time limit but still be deemed untimely if the court determines that it was not diligently filed. Benjamin v. Dalmo Manufacturing Co., 31 Cal.2d 523, 190 P.2d 593 (1948).

b. Mandatory Relief: Attorney Fault

If a defendant's motion is accompanied by an affidavit from an attorney attesting to the attorney's mistake, inadvertence, surprise, or neglect (excusable or not), the court *must* set aside any resulting default judgment or judgment of dismissal entered against the defendant. If the motion is made within six months of the entry of judgment, and the attorney's affidavit demonstrates that the judgment was actually caused by his conduct, relief from the judgment is mandatory. The court will require the attorney to pay reasonable legal fees and costs to the opposing counsel or parties. CCP § 473(b).

2. Void Judgments

CCP § 473(d) permits the court to set aside any void judgment or order upon a noticed motion by a party. In addition, the court has inherent power to set aside a judgment void on its face (if, for example, the court had no power or jurisdiction to enter the judgment or grant the relief).

3. Stipulated Vacation of Judgment

A trial court may vacate a judgment in order to "amend and control its process and orders so as to make them conform to law and justice." CCP § 128(a)(8). An appellate court, however, may not reverse or vacate a judgment based on stipulation of the parties unless: (a) "There is no reasonable possibility that the interests of nonparties or the public will be adversely affected by the reversal;" and (b) "The reasons of the parties for requesting reversal outweigh the erosion of public trust that may result from the nullification of a judgment and the risk that the availability of stipulated reversal will reduce the incentive for pretrial settlement." Id. The statutory language creates a presumption against stipulated reversals. Hardisty v. Hinton & Alfert, 124 Cal.App.4th 999, 21 Cal.Rptr.3d 835 (2004).

4. *Compare Federal Procedure*

FRCP 60 is similar to CCP § 473(b). In federal court, a party may be relieved from a final judgment, order, or proceeding on account of the following:

- mistake, inadvertence, surprise or excusable neglect;

- newly discovered evidence;
- fraud;
- void judgment;
- the judgment has been satisfied, released or discharged, the judgment is based on an earlier judgment that has been reversed or vacated, or applying the judgment prospectively is no longer equitable; or
- any other reason that justifies relief.

FRCP 60(b). In contrast to the California statute, FRCP 60 does not compel mandatory relief from judgment in the event of attorney neglect. All motions under FRCP 60 must be made within a reasonable time, and motions made on the first three grounds listed in FRCP 60 may be made no more than one year after the entry of the judgment or order or the date of the proceeding. FRCP 60(c)(1).

5. Illustration

Avery Overworked was a first year associate at the firm of Smith, Smith, Smith, Smith & Smith, LLP. He was assigned to prepare a CCP § 998 offer on behalf of his client Hal Hunter, who was suing the owner of Big Al's Cigarettes, Guns, Alcohol, and Explosives Emporium. The section 998 offer was supposed to propose settlement in favor of Hunter for $2,000,000. However, Overworked inadvertently proposed settlement *against* Hunter. Big Al's jumped at the offer, and the trial court entered the judgment accordingly. Hunter fired the Smith firm and sought immediate discretionary relief from the judgment under CCP § 473(b). The trial court will likely grant the motion because the judgment was entered due to Overworked's mistake and excusable neglect, and the motion was timely filed. Because Overworked did not file an affidavit attesting to his neglect, the court is not required to set aside the judgment. Zamora v. Clayborn Contracting Group, Inc., 28 Cal.4th 249, 121 Cal.Rptr.2d 187, 47 P.3d 1056 (2002).

VI. COURT TRIAL

A. Judge as Trier of Fact

If there is no request for a jury trial, or a jury is not appropriate, the judge serves as the trier of fact. In that role, the judge evaluates conflicts in the evidence and assesses the credibility of witnesses. Generally, a court trial proceeds in the same order as a jury trial. CCP § 607.

B. Motion for Judgment

After a party's presentation of evidence, the opposing party may move for judgment. CCP § 631.8(a). The judge is not limited to considering only the legal sufficiency of the opponent's evidence, as she would be in a nonsuit, directed verdict, or motion for JNOV in a jury trial. The judge may weigh the evidence and decide issues of credibility. If the judge grants the motion and enters judgment, she must issue a statement of decision. If the court denies the motion, the moving party may proceed with its presentation of evidence.

C. Statement of Decision

1. Tentative Decision

In a court trial lasting longer than one day, the court must render a tentative decision, orally or in writing. The tentative decision is not the judgment itself and is not binding on the court. The court may ultimately render a different judgment. CRC 3.1590.

2. Timing and Contents of Statement of Decision

The trial court is not required to issue a statement of decision unless requested by a party within ten days of the court's announcement of its tentative decision. CCP § 632. The court is not required to prepare findings of fact and conclusions of law. The statement of decision sets forth the court's explanation of the legal and factual basis for the court's decision on each major disputed issue. Any objections to the statement of decision must be presented to the court in a timely fashion. CCP § 634.

3. *Compare Federal Procedure*

FRCP 52(a)(1) requires the judge in a court trial to make findings of fact and conclusions of law, without need of a request from a party. The court then enters judgment under FRCP 58. A court may enter judgment on partial findings as a matter of law against a party in a court trial if the "party has been fully heard on an issue . . . and the court finds against the party on that issue." FRCP 52(c).

4. Illustration

Plum sued Doug in Inyo County Superior Court for specific performance of a real estate contract. The case was tried to the court without a jury, and the court entered judgment for Plum. Doug made an oral request for a written statement of decision from the judge. The judge stated that he had provided the parties with the statement of decision in the form of oral discussion between the parties and the court during post-trial proceedings and the court reporter's transcript from those proceedings. These items will not suffice. Upon the request of a party, the trial court must prepare a single document constituting a written statement of decision. Failure to do so results in reversible error. Whittington v. McKinney, 234 Cal.App.3d 123, 285 Cal.Rptr. 586 (1991).

CHAPTER 6

SAMPLE EXAM QUESTIONS

OBJECTIVE QUESTIONS

The questions in this section are based on the following hypothetical:

Quinn sued Dump Co. in San Joaquin County Superior Court arising from the emission of allegedly toxic fumes from Dump Co.'s manufacturing plant located near Quinn's residence in Manteca. Quinn's suit seeks damages for his respiratory and other bodily injuries, as well as a permanent injunction requiring Dump Co. to reduce or eliminate the toxicity of its emissions. Quinn has requested a jury trial.

---

(1) True or False: In cases like Quinn's, involving both legal and equitable causes of action, California follows the federal practice in which Quinn's claim for damages must be tried first before a jury, and the claim for injunctive relief will be tried later before the judge.

(2) Unless Quinn and Dump Co. agree to fewer jurors, the jury must have at least ____ jurors on it:

a. 6;

b. 8;

c. 10;

d. 12.

(3) True or False: Quinn and Dump Co. have three peremptory juror challenges each.

(4) Which of the following is a permissible reason for Dump Co. to use one of its peremptory challenges to remove a juror:

a. The juror's race;

b. The juror's gender;

c. The juror's sexual orientation;

d. The juror's age.

(5) True or False: Dump Co.'s peremptory challenge of the trial judge may be made orally with no advance notice.

(6) True or False: Quinn's attorney may submit proposed jury instructions at any time prior to the delivery of closing arguments.

(7) If Dump Co. wishes to move for a nonsuit based on Quinn's opening statement, Dump Co.:

a. Must wait until after Quinn and Dump Co. both have presented their respective evidence;

b. Must wait until after the jury has returned a verdict;

c. May move at the conclusion of Quinn's opening statement on the ground that the facts Quinn summarized in his opening statement are legally insufficient to support a jury finding in Quinn's favor;

d. None of the above.

(8) True or False: Quinn does not have to move for a directed verdict in order to preserve the right to move for a judgment notwithstanding the verdict (JNOV).

(9) The trial judge may grant a motion for a new trial for Dump Co. on which of the following grounds:

a. Dump Co.'s discovery of new material evidence, as long as the evidence could not reasonably have been discovered before trial;

b. Misconduct by a juror;

c. Excessive amount of damages awarded to Quinn by the jury;

d. All of the above.

(10) Assume that the trial judge granted Dump Co.'s motion for nonsuit and entered a judgment of dismissal. Quinn wishes to submit an application for relief from the judgment, accompanied by an affidavit of his attorney stating that the attorney neglected to mention in his opening statement some key evidence that Quinn would have introduced at the trial in support of his claim for damages. The motion:

a. Must be filed within a reasonable time after the entry of judgment, but in no case later than six months after entry of judgment;

b. Will be granted in the court's discretion as long as it is timely and the attorney's neglect was excusable;

c. Must be granted as long as it is timely, even if the attorney's negligence was inexcusable;

d. Must be accompanied by the text of the amended opening statement the attorney seeks to deliver.

(11) True or False: If Quinn's suit is tried by the court instead of by a jury, the judge is required to issue a statement of decision after rendering her tentative decision, even if neither Quinn nor Dump Co. requests the statement.

(12) True or False: If Quinn waived his right to a jury trial by failing to deposit advance jury fees, the court has discretion to relieve Quinn of his waiver.

(13) True or False: If Quinn establishes an absolute disparity of 12% between the percentage of Latino jurors in the jury venire as compared to the percentage of Latino individuals in San Joaquin County, that showing is sufficient for Quinn to establish a systematic exclusion of Latino jurors.

(14) True or False: A jury verdict in favor of Dump Co. need not be unanimous.

(15) True or False: If Quinn and Dump Co. enter a stipulation to vacate the trial court's judgment, the stipulation will be presumed valid and the appellate court will give effect to the stipulation unless the presumption is rebutted.

Answers to Objective Questions

(1) **False**. California has rejected the federal practice of trying legal claims to a jury before trying equitable claims to the court. California generally follows the "equity first" doctrine, whereby equitable claims are first tried before the judge, and then legal claims are tried before the jury. However, the court has discretion to have the jury decide the legal claims first.

(2) **b.** Article I, section 16 of the California Constitution permits the Legislature to provide that civil juries must contain at least eight people, unless both parties consent to fewer jurors. CCP § 220 allows the parties to agree to 12 or fewer jurors.

(3) **False**. In California, each side in an action involving two parties is entitled to six peremptory challenges. CCP § 231(c). In federal court, each side is entitled to three.

(4) **d.** A juror may not be removed because of the juror's "race, color, religion, sex, national origin, sexual orientation, or similar grounds." CCP § 231.5. Age is an

acceptable basis on which to exercise a peremptory challenge.

(5) **True**. Under CCP § 170.6(b), a party may exercise one peremptory challenge of a judge, either orally or in writing, without any advance notice.

(6) **False**. Each party must submit proposed jury instructions to the trial judge in writing before the first witness is sworn. Quinn may submit additional proposed instructions before closing arguments begin if the evidence introduced additional issues that were not adequately addressed by the earlier submission of proposed instructions. CCP § 607a.

(7) **c.** CCP § 581c(a) permits a defendant to move for a nonsuit after the completion of the plaintiff's opening statement. (Alternatively, Dump Co. could wait until after Quinn presents his evidence.) The court must determine whether the facts that Quinn's attorney presented in the opening statement are legally insufficient.

(8) **True.** Unlike federal practice, California law does not require that a party must have moved for directed verdict before filing a motion for JNOV.

(9) **d.** All of the grounds listed are among those set out in CCP § 657.

(10) **c.** If a timely motion to set aside the judgment is accompanied by a declaration attesting to the attorney's fault (including inexcusable neglect), the court must grant the motion. CCP § 473(b).

(11) **False**. The trial court is not required to issue a statement of decision unless Quinn or Dump Co. requests one within ten days of the court's announcement of its tentative decision. CCP § 632.

(12) **True**. Failure to deposit advance jury fees waives the right to a jury trial. CCP § 631(d)(5). The court, however, has discretion "upon just terms" to relieve Quinn of his waiver. CCP § 631(e).

(13) **False**. Absolute disparity is an example of one of the tests applied by the courts to satisfy the second prong of the *Duren* analysis (whether the representation of Latinos in the jury venire was not "fair and reasonable" when compared to the number of Latinos in the community). Even assuming that a 12 percent absolute disparity is sufficient to meet prong two, Quinn must still satisfy prong three: the disparity must be due to a systematic exclusion of Latinos from the jury venire.

(14) **True**. California does not require unanimous verdicts in civil cases. Three-fourths of the jurors may render a verdict.

(15) **False**. The court disfavors stipulated judgments.

CHAPTER 6

ESSAY QUESTIONS

A. Sam filed suit in Sacramento County Superior Court against his former employer, Regal–Mart, for wrongful termination and breach of contract. Sam is seeking damages and back pay, as well as an injunction ordering Regal–Mart to give Sam his job back. The litigation is well into the discovery process, and Regal–Mart's summary judgment hearing is scheduled in three weeks. Although the case is set for trial in three months, neither party has requested a jury trial.

(1) You are the chief legal counsel for Regal–Mart. You suspect that Sam will want his case tried before a jury and that he will make that request if Regal–Mart's summary judgment motion is denied and the case progresses to trial. You believe that it is more advantageous to Regal–Mart to have the case tried before the judge. What arguments might you make to limit Sam's access to a jury trial, should he request one?

(2) Assume that Sam's case has been set for a jury trial. The jury panel is undergoing the process of voir dire. Counsel for Regal–Mart has exercised peremptory challenges to remove all divorced people from the jury. Discuss whether these challenges are proper under California law.

B. Kate was severely injured in a car accident while driving near Redding. The initial police report stated that the accident was a result of rainy weather and slippery roads. Despite the findings in the accident report, Kate's attorney, Gil, filed suit in Shasta County Superior Court against Auto Group, the car's manufacturer, alleging that malfunctioning brakes and various design defects in the car caused the accident.

During the opening statement, Gil described his client's theory that the accident was, in fact, caused by the car's defects. After Gil presented his opening statement, Auto Group's attorney, Zev, moved for a nonsuit, which the judge denied. Gil then proceeded with the presentation of Kate's case. Gil, however, did not offer any expert testimony or other evidence that might establish that a design defect caused Kate's accident. Zev moved for a directed verdict on behalf of Auto Group, which the judge denied.

After jury deliberations, the jury returned a verdict in favor of Kate, awarding her $3,000,000 in damages. Promptly following the jury verdict, Zev filed two motions: one for judgment notwithstanding the verdict (JNOV), and alternatively one for new trial based on excessive damages. The judge denied the JNOV motion. The judge granted the motion for new trial on the condition that Kate accept a reduced damages judgment of $500,000.

Discuss whether the judge's ruling on each of the four motions (nonsuit, directed verdict, JNOV and new trial) was correct.

Answers to Essay Questions

Essay A

(1) Right to Jury Trial

- Sam's entitlement to jury trial:
    - Right does not come from the U.S. Constitution's Seventh Amendment, but rather from California Constitution, art. I, § 16.
    - Sam has brought both a legal cause of action and an equitable cause of action. Parties are entitled to a jury on legal claims, but not on equitable claims. In California, equitable claims are generally tried first, then legal claims (but the court has discretion to reverse the order).
    - The request for an injunction stemming out of the wrongful termination allegation will likely be tried first before the judge. Then the jury will try the legal issues, including entitlement to back pay. The jury will be bound by the judge's findings.
    - If Sam's damages and injunctive claims are so intertwined that they cannot be easily separated, the court will determine the "gist of the action." If the court decides that the gist is legal, the jury will try all claims. If the gist is equitable, the court will try all claims.
- Waiver of right to jury trial:
    - Party must request jury trial in a timely manner—usually in the complaint or answer, but at least at or shortly after the time the case is set for trial. CCP § 631(d)(4). The requesting party also must place a deposit for the cost of the first day (and after each day of trial must place an additional deposit). CCP § 631(b)–(c).
    - Waiver can include: failing to timely demand jury trial; written or oral consent; failure to deposit jury fees. CCP § 631(d).
    - The court has discretion to relieve a party of a jury trial waiver on just terms. CCP § 631(e).
    - Sam's case has been set for trial, the discovery process has been ongoing, and a summary judgment motion is on calendar. Sam has not demanded a jury trial at any stage. Sam appears to have waived his right to a jury trial. But the court may relieve him of the waiver in its discretion.

(2) Regal-Mart's Peremptory Challenges

- Regal–Mart may not use its peremptory challenges to remove jurors based on race, color, religion, sex, national origin, sexual orientation, or similar grounds. CCP § 231.5. Marital status is not specifically included in the statute, and it does not appear that marital status is a "similar ground" under the statute.

- The jury must be drawn from a representative cross-section of the community. To determine whether removing divorced people is a constitutionally impermissible ground for the exercise of peremptory challenges, the court must determine whether divorced people constitute a distinctive or cognizable group in the community.

- The cognizable group test is whether:

  - the members of the group share a common perspective arising from their life experience in the group; and

  - no other members of the community can adequately represent the perspective of the group.

    - Divorced people probably do not share a common perspective. People obtain divorces for a variety of reasons, the length of marriages differs widely, and there are many kinds of consequences of divorce on the individuals and children. Although some people may experience discrimination based on their divorce, divorced persons do not generally have a history of persecution.

    - Other members of the community who have been in committed nonmarital relationships that terminated may be able to represent the perspective of divorced people on the jury.

- Based on this test, the peremptory challenges are likely permissible because divorced people do not constitute a cognizable or distinctive group in the community.

Essay B

- Nonsuit:

  - Standard: nonsuit is granted if the plaintiff's opening statement has failed to present a prima facie case of each element of the plaintiff's causes of action. The motion may be granted only if it is certain that the facts stated would be insufficient to support a jury verdict in the plaintiff's favor.

  - Only a defendant may move for nonsuit, either after the plaintiff's opening statement or after the plaintiff's presentation of evidence. CCP § 581c(a).

- Defendant Auto Group timely moved for nonsuit after Gil's opening statement on behalf of Kate.

  - During opening statement, Gil told the jury about the evidence he planned to present on the theory that design defects in the car caused the accident.

  - The court properly denied the nonsuit.

  - Even if nonsuit were appropriate, the court would likely give Gil an opportunity to amend the opening statement rather than grant nonsuit at this stage.

- Directed verdict:

  - Standard: a directed verdict will be granted if, disregarding conflicting evidence and viewing the evidence in the light most favorable to the nonmoving party, the evidence is legally insufficient to support a verdict in favor of the nonmoving party.

    - The standard is same as that for nonsuit, but a directed verdict motion may be made by either the plaintiff or defendant after both sides have presented their evidence. CCP § 630(a).

  - Auto Group moved for a directed verdict at the conclusion of Kate's evidence. The motion is premature under California law, but would be timely under FRCP 50.

  - If the directed verdict motion had been timely, the court probably should have granted it. Gil failed to introduce any evidence suggesting that a design defect caused by Auto Group was the cause of the accident.

- JNOV:

  - Standard: JNOV should be granted when the nonmoving party's evidence is insufficient to support a verdict in its favor, and no reasonable jury could have returned the verdict that was rendered.

    - Either party may move for JNOV after the jury's verdict. CCP § 629. The timing is the same as that for a motion for new trial. CCP §§ 629, 659.

    - The standard is the same as that for nonsuit and directed verdict, but the JNOV motion is made after the jury's verdict.

    - JNOV motions are often combined with motions for new trial.

  - Kate's evidence was insufficient to prove that a design defect caused her accident. Even if the judge denied the directed verdict motion, the JNOV motion should have been granted.

- New trial:

  - Standard: the court may grant a new trial on one or more of the statutory grounds in CCP § 657. The trial court proceedings must have resulted in a "miscarriage of justice." Cal. Const., art VI, § 13.

    - A new trial may be granted on the ground of excessive damages. CCP § 657(5). The court may make its new trial order conditional on Kate's acceptance of a lower amount of damages (remittitur), as long as the reduced amount is fair and reasonable. CCP § 662.5.

    - The timing requirements for bringing a motion for new trial are jurisdictional. CCP § 659.

  - The court will order a conditional new trial on the ground that the jury awarded Kate excessive damages based on the lack of proof that the design defect caused her accident. If Kate refuses the reduced award, the court will grant Auto Group's motion for a new trial.

CHAPTER 7

SECURING AND ENFORCING JUDGMENTS

I. PROVISIONAL REMEDIES FOR SECURING JUDGMENTS

Provisional remedies are pretrial procedures that help assure that a defendant will be able to satisfy a judgment if the plaintiff prevails.

A. Attachment for Security

Attachment for security is a statutory tool allowing a plaintiff to secure a defendant's/potential debtor's property prior to the resolution of litigation. Attachment serves as security against any potential damages the plaintiff might be awarded at the conclusion of litigation and ensures that the plaintiff will actually recover those damages. See CCP §§ 482.010 et seq.

1. Claims Subject to Attachment

Attachment applies only to:

- a claim for money based on a contract;
- a claim of a fixed or readily ascertainable amount of $500 or more;
- an unsecured claim or one secured by personal (not real) property; and
- a commercial claim (arising out of the conduct of an individual in a trade, business or profession).

CCP § 483.010.

2. Right to Attach Order

The court must enter a right to attach order authorizing a writ of attachment. The right to attach order is ordinarily issued after notice and hearing, but in cases of great or irreparable injury to the plaintiff, the court may issue an ex parte order. CCP §§ 484.010, 484.040, 485.220. See also Western Steel and Ship Repair, Inc. v. RMI, Inc., 176 Cal.App.3d 1108, 222 Cal.Rptr. 556 (1986).

3. Property Subject to Attachment

Any property of a corporation or other business entity may be attached. CCP § 487.010. As to an individual defendant, only non-exempt property (such as real property, accounts receivable or equipment) may be attached. CCP § 487.010. All other property of an individual is exempt. CCP § 487.020.

4. *Compare Federal Procedure*

Federal courts also use attachment procedures. FRCP 64(a) authorizes federal courts to follow the attachment laws of the state in which the court is located in order to seize and secure property to satisfy a judgment. The U.S. Supreme Court has emphasized the importance of providing a defendant with advance notice and an opportunity to be heard as means of protecting the defendant's due process rights. United States v. James Daniel Good Real Property, 510 U.S. 43, 114 S.Ct. 492, 126 L.Ed.2d 490 (1993); Connecticut v. Doehr, 501 U.S. 1, 111 S.Ct. 2105, 115 L.Ed.2d 1 (1991).

5. Illustration

Lisa Landlord filed suit in Yolo County Superior Court against two tenants, Tom and Tessa, for breach of a commercial lease agreement. Lisa applied for a right to attach order for $60,000 to cover the amount of money Tom and Tessa still owed under their lease. Tom and Tessa filed an opposition to the request for attachment. Lisa's reply papers set out several new legal arguments. The court issued the right to attach order without a hearing. The court does not have discretion to issue the order without a hearing. CCP § 484.040. Tom and Tessa must be given a chance to respond to the new arguments set forth in Lisa's reply papers. Hobbs v. Weiss, 73 Cal.App.4th 76, 86 Cal.Rptr.2d 146 (1999).

B. Preliminary Injunctions and Temporary Restraining Orders

1. Preliminary Injunctions

A preliminary injunction allows a court to preserve the status quo pending the final determination of an underlying action at trial. See generally CCP §§ 526, 527.

a. Requirements for Preliminary Injunction

Notice and an opportunity to be heard are absolute requirements for the issuance of a preliminary injunction. In addition, injunctive relief involves consideration of two core matters by the court:

- the inadequacy of any existing remedies at law, including whether the moving party will suffer irreparable harm before the case can been fully adjudicated; and

- the likelihood that the moving party (usually the plaintiff) will succeed on the merits of the underlying action.

The court then balances the harm likely to be suffered by the moving party if the injunction is denied versus the harm to be suffered by the non-moving party if the injunction is granted. O'Connell v. Superior Court, 141 Cal.App.4th 1452, 47 Cal.Rptr.3d 147 (2006).

1) Inadequacy of Existing Remedies at Law and Irreparable Harm

The moving party must show that money damages will provide inadequate redress for any pending harm. Pacific Decision Sciences Corp. v. Superior Court, 121 Cal.App.4th 1100, 18 Cal.Rptr.3d 104 (2004). If money damages can provide sufficient redress, the movant will not suffer irreparable harm and cannot obtain injunctive relief. Irreparable harm is presumed where constitutional rights or property rights are involved.

2) Probability of Success

The moving party has the burden to demonstrate facts sufficient to show a "reasonable probability" of success on the merits. Fleishman v. Superior Court, 102 Cal.App.4th 350, 125 Cal.Rptr.2d 383 (2002). The court must make credibility assessments and weigh the evidence, even though a full factual record does not yet exist. If it clearly appears that the moving party cannot succeed on the underlying action, the injunction will be denied.

3) Balancing Comparative Harms

The court must weigh the respective harms to the parties. "If the denial of an injunction would result in great harm to the plaintiff, and the defendants would suffer little harm if it were granted, then it is an abuse of discretion to fail to grant the preliminary injunction." Robbins v. Superior Court, 38 Cal.3d 199, 205, 211 Cal.Rptr. 398, 401, 695 P.2d 695 (1985). Because of the inherently equitable nature of injunctive relief, the outcome of an application for an injunction often turns on the relative harm to each party.

b. Types of Preliminary Injunctions

1) Mandatory and Prohibitory Injunctions

Mandatory injunctions command a party to perform (or continue to perform) a particular action. Prohibitory injunctions, which are more common, command a party to cease or refrain from a particular action. Whether an injunction is mandatory or prohibitory depends not on its label as such, but on its effect. Because mandatory injunctions compel a party to act, they may be stayed pending appeal of the injunction. Prohibitory injunctions may not be stayed on appeal.

2) Statutory Injunctions

Various statutory claims give rise to injunctive relief. Among these are claims of harassment, group violence, restraint of trade, and misappropriation of trade secrets. The moving party seeking a statutory injunction must show a likelihood of success on the merits and that it will suffer greater harm if the injunction is denied than the non-moving party will suffer if the injunction is granted. However, the inadequacy of legal remedies is effectively already established by the applicable statutory provisions.

c. Undertaking

The moving party is required to post a bond—called an "undertaking"—if the court grants its request for a preliminary injunction. CCP § 529(a). This bond is designed to cover any damages that the non-moving party incurs as a result of the injunction if it turns out to have been incorrectly issued. The injunction is not effective until the undertaking is posted. Certain parties are exempt from the bond requirement, including indigent parties, parties in a domestic relations dispute, and governmental entities. CCP § 529(b).

2. Temporary Restraining Orders

A temporary restraining order (TRO) requires the same showing by the moving party as needed for a preliminary injunction: inadequate remedies at law and irreparable harm; a reasonable probability of success on the merits; and a balancing of comparative harms. TROs, however, are short in duration (typically 10–15 days), although they can be extended upon notice to the opposing party. TROs are normally issued pending a hearing on a preliminary injunction. Further, TROs, unlike preliminary injunctions, can be issued ex parte on a showing both that the moving party will suffer great harm before the matter can be heard with notice to the non-moving party, and that the moving party attempted to give the opposing party notice. CCP § 527(c). A bond may be required, but is not mandatory, for a TRO to issue.

3. *Compare Federal Procedure*

The test for granting preliminary injunctive relief in the federal system is largely the same as in California. As an additional threshold matter, before a preliminary injunction may issue in federal court, the plaintiff must make a showing that subject matter jurisdiction exists. Moreover, the federal courts consider whether an injunction would be against the public interest; if so, the court has the discretion to deny the injunction. The Ninth Circuit has sometimes applied an alternate test, based on an analysis of only the probability of success on the merits and the likelihood the movant will suffer irreparable harm. If these factors are disputed, the court will then also analyze the balance of the comparative hardships and the public interest affected by the potential injunction. Southwest Voter Registration Education Project v. Shelley, 344 F.3d 914 (9th Cir. 2003). FRCP 65(c) requires the posting of an undertaking in order to obtain a TRO or preliminary injunction, in an amount the court deems proper.

4. Illustration

Dutton allegedly stole proprietary information from his employer, Prince Properties, including sales contact lists and databases. Dutton was subsequently fired. Dutton had signed an agreement not to compete with Prince Properties. Despite his signing the agreement, Dutton intended to start his own company in direct competition with his former employer, and he solicited other

> employees of Prince Properties to join him. Prince Properties got wind of Dutton's plan and applied to the Amador County Superior Court for a preliminary injunction against Dutton. Because Prince Properties was likely to succeed on the merits to prohibit Dutton from using its proprietary information to compete against it, and because Prince Properties would suffer irreparable harm to its business from the disclosure of trade secret information, an injunction was properly issued. ReadyLink Healthcare v. Cotton, 126 Cal.App.4th 1006, 24 Cal.Rptr.3d 720 (2005).

II. ENFORCEMENT OF JUDGMENTS AND ORDERS

Once the plaintiff has obtained a judgment against the defendant, several statutory tools are available to the plaintiff to enforce and collect on the judgment.

A. Execution

1. California Money Judgments

Money judgments are not self-executing. Judgment creditors must follow detailed procedural steps set forth by state law to collect on money judgments. Judgments are enforceable for a period of ten years following the date of entry. CCP § 683.020. A judgment creditor may renew a judgment for additional ten-year periods by filing a renewal application before the current ten-year period has expired. CCP §§ 683.120, 683.180. The judgment creditor often records the judgment in the counties where the judgment debtor owns property in order to create a lien.

a. Writ of Execution

The judgment creditor may apply to the court clerk to issue a writ of execution to enforce a money judgment. CCP § 699.510. Once the judgment creditor obtains a writ of execution, the creditor then compels the levying officer (typically the sheriff) to enforce the judgment. CCP § 699.510. A levy creates an execution lien that is satisfied by selling or taking possession of the judgment debtor's property (real or personal). CCP §§ 697.710, 701.510. The judgment debtor must be served with notice of the levy. The notice should identify the property subject to the levy and inform the judgment debtor of its rights and duties under the levy. CCP §§ 700.010, 703.010.

b. Property Exempt from Writ of Execution

All of the judgment debtor's property (personal and real) is subject to levy under a writ of execution unless the property is exempt. CCP §§ 695.010(a), 699.710. Examples of exempt property include motor vehicles up to $2,300 (CCP § 704.010), "reasonably necessary" household furnishings (CCP § 704.020), and jewelry, heirlooms, and works of art up to $6,075 (CCP § 704.040). Perhaps most importantly, a judgment debtor may claim a "homestead" exemption on his principal dwelling from $50,000 to $150,000 depending on several factors including the judgment debtor's age, martial status, and income level. CCP §§ 704.710–.780. Exemptions not claimed in a timely manner are waived, subjecting the property to enforcement of the judgment. CCP § 703.030(a).

c. Sale of Seized Property

A judgment creditor may sell levied property in order to satisfy a money judgment. CCP § 701.510. The judgment creditor must first serve notice of the intended sale on the judgment debtor, either personally or by mail. CCP § 701.530. The proceeds of the sale must be distributed in order of priority until the money is exhausted. Certain creditors, such as tax authorities or mechanic's lien holders, may be entitled to higher priority to the proceeds.

2. Enforcement of Sister State Money Judgments

The enforcement in California of money judgments rendered in other states is accomplished via the expedited procedures of the Sister State Money–Judgments Act. CCP §§ 1710.10 et seq.; Kahn v. Berman, 198 Cal.App.3d 1499, 244 Cal.Rptr. 575 (1988). The judgment creditor files an application for entry in the Superior Court in the county where the judgment debtor resides, or in any county if the judgment debtor is not a resident of California. CCP §§ 1710.15, 1710.20. The court clerk enters the judgment pursuant to the same procedures as California money judgments. CCP § 1710.25. The judgment creditor then serves the notice of entry of the judgment on the judgment debtor. CCP § 1710.30. The sister state judgment has the same effect as a judgment entered originally in California. CCP § 1710.35.

3. Enforcement of Foreign Money Judgments

Under California's Uniform Foreign Country Money Judgments Recognition Act (CCP §§ 1713 et seq.), a judgment creditor cannot enforce a money judgment from a foreign country in the expedited manner permitted for enforcement of sister state judgments. A foreign judgment may be enforced only by filing an original action and providing proper service of process. CCP § 1718; Renoir v. Redstar Corp., 123 Cal.App.4th 1145, 20 Cal.Rptr.3d 603 (2004).

4. Enforcement of Arbitration Awards

Arbitration awards rendered in California or in another state may be enforced even if they are not reduced to a judgment. A foreign arbitration award is enforceable pursuant to treaty. Dial 800 v. Fesbinder, 118 Cal.App.4th 32, 12 Cal.Rptr.3d 711 (2004).

5. *Compare Federal Procedure*

Federal law provides that "[e]very judgment rendered by a district court within a State shall be a lien on the property located in such State in the same manner, to the same extent and under the same conditions as a judgment of a court of general jurisdiction in such State, and shall cease to be a lien in the same manner and time." 28 USC § 1962. Thus, with some exceptions, federal courts sitting in California will follow the state's enforcement of judgments law as long as the judgment debtor resides within the state. See also FRCP 64(a) (federal courts may apply state enforcement of judgments law); and FRCP 69(a)(1) (state law governs the enforcement of judgment in federal courts unless a federal statute applies). State court judgments are accorded full faith and credit in the federal courts. 28 USC § 1738.

6. Illustration

Pip won a money judgment against Dub in Mariposa County Superior Court. Pip properly followed all procedures for enforcing the judgment via a writ of execution. In response, Dub listed several pieces of personal property as exempt from execution. Specifically, he claimed that an oak frame mirror, frosted glass vase, crystal bowl, hand-made drum, antique secretary's desk, and sterling silver hunting knife constituted "household furnishings" under CCP § 704.020. If these items are "reasonably necessary" for Dub's use at his residence, they will be subject to a full and unlimited exemption. Pip contends that if these items are exempt at all, they are subject to CCP § 704.040's exemption ceiling of $6,075 because they are "works of art." The court is likely to find that the items are household furnishings and not works of art. "They contribute to the pleasure and comfort of the owner and perhaps to his pride of ownership. In the eyes of the law, they are no less necessary than a chair or rug." In re Crosby, 162 B.R. 276 (Bkrtcy C.D. Cal. 1993).

B. Receivers

1. Appointment of Receiver

Receivers serve as officers of the court to collect money to satisfy a judgment or to manage property during pending litigation when there is a chance the property might be transferred or reduced in value before the conclusion of the action. The court may appoint a receiver after a judgment has been rendered if the judgment creditor establishes that a receivership is a "reasonable method to obtain the fair and orderly satisfaction of the judgment." CCP § 708.620. Alternatively, the court may appoint a receiver during the litigation. CCP § 564. The receiver serves as a fiduciary of both parties and must exercise great care when managing the given property. If a receiver breaches her fiduciary duty, she may be held personally liable. City and County of San Francisco v. Daley, 16 Cal.App.4th 734, 20 Cal.Rptr.2d 256 (1993).

2. *Compare Federal Procedure*

Federal courts may also appoint receivers. FRCP 66. The appointment of a receiver is an extraordinary remedy.

3. Illustration

Pepper sued Diana in Sonoma County Superior Court for breach of a lease agreement. Pepper obtained a judgment for $28,000. Pepper placed a lien on Diana's bank account, but it only had a balance of $2,000. Diana operates a successful cosmetic surgery practice in Santa Rosa. Although Pepper suspected that Diana had interests in several rental properties, Diana stated her interests were subject to a trust agreement whereby Diana's mother-in-law received the rents from those properties. Given the difficulty Pepper experienced in tracking down Diana's properties and assessing her interests, the court will likely grant Pepper's request that it appoint a receiver to oversee the collection of the remaining $26,000 of the judgment out of the income generated from Diana's cosmetic surgery practice. Olsan v. Comora, 73 Cal.App.3d 642, 140 Cal.Rptr. 835 (1977).

C. Contempt

A court order entered against a party may be enforced by contempt proceedings in the event the order is disobeyed. A party may behave in other ways that constitute contempt, such as unlawfully interfering with the court's process or proceedings, disorderly conduct toward a judge during a proceeding, or unlawfully detaining a witness or party going to court. CCP § 1209. Contempt may be either direct (conduct in the presence of the court) or indirect (conduct outside the presence of the court). CCP § 1211. In addition to statutory contempt measures, a court has inherent power to punish a party for conduct that interferes with the orderly proceedings of the court. CCP § 128(a)(3).

1. Elements of Contempt

To find contempt, the following elements must be established:

- entry of a valid order;
- actual knowledge of the order;
- ability to comply with the order; and
- willful failure to comply with the order.

In re Ivey, 85 Cal.App.4th 793, 102 Cal.Rptr.2d 447 (2000).

2. Types of Contempt

a. Civil Contempt

A party commits civil contempt when she disobeys a court order benefiting another party. Typically, civil contempt proceedings are coercive in nature—the contempt order is intended to persuade the disobedient party to comply with the court order by imposing either a fine or jail time until the party complies. CCP § 1219(a). Civil contempt may also be punitive in nature. California law permits the punishment for each act of civil contempt to a maximum $1,000 fine or up to five days in jail. CCP § 1218(a).

b. Criminal Contempt

Criminal contempt occurs when a party willfully disobeys a court order or is disrespectful toward the court or a judge. The purposes of punishing the contemptuous party in this context are to preserve the integrity of the court and to protect the administration of justice. Willful disobedience of a court order may constitute a misdemeanor under Cal. Penal Code § 166(a)(4).

3. Contempt Proceedings

a. Protections

Several constitutional protections are available to the contemnor because of the quasi-criminal nature of civil contempt proceedings. Such protections include a presumption of innocence, right to cross-examine adverse witnesses, and assistance of counsel. A right to a jury trial exists only if the fixed sentence to be imposed exceeds six months imprisonment.

b. Due Process

Whether a contempt order violates a contemnor's federal due process rights depends on the punishment. If the court's punishment is conditioned on compliance with the original order—e.g. the party shall be incarcerated until she complies—the order is not criminal in nature. The proceeding need only comply with *civil* due process requirements, such as providing notice to the party and affording an opportunity to be heard. However, if the court's punishment is not conditioned on compliance, but rather is entirely punitive (e.g., the party must pay a $15,000 fine), the contempt is considered criminal, and the allegedly contemptuous party is entitled to *criminal* due process protections. Hicks v. Feiock, 485 U.S. 624, 108 S.Ct. 1423, 99 L.Ed.2d 721 (1988).

4. *Compare Federal Procedure*

Federal contempt proceedings are similar to California's and are subject to the same due process limitations. Notably, however, federal contempt sanctions usually are not subject to the strict fine and jail time limitations imposed in California by statute. Some federal courts have imposed multi-million dollar fines as well as lengthy terms of imprisonment. See American Airlines, Inc. v. Allied Pilots Association, 228 F.3d 574 (5th Cir. 2000) (affirming contempt fine of $45.5 million). But see International Union, United Mine Workers of America v. Bagwell, 512 U.S. 821, 114 S.Ct. 2552, 129 L.Ed.2d 642 (1994) (contempt fine exceeding $50 million considered criminal in nature and can be imposed only through jury trial).

> **5. Illustration**
>
> Wiley is a California attorney and is the managing partner of his firm. Wiley represented a client on a matter that was currently pending before the California Supreme Court. The Court had scheduled oral argument, and Wiley had been notified of the date. However, on the scheduled date, he did not appear. The Supreme Court found that Wiley had falsely claimed that he was not aware of the date of the hearing. Moreover, the Court found that Wiley made the intentional decision to not assign another attorney from his office to appear for oral argument. The Court held Wiley in contempt under CCP § 1209(a), fined him $1,000, and referred the matter to the State Bar of California for further investigation and possible disciplinary proceedings. In re Aguilar, 34 Cal.4th 386, 18 Cal.Rptr.3d 874, 97 P.3d 815 (2004).

III. COSTS AND ATTORNEY'S FEES

An important post-litigation matter is the recovery of the costs of suit and attorney's fees.

A. Costs

1. Right to Costs

The right to recover costs of suit is created by statute. Historically, the "American Rule" has required that costs, like attorney's fees, be borne by each party. Today, however, the governing statutes have effectively reversed the historical presumption. The main costs statute, CCP § 1032(b), provides that the "prevailing party" is entitled to costs as a matter of right unless a statutory exception applies.

2. Prevailing Party

a. Statutory Definitions

The prevailing party, who is entitled to recovery of costs as a matter of right, is statutorily defined as:

- the party with a net monetary recovery;
- a defendant in whose favor a dismissal is entered;
- a defendant where neither the plaintiff nor the defendant obtains any relief; or

- a defendant as against those plaintiffs who do not recover any relief against that defendant.

CCP § 1032(a)(4).

b. Court's Discretion

If a party's recovery is nonmonetary or otherwise does not fit into one of the statutory definitions, the court must designate the prevailing party. Under these circumstances, the court must exercise its discretion to allow costs or not. If it does allow costs, it may apportion them between the parties. CCP § 1032(a)(4); Lincoln v. Schurgin, 39 Cal.App.4th 100, 45 Cal.Rptr.2d 874 (1995).

3. Recovery of Costs

a. Allowable Costs

Costs must be "allowable" as defined by CCP § 1033.5. Allowable costs include: filing, motion and jury fees; juror expenses; deposition fees; regular witness fees; and court reporter fees. CCP § 1033.5(a). Expert witness fees are not allowable costs, unless ordered by the court. CCP § 1033.5(a)(8), (b)(1). Cost items that are expressly not allowable include investigation expenses in preparing for trial and transcripts of court proceedings not ordered by the court. CCP § 1033.5(b). Costs for other items not expressly addressed by statute may be allowed at the discretion of the court. CCP § 1033.5(c)(4).

b. Other Requirements

Any expenses, including those expressly allowed by law, must:

- be actually incurred;
- be reasonably necessary to the conduct of the litigation (rather than merely convenient or beneficial to its preparation); and
- not exceed a reasonable amount.

CCP § 1033.5(c).

4. Attorney's Fees as Costs

Attorney's fees are considered an allowable cost when authorized by contract, statute or law. CCP § 1033.5(a)(10). Statutes providing for "costs and attorney's fees" are uniformly read to allow the recovery of attorney's fees as a component of the costs if allowed under CCP § 1033.5(a)(10)(B). CCP § 1033.5(c)(5).

5. *Compare Federal Procedure*

Under FRCP 54(d)(1), a federal district court "should" award costs to the prevailing party. Unlike California, the district court does not award costs as a matter of right to the prevailing party. The federal court retains substantial discretion. The applicable federal statute lists more limited categories of allowable costs. 28 USC § 1920. The entitlement to an award of attorney's fees as costs is less clear under federal law than California law. An example of the confusion is the provision in FRCP 68 for shifting costs based on an offer of judgment. The cost award varies depending upon the definition of "costs" in the underlying federal statute involved in the suit. Marek v. Chesny, 473 U.S. 1, 105 S.Ct. 3012, 87 L.Ed.2d 1 (1985).

6. Illustration

Peony was fired from her job and sued her employer, Dolly's Diner, Inc., for wrongful termination in Plumas County Superior Court. The case went to trial, and the jury found for Dolly's Diner. Pursuant to CCP § 1032, Dolly's Diner sought recovery of various costs. Among them were the costs of videotaping Peony's deposition and photocopying exhibits—none of which were used at trial. Peony opposed these costs. Videotaping the deposition was an allowable cost under CCP § 1033.5(a)(3) because it was reasonably necessary for preparation of cross-examination and trial strategy. Dolly's Diner may recover the cost of copying exhibits only if the exhibits were "reasonably helpful to aid the trier of fact." CCP § 1033.5(a)(12). The unused exhibits are not an allowable cost. Seever v. Copley Press, Inc., 141 Cal.App.4th 1550, 47 Cal.Rptr.3d 206 (2006).

B. Attorney's Fees

1. Right to Recover Attorney's Fees

California follows the "American Rule," under which each side bears its own attorney's fees unless a law or the parties' agreement provides otherwise. CCP § 1021. However, California recognizes important exceptions based on fee-shifting statutes, contractual fee provisions, and equitable doctrines. CCP § 1033.5(a)(10).

a. Statutory Fee-Shifting

Several California statutes provide for the shifting of the recovery of attorney's fees to the prevailing party.

1) Private Attorney General

California's "private attorney general" statute is a key fee-shifting statute. It encourages parties to bring lawsuits to vindicate the public interest by awarding attorney's fees to the successful party in an action that resulted in the "enforcement of an important right affecting the public interest" if:

- a significant benefit has been conferred on the general public or a large class of people (beyond the litigating party);
- "the necessity and financial burden of private enforcement" make a fee award appropriate; and
- the fee is not paid out of the recovery.

CCP § 1021.5. A plaintiff is typically considered the successful party if she served as a "catalyst motivating defendants to provide the primary relief sought" or "activat[ed] defendants to modify their behavior." Graham v. Daimler-Chrysler Corp., 34 Cal.4th 553, 567, 21 Cal.Rptr.3d 331, 341, 101 P.3d 140 (2004). It is not necessary that the plaintiff have obtained all of the relief she sought in the lawsuit.

2) Other Fee-Shifting Statutes

Some fee-shifting statutes provide that the losing party must pay the prevailing party's attorney's fees. Others are "one-way," providing fees to a prevailing plaintiff, but not to a prevailing defendant. Compare, e.g., Cal. Lab. Code § 218.5 (two-way fee-shifting statute for actions to recover unpaid wages, fringe benefits, or health and welfare or pension fund contributions) with Cal. Lab. Code § 1194 (one-way fee-shifting statute for actions to recover unpaid minimum wage or overtime compensation).

b. Contractual Fee-Shifting

Parties to a contract are free to provide for the shifting of attorney's fees by agreement. CCP § 1021. One-way fee provisions in a contract, awarding fees to one specified party or the other in an action on the contract, are interpreted by California courts as two-way provisions in which the prevailing party is entitled to recover fees. Cal. Civ. Code § 1717(a).

1) Prevailing Party on the Contract

The fee-shifting provision of Cal. Civ. Code § 1717 and permits an award of fees to the "party prevailing on the contract." The prevailing party is defined as "the party who recovered a greater relief in the action on the contract." The court has discretion to determine that there is no party prevailing on the contract. In addition, there is no prevailing party if the action has been dismissed voluntarily or pursuant to settlement. Cal. Civ. Code § 1717(b).

2) Prevailing Party on Non-Contract Claims

A prevailing party's entitlement to recovery of attorney's fees under Cal. Civ. Code § 1717 for noncontractual (e.g., tort) claims that are conjoined with contractual claims must be determined under the terms of the contract's attorney's fee provision. Erickson v. R.E.M. Concepts, Inc., 126 Cal.App.4th 1073, 25 Cal.Rptr.3d 39 (2005).

c. Equitable Fee-Shifting

California recognizes a few equitable exceptions to the American Rule. One significant exception is "common fund." Where a party brings an action to preserve a common fund of money, often in a class action, that party is entitled to attorney's fees paid out of the fund. The California Supreme Court created another exception in Brandt v. Superior Court, 37 Cal.3d 813, 210 Cal.Rptr. 211, 693 P.2d 796 (1985), where the court held attorney's fees to be a compensable form of damages when an insurer refused in bad faith to pay policy benefits. California courts retain the authority to recognize new equitable exceptions. Serrano v. Priest, 20 Cal.3d 25, 141 Cal.Rptr. 315, 569 P.2d 1303 (1977).

2. Calculating Attorney's Fees

Whether based on statutory or contractual fee-shifting, California generally determines the appropriate amount of attorney's fees by multiplying the reasonable hourly rate for comparable work in the legal community by the reasonable number of hours expended, arriving at a figure known as the "lodestar." The trial court has wide discretion in determining the actual fee, and it may adjust the lodestar up for novel and difficult questions, particular skill in litigation, the extent to which the case precluded the attorneys from working on other cases, and the "contingent nature of the fee award." Ketchum v. Moses, 24 Cal.4th 1122, 1132, 104 Cal.Rptr.2d 377, 384, 17 P.3d 735 (2001). The lodestar method of calculating attorney's fees is contrasted with the "cost plus" method, in which the actual number of hours expended is multiplied by the attorney's actual hourly rate.

3. *Compare Federal Procedure*

The U.S. Supreme Court has held that most exceptions to the American Rule under federal law must be created by Congress. Alyeska Pipeline Service Co. v. Wilderness Society, 421 U.S. 240, 95 S.Ct. 1612, 44 L.Ed.2d 141 (1975). As a result, there are many federal fee-shifting provisions tied to specific statutes. Unlike California's private attorney general statute—CCP § 1021.5—there is no federal omnibus private attorney general statute. The party must prevail on a cause of action that specifically allows the award of fees. Moreover, federal law does not recognize the "catalyst" theory in determining whether the plaintiff was the prevailing party under a statute. Rather, the plaintiff must have obtained a judgment on the merits or a court-sanctioned consent decree. Buckhannon Board & Care Home, Inc. v. West Virginia Department of Health & Human Resources, 532 U.S. 598, 121 S.Ct. 1835, 149 L.Ed.2d 855 (2001). In calculating the amount of attorney's fees to be awarded, enhancements to the basic lodestar figure are disapproved in federal law. The lodestar alone is considered the reasonable fee. Pennsylvania v. Delaware Valley Citizens' Council for Clean Air, 478 U.S. 546, 106 S.Ct. 3088, 92 L.Ed.2d 439 (1986).

4. Illustration

Not Here Buddy! (NHB) was formed by a group of concerned homeowners who want to keep the City of Berkeley (City) from building a high-rise housing development for senior citizens in their neighborhood. The City held a hearing and granted approval for the development. NHB brought suit in Alameda County Superior Court against the City, alleging due process violations because the City did not give NHB a fair hearing, and attacking the project on various environmental and zoning grounds. The court agreed that NHB did not receive a fair hearing and ordered the City to hold a rehearing. The court reserved the other issues. After the rehearing, the City again approved the project. NHB then returned to court to challenge the project on the environmental and zoning grounds, but it was unsuccessful. NHB now seeks to recover its attorney's fees under CCP § 1021.5, California's private attorney general statute. The requirements of CCP § 1021.5 have been satisfied. Although NHB was unsuccessful in preventing the project from going forward, it accomplished other worthy outcomes. The lawsuit resulted in additional public input, increased City-wide accountability, and improvements to the hearing process. Bowman v. City of Berkeley, 131 Cal.App.4th 173, 31 Cal.Rptr.3d 447 (2005).

SAMPLE EXAM QUESTIONS

OBJECTIVE QUESTIONS

The questions in this section are based on the following hypothetical:

Lenny Landlord owned several houses in Imperial County. Two of these houses had been vacant for some time, and they became sites of drug use and dealing by nonresidents of the neighborhood. Ned Neighbor brought a lawsuit against Landlord for maintaining a nuisance. Neighbor sought damages as well as a preliminary and a permanent injunction mandating that Landlord abate the nuisance and provide adequate maintenance and supervision of his properties.

---

(1) True or False: Neighbor may seek prejudgment attachment of Landlord's property to ensure that Landlord will be able to satisfy any possible judgment in Neighbor's favor.

(2) In deciding whether to grant Neighbor's application for a preliminary injunction, which of the following must the court consider:

a. Neighbor's likelihood of success on the merits;

b. Whether there is an inadequate remedy at law, so that Neighbor will suffer irreparable harm before the case can be fully heard;

c. The harm that Neighbor will suffer if the injunction is denied balanced against the harm that Landlord will suffer if the injunction is granted;

d. All of the above.

(3) True or False: Due process requires that Landlord must receive notice before the court issues a preliminary injunction against him.

(4) True or False: If Neighbor is designated the prevailing party after trial, he may recover only those costs specifically allowable by statute.

(5) In the *Neighbor v. Landlord* litigation, who will be designated a prevailing party entitled to an award of costs as of right:

a. Landlord, if Neighbor voluntarily dismissed him from the action;

b. Neighbor, if he won a permanent injunction against Landlord;

c. Neither Neighbor nor Landlord, because an award of costs as of right is permitted only when the litigation arises from a contract which entitles the prevailing party to recover costs under the contract;

d. Neither Neighbor nor Landlord, because the litigation did not arise from a statutory claim for which an award of costs to the prevailing party is statutorily required.

(6) The court is considering whether Landlord has committed contempt. Which of the following most accurately describes the difference between the concepts of civil and criminal contempt?

a. Civil contempt is a violation of an order issued in civil proceedings, while criminal content is a violation of an order issued in criminal proceedings;

b. Civil contempt occurs when one party fails to comply with a court order benefiting another party, while criminal contempt remedies acts of disrespect and disobedience against the court;

c. A judge may impose fines payable to the court in civil contempt proceedings but may order only jail in criminal contempt proceedings;

d. None of the above.

(7) True or False: Neighbor may request the court to appoint a receiver either during the pendency of the lawsuit or after he wins a judgment.

(8) True or False: The court may not issue a temporary restraining order against Landlord unless Neighbor posts an undertaking.

(9) True or False: Neighbor may recover attorney's fees under the private attorney general statute even if he did not obtain all of the relief he was seeking.

(10) If Neighbor wins a judgment for damages against Landlord and then seeks to enforce the judgment:

a. Landlord's own place of dwelling is automatically exempt from execution of the judgment;

b. The procedures governing enforcement of Neighbor's California money judgment are identical to those governing enforcement of foreign money judgments;

c. Neighbor must serve Landlord with a notice that his property is subject to a levy;

d. Neighbor's judgment will expire after ten years and may not be renewed.

Answers to Objective Questions

(1) **False**. CCP § 483.010 provides that prejudgment attachments may only issue in contract actions from which a claim for money arises. Neighbor's lawsuit is a tort action.

(2) **d.** The court will order injunctive relief only if all of these requirements are satisfied.

(3) **True**. The court may grant a preliminary injunction only after Landlord has been notified and given an opportunity to respond. In contrast, a temporary restraining order may be issued without notice.

(4) **False**. Items of costs that are not specifically included in the listing of allowable costs of CCP § 1033.5(a) may nevertheless be allowed in the court's discretion. CCP § 1033.5(c)(4).

(5) **a.** CCP § 1032(a)(4) sets out the definitions of a prevailing party who may recover costs as a matter of right. One of those definitions is "a defendant in whose favor a dismissal is entered."

(6) **b.** Civil contempt orders are intended to force a party to comply with an adverse order that benefits another party. Criminal contempt orders punish disobedience or disrespect directed at the court, often by requiring the contemnor to pay a fine to the court.

(7) **True**. The court may appoint a receiver either during the litigation (CCP § 564) or after judgment (CCP § 708.620).

(8) **False**. Unlike preliminary injunctions, where an undertaking is required, the plaintiff need not post a bond when the court grants a temporary restraining order unless the court orders otherwise.

(9) **True**. If Neighbor obtained limited relief, he may recover a lower amount of attorney's fees. In addition, if Neighbor acted as a catalyst that motivated Landlord to change his behavior, Neighbor will be considered to be the prevailing party entitled to attorney's fees.

(10) **c.** Notice to the judgment debtor of the levy is required. CCP §§ 700.010, 703.010. The homestead exemption is not automatic; it must be claimed. The

enforcement of foreign money judgments involves the filing of an original action and the service of process. A judgment expires ten years after its entry, but it may be renewed for additional ten-year periods. CCP §§ 683.120, 683.180.

ESSAY QUESTION

Mike and Kyle grew up in South Lake Tahoe. Mike and Kyle inherited from their parents a substantial estate consisting of a large home and guesthouse on a six-acre plot of land. The title to the property is in the names of both Mike and Kyle. Kyle, a somewhat underhanded businessman, sold the estate without Mike's consent to DOG Properties, a strip mall developer who planned to demolish the home and guesthouse and build a shopping center. Mike sued both Kyle and DOG Properties in El Dorado County Superior Court for damages as well as to recover the family property (to which Mike has great sentimental attachment).

DOG Properties is eager to begin development. Mike has requested a temporary restraining order and preliminary injunction to prevent DOG from demolishing the property pending adjudication of the propriety of the transfer of the property to DOG.

(1) Should the court grant the temporary restraining order? Should the court grant the preliminary injunction? Discuss the analysis the court must undertake for each form of relief.

(2) Assume Mike ultimately prevails in the lawsuit and obtains a judgment for damages from DOG and Kyle for wrongful transfer. Discuss what steps Mike might take to enforce the judgment.

(3) Assume that before trial, Mike decides to voluntarily dismiss his lawsuit against Kyle, and the court enters a judgment of dismissal as to Kyle. Mike's action against DOG proceeds through trial, where Mike obtains a judgment for damages. Discuss the entitlement of Kyle and Mike to recover their respective costs and attorney's fees.

Answer to Essay Question

(1) Temporary Restraining Order and Preliminary Injunction

- Temporary Restraining Order:
  - TRO will be issued if irreparable injury will occur before a preliminary injunction hearing can be held.
    - The court will issue a TRO for a period of 15 days if no notice is provided to DOG.

- Mike must show:
    - Irreparable injury will occur without the issuance of the TRO;
    - No adequate remedy at law;
    - Reasonable probability that Mike will prevail on his cause of action against DOG.
    - The harm to Mike if the TRO is denied outweighs the harm to DOG and Kyle if the TRO is issued.
- Mike may obtain the TRO ex parte if he would suffer irreparable harm if the matter had to wait to be heard on notice to DOG and Kyle.
- The court may require an undertaking from Mike.
- Application:
    - Irreparable injury: Mike likely has a successful argument for irreparable injury. DOG seems eager to begin bulldozing. Mike also has great sentimental attachment to the property, so if DOG demolishes the property, it is likely irreplaceable to Mike.
    - No adequate remedy: DOG will likely demolish some or all of the property before Mike can have the matter tried, and damages will be inadequate to compensate for the unique irreplaceable property.
    - Probability of prevailing: Mike will probably be able to make a prima facie showing of the elements of his cause of action against DOG and Kyle. Mike is a rightful owner of his parents' estate and did not consent to its sale. Further, the facts indicate that DOG and Kyle were acting in bad faith.
    - Balance of harms: Mike's harm would be the destruction of the house, whereas DOG's harm would be monetary in the sense that his construction project would be delayed. Therefore, Mike's harm probably outweighs DOG's harm.
    - Notice: Mike will probably argue that providing notice of the TRO might provoke DOG to bulldoze the property faster and thus could cause more damage.

- Undertaking: The court may require Mike to post a bond before it will issue the TRO. However, that is within the judge's discretion to decide.

- Preliminary Injunction:

  - The court will apply the elements listed above for a TRO.

  - The court will not issue a preliminary injunction in the absence of notice to DOG and Kyle.

  - Mike will be required to provide an undertaking before the preliminary injunction will issue.

(2) Enforcement

- Alternatives:

  - Writ of Execution: Mike may apply for a writ of execution to enforce the judgment. Property belonging to DOG and Kyle may then be sold by the levying officer to satisfy the judgment. DOG and Kyle may be able to claim various exemptions.

  - Request the appointment of a receiver: Mike could request the appointment of a receiver to collect money from DOG's or Kyle's businesses. However, this is an extraordinary remedy, and likely a last resort.

(3) Costs and Attorney's Fees

- Kyle's Costs and Fees:

  - Kyle is entitled to recover his costs as the prevailing party because he is a defendant in whose favor a dismissal was entered. CCP § 1032(a)(4).

  - Kyle is not entitled to recover his attorney's fees under any statute, contract or law. CCP § 1033.5(a)(10). Mike's lawsuit was not an action on a contract, so there is no fee-shifting available under Cal. Civ. Code § 1717. Even if section 1717 applied to Mike's action, Kyle would still not be entitled to his attorney's fees because a party who is voluntarily dismissed from the action is not considered a prevailing party.

- Mike's Costs and Fees:

  - Mike is entitled to recover his costs as the prevailing party because he received a net monetary recovery against DOG. CCP § 1032(a)(4).

  - Mike is not entitled to recover his attorney's fees under any statute, contract or law. CCP § 1033.5(a)(10). The American Rule applies, requiring Mike to bear his own attorney's fees.

*

CHAPTER 8

APPELLATE REVIEW

I. RIGHT OF APPEAL

The California Constitution sets out the jurisdiction (powers) of the appellate courts. See Cal. Const., art. VI, §§ 11, 12. But statutory law largely determines the types of judgments and orders from which a party has the right to take an appeal. CCP § 904.1. In addition, judicially-created doctrines and exceptions (see section (III)(A)(2), below) have expanded the appellate right beyond what is provided by statute. The right to appeal may not be conferred by stipulation, consent, estoppel or waiver. Besides filing an appeal, a party may seek review via a petition for extraordinary writ (see section (III)(B)(1), below).

A. Review by Superior Court Appellate Division

1. Limited Civil Cases

A party to a limited civil case has a right to appeal from a judgment, but only to the Appellate Division of the Superior Court. CCP §§ 77(e), 904.2. The Court of Appeal may hear an appeal of a limited civil case judgment only if the Superior Court certifies the appeal, or if the Court of Appeal determines, on its own motion, that the transfer is appropriate. CCP § 911.

2. Small Claims Cases

A defendant (but not a plaintiff) may "appeal" a small claims judgment to the Superior Court. The Superior Court proceedings are not actually an appeal. Instead, the Superior Court conducts a trial de novo. The judgment of the Superior Court is not appealable. CCP § 116.780. Postjudgment orders rendered by the Superior Court to enforce the judgment are reviewable by that court's Appellate Division. General Electric Capital Auto Financial Services, Inc. v. Appellate Division of Superior Court, 88 Cal.App.4th 136, 105 Cal.Rptr.2d 552 (2001).

B. Review by Court of Appeal

1. Superior Court Rulings in Unlimited Civil Cases

Appealable judgments and orders rendered by the Superior Court in unlimited civil cases may be appealed to the Court of Appeal. CCP § 904.1.

2. Administrative Rulings

The Court of Appeal has jurisdiction over appeals and writ proceedings from decisions of the Workers' Compensation Appeals Board, Agricultural Relations Appeals Board, and Public Employment Relations Board, as well as certain decisions of the Public Utilities Commission.

C. Review by California Supreme Court

1. Civil Cases

California Supreme Court review of civil decisions of the Court of Appeal is discretionary. Grounds for review include securing uniformity of decisions or settling important questions of law. CRC 8.500(b)(1). The process of appeal to the Supreme Court is initiated by the filing of a petition for review within ten days after the decision of the Court of Appeal becomes final. CRC 8.500(a), (e). The Supreme Court grants review in fewer than five percent of the civil matters in which a petition is filed.

2. Criminal Cases

The California Supreme Court has discretion to review decisions of the Court of Appeal in criminal matters. However, all criminal judgments imposing the death penalty are automatically appealed directly from the superior courts to the Supreme Court.

3. Administrative Rulings

The Supreme Court has original jurisdiction over review of certain decisions of the Public Utilities Commission, recommendations of the State Bar on attorney admission and disciplinary proceedings, and recommendations from the Commission on Judicial Performance on disciplinary proceedings regarding judges.

II. NATURE OF REVIEW BY COURT OF APPEAL

The purpose of review by the Court of Appeal is to correct prejudicial error committed by the trial court. (See section (VI), below.) The Court of Appeal does not retry the trial court action. It bases its review on the trial court record, applying the appropriate standard of review (see section (V), below).

A. Presumption of Correctness

The trial court's judgment or order is generally presumed to be correct. Denham v. Superior Court, 2 Cal.3d 557, 86 Cal.Rptr. 65, 468 P.2d 193 (1970). Ambiguities in the trial court record are resolved in favor of affirming the trial court order or judgment. The trial court's disposition will be affirmed as long as it was correct, even if the court's reasoning was incorrect.

B. Trial Court Record and Appellant's Burden

It is the appellant's burden to demonstrate prejudicial error through an adequate trial court record. The central role played by the record in the appellate process compels trial attorneys to be mindful of creating an adequate record in which grounds for appeal have been preserved. The record should reflect that the appellant interposed timely and proper objections during the trial court proceedings in order to prevent waiver of those objections on appeal. Generally, the appellant is not permitted to raise matters before the Court of Appeal that were not included and preserved in the trial court record.

C. Statement of Decision

In a nonjury (bench) trial, a party may request the trial court to issue a statement of decision explaining the legal and factual bases for its decision as to each controverted issue. CCP §§ 632, 634. (See Chapter 6(VI)(C).) The Court of Appeal may use the statement of decision in its review of the trial court judgment to determine if the decision is both factually and legally supported. If the appellant fails to request a statement of decision, the Court of Appeal will imply findings in support of the judgment. Fladeboe v. American Isuzu Motors Inc., 150 Cal.App.4th 42, 58 Cal.Rptr.3d 225 (2007).

D. Appellate Court Dispositions

An appellate court "may affirm, reverse, or modify" the trial court judgment or order, and may "direct the proper judgment or order to be entered." CCP § 43.Alternatively it may order a new trial or other further proceedings.

III. APPEALABILITY

The threshold issue for an appellate court is whether the judgment or order before it is appealable. This can be a difficult inquiry, one with serious jurisdictional consequences. If a party fails to file a timely notice of appeal from an appealable judgment or order, the chance to obtain appellate review is forfeited. If an appeal is taken from a nonappealable judgment or order, the appellate court must dismiss the appeal, unless it exercises its discretion to treat the infirm appeal as a petition for an extraordinary writ.

A. Appealable Judgments and Orders

1. One Final Judgment Rule

a. Appeal from Judgment

CCP § 904.1(a)(1) codifies the one final judgment rule, permitting an appeal from "a judgment" in the action. A judgment is defined as "the final determination of the rights of the parties in an action or proceeding." CCP § 577. Only one final judgment is rendered by the trial court. The appellate court seeks to avoid piecemeal appeals of non-final trial court orders or judgments.

b. Finality

An order or judgment is considered final "when it terminates the litigation between the parties on the merits of the case and leaves nothing to be done but to enforce by execution what has been determined." Public Defenders' Organization v. County of Riverside, 106 Cal.App.4th 1403, 1409–1410, 132 Cal.Rptr.2d 81, 85 (2003). Labeling a judgment or order as final is not determinative. The appellate court considers the actual content and effect of the disposition.

c. *Compare Federal Procedure*

Federal appellate courts review "final decisions" of the district courts. 28 USC § 1291. Similar to the California standard, a final decision is one that "ends the litigation on the merits and leaves nothing for the court to do but execute the judgment." Quackenbush v. Allstate Insurance Co., 517 U.S. 706, 712, 116 S.Ct. 1712, 1718, 135 L.Ed.2d 1 (1996).

d. Illustration

Ally, Billy and Cally were partners in the ownership and operation of an apartment building in Rocklin. Ally accused

> Billy and Cally of violating the partnership agreement by failing to maintain accurate records and properly account for profits. Ally brought suit in Placer County Superior Court to dissolve the partnership and sell the assets. The trial court entered judgment for dissolution of the partnership and sale of the apartment building. The judgment did not specify the ownership interests of each partner, did not completely provide for the allocation of sale proceeds, and did not state how partnership costs and expenses would be allocated among the partners. Billy and Cally filed a notice of appeal from the judgment. The appeal will be dismissed because it was not taken from a final judgment. The judgment did not resolve several matters, requiring the trial court to conduct additional proceedings. Because piecemeal appeals are disfavored, Billy and Cally must wait to appeal until after the trial court enters a single, complete and final resolution of the issues. Kinoshita v. Horio, 186 Cal.App.3d 959, 231 Cal.Rptr. 241 (1986).

2. Judicially-Created Exceptions to One Final Judgment Rule

a. Actions Involving Multiple Parties or Causes of Action

1) Judgment Final as to Party

In actions involving multiple plaintiffs or defendants, a judgment is considered final if it leaves no issue for further determination as to a particular plaintiff or defendant, even if further proceedings are pending against other parties. Justus v. Atchison, 19 Cal.3d 564, 139 Cal.Rptr. 97, 565 P.2d 122 (1977).

2) Compare: Multiple Causes of Action

In contrast, in actions involving multiple causes of action, there is no appealable judgment until all causes of action are finally determined. If some causes of action are ordered to be tried separately and reach final determination, but additional causes of action remain for disposition, an appeal from a judgment adjudicating the separately tried causes of action is premature. Morehart v. County of Santa Barbara, 7 Cal.4th 725, 29 Cal.Rptr.2d 804, 872 P.2d 143 (1994).

3) *Compare Federal Procedure*

Under FRCP 54(b), a district court may enter a judgment as to fewer than all parties *and* claims, as long as the court expressly determines that there is no just reason for delay and directs the entry of a partial final judgment. If the court does not make this express determination and direction, any judgment as to fewer than all parties or claims is not considered a final judgment and is thus not appealable.

4) Illustration

An ExpressMail Co.'s truck driver hit Polka's car in Oroville while making deliveries under a contract with Fedecks. Polka sued both ExpressMail Co. and Fedecks for damages in Butte County Superior Court. The trial court entered summary judgment for Fedecks and dismissed it from the lawsuit. Polka's lawsuit against ExpressMail Co. continued. Two months later, the trial court entered summary judgment for ExpressMail Co. One month later, Polka filed a notice of appeal from the judgments entered for Fedecks and ExpressMail Co. The appeal from the judgment for Fedecks was untimely. The trial court rendered a final appealable judgment as to Fedecks separately from the judgment for ExpressMail Co., and Polka should not have waited until the second judgment to seek appeal as to both defendants. The judgment for Fedecks was final as to that party because it left no further issues to be resolved and was not dependent on the court's ruling as to ExpressMail Co. Therefore, the untimely appeal from the judgment for Fedecks should be dismissed. Millsap v. Federal Express Corp., 227 Cal.App.3d 425, 277 Cal.Rptr. 807 (1991).

b. Collateral Order Doctrine

1) Appealability of Collateral Orders

The collateral order doctrine is a judicially-created exception to the one final judgment rule. To be immediately appealable under this doctrine, an order must:

- involve a matter truly collateral to the merits of the litigation;
- be final as to the collateral matter; and
- direct the payment of money by the appellant or the performance of an act by or against the appellant.

Sjoberg v. Hastorf, 33 Cal.2d 116, 199 P.2d 668 (1948).

a) Collateral Matter

A matter is collateral if it is distinct from the subject matter or merits of the litigation. It is not considered collateral if it is a "necessary step" in determining the merits of the case. Union Oil Co. v. Reconstruction Oil Co., 4 Cal.2d 541, 545, 51 P.2d 81, 83 (1935). This requirement is construed narrowly in order to keep the collateral order doctrine from swallowing the one final judgment rule.

b) Final

An order is final if no further adjudication is required on the issues addressed by the order.

c) Payment or Performance

Most courts mandate that the collateral order must require the payment of money by the appellant or the performance of an act by or against the appellant. Ponce–Bran v. Trustees of the California State University and Colleges, 48 Cal.App.4th 1656, 56 Cal.Rptr.2d 358 (1996); but see Meehan v. Hopps, 45 Cal.2d 213, 288 P.2d 267 (1955) (no requirement of payment or performance). Examples of orders reviewed under the collateral order doctrine are those requiring payment of attorney's or arbitrator's fees, ordering the payment of a creditor's lien, or directing the sealing or unsealing of court filings.

2) *Compare Federal Procedure*

The collateral order doctrine is recognized in federal courts, but it is narrowly applied so as to be consistent with 28 USC § 1291, which permits appeal only from "final decisions of the district courts." To qualify for immediate appeal as a collateral order, a district court disposition must be conclusive, must resolve an important issue (one completely distinct from the merits), and must otherwise be unreviewable on appeal from the final judgment. Will v. Hallock, 546 U.S. 345, 126 S.Ct. 952, 163 L.Ed.2d 836 (2006). There is no requirement of payment of money or performance of an act, as there is in California procedure.

> **3) Illustration**
>
> Pavel and Dora had a brief but intense relationship in Crescent City, and Dora became pregnant. Dora told Pavel that she wanted to raise the child on her own with no participation from Pavel, but Pavel wanted joint legal and physical custody. Pavel sought custody and visitation orders from the family law court in Del Norte County. The court entered a pretrial order spelling out the custody arrangements until a full trial could be held. Pavel filed a notice of appeal from the custody order, contending that it was an appealable collateral order. The order is not appealable under the collateral order doctrine. First, the order is not collateral to the merits of the action, which center exclusively on the custody arrangements between Dora and Pavel. Second, the custody order does not direct the payment of money or the performance of an act. While the order sets out the terms for custody and visitation, it did not require Pavel to see his child at those times—it merely gave him the opportunity to do so if he chose. Therefore, Pavel must await entry of a final judgment on custody and appeal from that judgment. Lester v. Lennane, 84 Cal.App.4th 536, 101 Cal.Rptr.2d 86 (2000).

3. Interlocutory Judgments and Orders

a. Appealability

There is no general right of appeal from an interlocutory (non-final) judgment or order (a ruling disposing of a party's motion or application to the trial court). CCP § 904.1, however, does permit immediate appeal from a limited number of specific interlocutory judgments and orders. Examples include:

- an order made after an appealable judgment has been entered;
- an order granting a motion to quash service of summons;
- an order to stay or dismiss an action on grounds of forum non conveniens;
- an order granting a new trial or denying a motion for judgment notwithstanding the verdict;

- an order granting or refusing to grant an injunction;
- an interlocutory judgment directing a partition;
- an interlocutory judgment or order for payment of monetary sanctions exceeding $5,000; and
- an order granting or denying an anti-SLAPP motion.

b. ***Compare Federal Procedure***

The circuit courts of appeals have authority to review a narrow range of interlocutory orders and decrees. Examples include: (1) orders granting, continuing, modifying, refusing or dissolving an injunction; (2) orders appointing receivers; and (3) decrees determining the rights and liabilities of the parties to admiralty cases. 28 USC § 1292(a). In addition, if the district court believes an otherwise nonappealable order involves an uncertain but "controlling question of law," and an immediate appeal will materially advance the litigation, the district judge may certify the order for appeal. The Court of Appeals then may, in its discretion, permit the appeal. 28 USC § 1292(b). No similar certification procedure exists under California law.

c. Illustration

Polly purchased a heavy-duty truck from DieHard Truck Co. for use in her hauling business in Los Banos. Soon after purchase, Polly's drivers began to experience serious mechanical problems with the truck, and Polly eventually had to cease using it. She sued DieHard in Merced County Superior Court for breach of warranty damages. At trial, the jury reached a verdict for Polly and awarded her damages of $50,000. DieHard brought a motion for judgment notwithstanding the verdict (JNOV) and alternatively for new trial. The trial court denied the JNOV motion and granted the new trial motion. Polly appealed from the order granting the new trial, but DieHard did not appeal from the order denying the JNOV motion. It instead argued in its responding brief to Polly's appeal that the trial court improperly denied the JNOV motion. Under CCP § 904.1(a)(4), the Court of Appeal has jurisdiction over Polly's immediate appeal from the order granting the new trial because it is an appealable interlocutory order. The order denying the JNOV motion is also an appealable interlocutory order under CCP § 904.1(a)(4).

> DieHard's failure to properly appeal from that order deprives the court of jurisdiction to review it in conjunction with Polly's appeal of the new trial order. Berge v. International Harvester Co., 142 Cal.App.3d 152, 190 Cal.Rptr. 815 (1983).

B. Nonappealable Judgments and Orders

If a judgment or order is not immediately appealable under any of the principles discussed above, a party ordinarily has two choices: wait until the trial court enters a final or otherwise appealable judgment in the action; or file a petition for an extraordinary writ. In some cases, the Court of Appeal may treat an "infirm" appeal as an application for an extraordinary writ, even if the party seeking review has not filed a writ petition. In rare cases, the court it might "save" the infirm or premature appeal.

1. Review by Extraordinary Writ

a. Nature of Writ Review

An extraordinary writ is an order from a reviewing court to a trial court requiring it to act or prohibiting it from acting in a particular way. Extraordinary writs provide a vehicle for the Court of Appeal to exercise its discretion to provide immediate review of nonappealable trial court judgments and orders. Because writs are considered an extraordinary remedy, requests for them are frequently summarily denied by reviewing courts. The courts of appeal have original jurisdiction over "common law" writs: mandate, prohibition and certiorari. In addition, writ review may be authorized by statute for particular trial court rulings, such as an order granting or denying a motion for change of venue (CCP § 400), an order denying a motion for summary judgment (CCP § 437c(m)(1)), and an order denying a motion to quash service of summons (CCP § 418.10(c)).

b. Type of Writs

1) Writ of Mandate

A writ of mandate orders the trial court to take affirmative action. The writ corrects an abuse of discretion or compels the performance of a nondiscretionary duty by the trial court. CCP § 1085.

2) Writ of Prohibition

A writ of prohibition is preventative. It is used to restrain threatened judicial action that is without or in excess of jurisdiction. CCP § 1102.

3) **Writ of Certiorari**

A writ of certiorari (sometimes called writ of review) is used to review completed (as opposed to threatened) judicial acts taken without or in excess of jurisdiction. CCP §§ 1067, 1068. Examples of matters reviewable by certiorari include certain contempt orders, judgments of the Appellate Division of the Superior Court, and nonappealable probate orders. The writ of certiorari is the exclusive means to seek review of decisions of the Public Utilities Commission.

4) **Compare: Writ of Supersedeas**

A writ of supersedeas is issued by the Court of Appeal to preserve the status quo in the trial court pending appeal. The writ suspends the trial court's power to order execution of the judgment or order being appealed. CCP § 923. While supersedeas is a form of common law writ, it is not a means to review action taken by the trial court (as do the writs of mandate, prohibition and certiorari).

5) **Compare: Writ of Coram Vobis**

The writ of coram vobis is issued by the Court of Appeal when, during the pendency of the appeal, the appellant learns of new evidence that might have resulted in a trial court order granting reconsideration or a new trial had it been discovered earlier. The writ compels the trial court to reconsider the appealed judgment or order in light of the newly discovered evidence. The writ is considered a drastic remedy and will be issued only upon a showing by the appellant that the new evidence was not discovered earlier because of extrinsic fraud that prevented a full hearing on the issue. Los Angeles Airways, Inc. v. Hughes Tool Co., 95 Cal.App.3d 1, 156 Cal.Rptr. 805 (1979).

c. **Alternative and Peremptory Writs**

Writs of mandate and prohibition may be issued as alternative or peremptory writs. An alternative writ directs the lower court to act or refrain from acting, or, alternatively, to show why it should not be required to perform or refrain from performing that act. A peremptory writ is a final directive to the lower court to act or refrain from acting. A peremptory writ may be issued either after an alternative writ or in the first instance.

d. **Requirements for Writ Relief**

In order to obtain any of the writs discussed above (except supersedeas and coram vobis), the petitioner must establish that there is not a plain, speedy, and adequate appellate remedy, and that the petitioner will suffer irreparable harm if the writ petition if denied. Omaha Indemnity Co. v. Superior Court, 209 Cal.App.3d 1266, 258 Cal.Rptr. 66 (1989).

1) No Adequate Remedy

Usually, awaiting final judgment and obtaining appellate review at that point is considered an adequate remedy. The adequacy of this remedy, however, depends on the circumstances of the particular case. The requirement of showing no adequate remedy is often satisfied by demonstrating that the remedy of direct appeal is not available, or that hardship or unusual circumstances make review by direct appeal inadequate.

2) Irreparable Harm

The petitioner must demonstrate that he will suffer some significant and irremediable damage or injury if the writ is not issued.

e. Treating Infirm Appeal as Extraordinary Writ

If a party attempts to appeal from a nonappealable judgment or order (an "infirm" appeal), the Court of Appeal ordinarily dismisses the appeal. However, if the purported appeal involves unusual circumstances, matters of public importance, and/or issues of first impression, the Court of Appeal may choose to treat the infirm appeal as a petition for extraordinary writ. The appellate court may be more inclined to grant this treatment where the issue of appealability is confusing or unclear, and where the merits of the issues already have been briefed in full so that judicial economy would not be served by waiting for the time for appeal. Morehart v. County of Santa Barbara, 7 Cal.4th 725, 29 Cal.Rptr.2d 804, 872 P.2d 143 (1994).

f. *Compare Federal Procedure*

Much like California, the federal system maintains the writ of mandate (or mandamus) / prohibition dichotomy. However, in many cases, the federal courts use the term "writ of mandamus" to address both mandate and prohibition situations. When deciding whether to issue a writ of mandamus or prohibition, courts balance such factors as whether: (1) other means of relief are available; (2) prejudice or damage exists that cannot be corrected on appeal; (3) the lower tribunal's order was clearly erroneous; (4) the lower tribunal's order was a recurring error; and (5) the lower tribunal's error brings up new and important problems or issues of first impression. Douglas v. United States District Court, 495 F.3d 1062 (9th Cir. 2007); FRAP 21. The federal writ of certiorari is commonly requested when a litigant seeks U.S. Supreme Court review of decisions rendered by the Court of Appeals. 28 USC § 1254. The writ of certiorari is also used as the Supreme Court's means to review decisions of a state's highest court involving issues of federal law. 28 USC § 1257(a).

g. Illustration

Platt regularly pickets and distributes leaflets outside of the Divisadero Women's Clinic. Platt filed suit in San Francisco County Superior Court against the Clinic, alleging that Clinic staff obstructed Platt from exercising his First Amendment rights. During the discovery phase of the lawsuit, Platt propounded interrogatories and document demands seeking identifying information for Clinic staff and volunteers who were not parties to the lawsuit. The Clinic refused to provide the information on the ground of privacy. Platt filed a motion to compel the disclosure. The trial court granted the motion. The Clinic filed a petition for an extraordinary writ with the Court of Appeal. Although discovery orders are typically reviewed upon appeal from a final judgment, the writ petition in this case is proper because: (1) it seeks immediate review of an issue of first impression concerning important privacy rights of third parties; and (2) the Clinic has no adequate remedy at law because the disclosure of names will have occurred before the matter could be heard on appeal after final judgment. Planned Parenthood Golden Gate v. Superior Court, 83 Cal.App.4th 347, 99 Cal.Rptr.2d 627 (2000).

2. Alternate Means of Review of Nonappealable Orders

a. "Saving" Erroneous or Premature Appeal

An erroneous appeal taken from a nonappealable order may be "saved" by the Court of Appeal. The court may exercise its discretion to wait until a notice of appeal is filed from the final judgment and construe the premature appeal as taken from the final judgment. However, some courts of appeal have expressed disapproval of this seeming attempt to bypass the requirements of CCP § 904.1. See Cohen v. Equitable Life Assurance Society, 196 Cal.App.3d 669, 242 Cal.Rptr. 84 (1987).

b. Immediate Review of Nonappealable Orders

If the trial court enters an interlocutory judgment or order made immediately appealable by CCP § 904.1, and that judgment or order is appealed, the Court of Appeal may review any other nonappealable ruling made by the trial court that "involves the merits or necessarily affects the judgment or order appealed from or which substantially affects the rights of a party." CCP § 906; Santa Barbara Pistachio Ranch v. Chowchilla Water District, 88 Cal.App.4th 439, 105 Cal.Rptr.2d 856 (2001).

IV. OTHER REQUIREMENTS FOR APPELLATE REVIEW

In addition to determining the appealability of a judgment or order, issues of standing to appeal and timeliness of the filing of the notice of appeal affect the Court of Appeal's ability to review the matter before it.

A. Standing

Standing to appeal is a jurisdictional requirement. Only a "party aggrieved" has standing to appeal from a judgment or order. CCP § 902.

1. "Party"

To be considered a party, a person generally must be a party of record (named party) to the action in the trial court. A person not named in the trial court action nevertheless might be considered a "party" for standing purposes if she would be bound by the judgment under principles of claim preclusion. Life v. County of Los Angeles, 218 Cal.App.3d 1287, 267 Cal.Rptr. 557 (1990).

2. "Aggrieved"

A party is aggrieved if her "immediate, pecuniary, and substantial" rights or interests are "injuriously affected by the judgment." County of Alameda v. Carleson, 5 Cal.3d 730, 736, 97 Cal.Rptr. 385, 389, 488 P.2d 953 (1971).

3. *Compare Federal Procedure*

Like a California appellant, only a party aggrieved by the district court judgment has standing to appeal in the federal circuit courts.

> **4. Illustration**
>
> Manny is the alleged biological father of Ike, although Manny is not named as such on Ike's birth certificate. Proceedings commenced in Placer County Superior Court to terminate parental rights as to Ike. Ike's mother was a named party in the proceedings, but Manny was not. Manny received notice of the proceedings but did not appear at the hearing. The court ordered the "parental rights of mother and the unknown father aka Manny" to be terminated. Manny filed a timely notice of appeal of the court's order. Manny does not have standing to appeal the order. The notice of the hearing presented Manny with the opportunity to attempt to join the action as a party, but he did not pursue intervention. Although Manny is aggrieved by the order terminating his parental rights, and he is referred to by name in the order, he had never become a party of record in the proceedings and thus lacked standing to appeal the order. In re Joseph G., 83 Cal.App.4th 712, 99 Cal.Rptr.2d 915 (2000).

B. Timeliness of Appeal

1. Filing Notice of Appeal

An aggrieved party triggers the Court of Appeal's jurisdiction by filing a timely notice of appeal.

2. Timeliness of Notice of Appeal

CRC 8.104 and 8.108 set out the time limits for filing this notice. These limits are considered jurisdictional—if a party files an untimely notice of appeal, the Court of Appeal has no choice but to dismiss the appeal. CRC 8.104(b). The court may not relieve or excuse a party from the consequences of filing an untimely notice of appeal, even if the party makes a showing of good cause. CRC 8.60(d).

a. Normal Time Limits

A notice must be filed on or before the earliest of the following times:

- 60 days after the Superior Court clerk mails a copy of the notice of entry of judgment or a file-stamped copy of the judgment;
- 60 days after appellant serves or is served with a copy of the notice of entry of judgment or a file-stamped copy of the judgment; or

- 180 days after entry of judgment.

CRC 8.104(a). "Judgment" includes an appealable order. CRC 8.104(f). The date of entry of a judgment is the date it is filed or entered in the book of judgments. The date of entry of an appealable order is the date it is entered in the minutes. However, if the order directs a written order to be prepared, the date of entry is the date the signed order is filed. The date of entry of an order not entered into the minutes is the date the signed order is filed. CRC 8.104(d).

b. Extended Time Limits

1) Post-Order or Post-Judgment Motions

CRC 8.108 extends the normal deadlines in CRC 8.104(a) for filing the notice of appeal in situations where certain post-order or post-judgment motions have been filed in the trial court. These include motions: (a) for new trial; (b) to vacate judgment; (c) for judgment notwithstanding the verdict; and (d) to reconsider an appealable order. These extensions give the would-be appellant additional time to file an appeal following the trial court's ruling on the motion, as long as the motion in the trial court was itself timely.

2) Cross-Appeals

If a party files a notice of appeal after another party has already filed an initial notice of appeal, the second notice of appeal is treated as a cross-appeal. The timely filing of the first notice of appeal extends the deadline for all cross-appeals for twenty days after the trial court mails notice of the filing of the first appeal. CRC 8.108(e)(1).

c. Premature Appeals

A notice of appeal filed after a judgment is rendered but before the judgment has been entered is a valid notice. The notice is treated as if it had been filed immediately after entry of judgment. CRC 8.104(e)(1). If the notice of appeal was filed before the judgment was actually rendered but after the announcement of the intended ruling, the Court of Appeal may, in its discretion, treat the notice of appeal as having been filed immediately after the entry of judgment. CRC 8.104(e)(2).

3. *Compare Federal Procedure*

Federal appeals are generally subject to shorter time limits than in California. In most cases, a notice of appeal must be filed with the district court clerk within 30 days after entry of the judgment or order being appealed. FRAP 4(a)(1)(A); 28 USC § 2107(a). This time limit may be extended when particular post-judgment motions have been filed. In those cases, the time to file the notice of appeal begins to run for all parties upon the entry of the order disposing of the last remaining motion. FRAP 4(a)(4). In marked contrast to California procedure, the district court may extend the time to file the notice of appeal if a party shows excusable neglect or good cause. FRAP 4(a)(5); 28 USC § 2107(c). The district court may also, upon motion of a party, reopen the time to file a notice of appeal if that party shows that it did not receive notice of the entry of the judgment or order. FRAP 4(a)(6); 28 USC § 2107(c).

4. Illustration

Pack bought an old-looking globe from Dana in St. Helena. Dana, an antiques dealer, represented that the globe was made in 1880, but Pack later learned (by taking it to a taping of "Antiques Road Show") that the globe was actually a reproduction made much later. Pack sued Dana for fraud in Napa County Superior Court. Dana filed a general demurrer to the complaint, which the trial court sustained without leave to amend. The court entered a judgment of dismissal on May 23. On June 1, Dana mailed a notice of entry of judgment to Pack's post office box, but he put an incorrect zip code on the envelope. On September 9, Pack filed a notice of appeal. Dana argued that the appeal should be dismissed as untimely, since Pack filed it more than 60 days after Dana served the notice of entry of judgment. However, notice sent to an incorrect address is not valid notice. Thus, Pack's notice of appeal was timely because it was filed within 180 days after entry of judgment. Moghaddam v. Bone, 142 Cal.App.4th 283, 47 Cal.Rptr.3d 602 (2006).

V. STANDARD OF REVIEW

A. Purpose and Types of Standards of Review

When the appellate court reviews the trial court record for prejudicial error, it must apply the appropriate standard of review. The standard of review affects the degree of deference the appellate court must give to the trial court's ruling. There are three principal standards of review: de novo (independent) review; abuse of discretion; and substantial evidence. In many cases, the reviewing court will apply more than one standard, depending on the nature of the trial court rulings. Whitlock v. Foster Wheeler, LLC, 160 Cal.App.4th 149, 72 Cal.Rptr.3d 369 (2008).

1. De Novo (Independent) Review Standard

De novo review accords no deference to the trial court's judgment. This standard is applied when the appellate court reviews pure questions of law. Examples of issues reviewed under this standard include: (a) interpretation of statutes; (b) determination of whether a duty of care is owed; (c) constitutional issues; and (d) the application of law to undisputed facts.

2. Abuse of Discretion Standard

If the trial court's ruling was based on the judge's exercise of discretion, the appellate court reviews that ruling under the abuse of discretion standard. The reviewing court will reverse the trial court judgment only if the exercise of discretion resulted in a "miscarriage of justice." The most common formulation of this standard is that the appellate court assesses whether the trial court's ruling exceeded "the bounds of reason." Walker v. Superior Court, 53 Cal.3d 257, 272, 279 Cal.Rptr. 576, 585, 807 P.2d 418 (1991). This standard offers great deference to the trial court's decision. Dozens of categories of trial court rulings are reviewed under the abuse of discretion standard, including discovery rulings, attorney's fee awards, injunctions, sanctions orders, and orders permitting amendment of pleadings.

3. Substantial Evidence Standard

a. Nature of Standard

The substantial evidence standard applies when the trial court ruling involves the resolution of factual disputes by either the jury or the court. The reviewing court determines, based on the whole record, whether substantial evidence supports the judgment. If so, it will affirm the judgment. This standard accords significant deference to the trial court's ruling.

b. Quality of Evidence

"Substantial evidence" is not a quantitative inquiry. The appellate court does not weigh the evidence. Instead, it focuses on the quality of the evidence in support of the judgment to determine if it is of a ponderable legal significance, credible, and solid. Very little evidence might be considered substantial if it is of a sound and firm nature; conversely, a great deal of weak evidence is not substantial. For example, the testimony of one credible witness may be considered substantial evidence of a fact, even though the testimony of several other less credible witnesses was contradictory. The substantial evidence standard is used to review such matters as interpretation of a contract where there is conflicting extrinsic evidence, and the underlying factual basis for the trial court's exercise of discretion.

B. *Compare Federal Procedure*

The federal circuit courts apply the same three standards of review discussed above. The substantial evidence standard, however, is used only to review factual resolutions by a jury. In reviewing a district court's findings of fact in a non-jury case, the federal appeals court applies a "clearly erroneous" standard instead. FRCP 52(a)(6). A ruling will be found clearly erroneous if "the reviewing court on the entire evidence is left with the definite and firm conviction that a mistake has been committed." United States v. United States Gypsum Co., 333 U.S. 364, 395, 68 S.Ct. 525, 542, 92 L.Ed. 746 (1948).

C. Illustration

Persis sued Dolan in Nevada County Superior Court for selling Persis a defective car. Dolan filed a motion to strike the complaint because it contained irrelevant allegations, but before the court's ruling, Persis filed an amended complaint. Thereafter, Persis was uncooperative in participating in discovery, and the court granted Dolan's request to appoint a special discovery master. Persis filed numerous motions against the special master, the judge and Dolan's attorney. The court issued an order declaring Persis a vexatious litigant under CCP § 391. (See Chapter 3(VIII)(B).) Persis appealed the order. The Court of Appeal's review of the order will involve the application of several standards of review. The court's exercise of discretion in declaring Persis a vexatious litigant is reviewed for abuse of discretion. The factual findings underlying the court's exercise of its discretion are reviewed under the substantial evidence standard. The Court of Appeal's interpretation of the requirements of and legislative intent behind the vexatious litigant statute is subject to de novo (independent) review. Bravo v. Ismaj, 99 Cal.App.4th 211, 120 Cal.Rptr.2d 879 (2002).

VI. PREJUDICIAL VERSUS HARMLESS ERROR

The Court of Appeal, applying the appropriate standard of review, reviews the trial court record for error. Only prejudicial error is sufficient to cause reversal or modification of the trial court judgment. A finding of harmless error results in affirmance of the judgment.

A. Definition of Prejudicial Error

Error must result in a "miscarriage of justice" in order to be deemed prejudicial. Cal. Const., art VI, § 13. A miscarriage of justice occurs when "it is reasonably probable that a result more favorable to the appealing party would have been reached in the absence of the error." Cassim v. Allstate Insurance Co., 33 Cal.4th 780, 800, 16 Cal.Rptr.3d 374, 388, 94 P.3d 513 (2004); see also CCP § 475, Cal. Evid. Code §§ 353–354. Any error not resulting in a miscarriage of justice is considered harmless.

1. Actual Error

Because a judgment is presumed to be correct, the appellant has the burden to show actual prejudicial error.

2. Reversible Error Per Se

In a very limited number of cases, error may be considered reversible per se, relieving the appellant of the requirement to prove prejudicial error. Examples of errors presumed to be prejudicial include erroneous denial of a request for a jury trial, erroneous restriction on the right of cross-examination, and judicial bias.

B. *Compare Federal Procedure*

The federal circuit courts may not reverse a district court judgment if the trial court committed only harmless error. FRCP 61; 28 USC § 2111. Under section 2111, the appellate court must exercise its judgment instead of automatically reversing upon the finding of any error. Under the harmless error statute, there is no automatic reversal for "errors that do not affect the essential fairness of a trial." McDonough Power Equipment, Inc. v. Greenwood, 464 U.S. 548, 553, 104 S.Ct. 845, 848, 78 L.Ed.2d 663 (1984).

C. Illustration

Powell sued Dr. Diablo in Mendocino County Superior Court for medical malpractice for leaving a sponge in Powell's chest after

> coronary bypass surgery. Toward the end of the trial, Powell's attorney made a motion to reopen the testimony of Dr. Diablo. In ruling on the motion, the trial judge stated: "Your motion is denied. This trial is going on its third week. I think the jury is getting tired of repeatedly hearing some of the same testimony. I am, too." On objection from Powell, the judge struck his comment from the record and admonished the jury to disregard it. The jury rendered a verdict for Dr. Diablo. On appeal from the judgment, Powell asserted that the judge's comment constituted prejudicial error. Except in unusual circumstances, comments of the trial judge do not result in reversible error, especially where the judge admonished the jury to disregard the comment. Aguayo v. Crompton & Knowles Corp., 183 Cal.App.3d 1032, 228 Cal.Rptr. 768 (1986).

VII. APPELLATE SANCTIONS

The appellate courts are authorized to impose sanctions in connection with appeals (CRC 8.276(a)) and writ petitions (CRC 8.490(n)).

A. Frivolous Appeal or Writ

The Court of Appeal may award sanctions to a respondent for an appellant's filing of a frivolous appeal or a petitioner's filing of a frivolous writ petition. CRC 8.276(a), 8.490(n). An appeal is deemed frivolous under a subjective standard when it is pursued for an improper purpose (such as to harass the respondent or delay the effect of an adverse judgment), or under an objective standard when it "indisputably has no merit" (when a "reasonable attorney would agree that the appeal is totally and completely without merit"). Olsen v. Harbison, 134 Cal.App.4th 278, 284, 35 Cal.Rptr.3d 909, 914 (2005). The reviewing court may add to the costs on appeal the attorney's fees and costs respondent incurred in responding to a frivolous appeal. CCP § 907.

B. Violation of Appellate Procedural Rules

CRC 8.276(a) and 8.490(n) authorize sanctions for unreasonable violations of rules of court governing appeals and writs, respectively. In re S.C., 138 Cal.App.4th 396, 41 Cal.Rptr.3d 453 (2006) (sanctioning appellant's counsel for a variety of violations in the preparation of appellant's opening brief, such as failure to cite to authority, to include relevant facts, and to state each point under a separate heading).

C. *Compare Federal Procedure*

FRAP 38 authorizes "an award of just damages and single or double costs to the appellee" for a frivolous appeal. An "appeal is frivolous if the results are obvious, or the arguments of error are wholly without merit." In re George, 322 F.3d 586, 591 (9th Cir. 2003). In addition, 28 USC § 1912 permits an award of damages and costs to the prevailing party "for his delay."

D. Illustration

Axel filed a notice of appeal from the trial court's judgment. Axel's opening appellate brief violated several appellate rules of court: (1) it did not organize each argument in a separate section with its own heading; (2) it did not summarize key facts restricted to the contents of the trial court record; (3) it did not include specific page cites to the record; and (4) its appendix included documents irrelevant to the matters on appeal. In addition, Axel's appeal was frivolous because he raised arguments that were "patently disingenuous" and that "distorted the law, the facts, and logic." The Court of Appeal may remand the case to the trial court for determination of the amount of sanctions to be imposed on Axel. Evans v. CenterStone Development Co., 134 Cal.App.4th 151, 35 Cal.Rptr.3d 745 (2005).

SAMPLE EXAM QUESTIONS

OBJECTIVE QUESTIONS

The questions in this section are based on the following hypothetical:

Gail sued Fred in Lassen County Superior Court for breach of contract, negligence, and fraud. Fred filed a general demurrer as to the breach of contract cause of action. The trial court issued an order sustaining Fred's demurrer without leave to amend. The court then conducted a jury trial of only the negligence cause of action. Judgment was entered for Fred on that cause of action. The fraud cause of action remained pending in the trial court.

---

(1) The right of appeal in California comes from:

a. The U.S. Constitution, consistent with U.S. Supreme Court precedent;

b. The California Constitution, consistent with California Supreme Court precedent;

c. California statute;

d. Both b and c.

(2) True or False: The order sustaining Fred's demurrer without leave to amend as to Gail's breach of contract cause of action is not immediately appealable.

(3) True or False: Gail may immediately appeal from the judgment entered for Fred on the negligence cause of action even though the fraud cause of action remains pending.

(4) Which of the following would NOT be immediately appealable under California statute:

a. An order denying Fred's motion to quash service of summons;

b. An order granting Fred's motion for a new trial or denying Fred's motion for judgment notwithstanding the verdict;

c. An interlocutory judgment requiring that Fred pay monetary sanctions exceeding $5,000;

d. An order granting or denying Fred's anti-SLAPP motion to strike.

(5) True or False: The Court of Appeal may permit Gail to file a late notice of appeal if she can show good cause.

(6) True or False: The Court of Appeal has discretion to treat Gail's appeal taken from a nonappealable order as a petition for an extraordinary writ.

(7) True or False: If the trial court found that Gail did not have standing to bring her action, she also does not have standing to appeal the trial court's finding of lack of standing.

(8) True or False: If the Court of Appeal applies the substantial evidence standard of review to Gail's appeal of the trial court's final judgment, the appellate court must affirm the judgment if the weight of the evidence favors Fred.

(9) True or False: The Court of Appeal will reverse the trial court's judgment in favor of Gail only if the judgment resulted in a miscarriage of justice.

(10) The Court of Appeal may issue sanctions against Gail if:

a. She has filed an appeal for an improper purpose;

b. She has filed a writ petition that indisputably has no merit;

c. She has filed a brief that does not comply with applicable appellate rules;

d. All of the above.

Answers to Objective Questions

(1) **c.** The right of appeal is statutory. Neither the California nor the U.S. Constitution confers a right of appeal.

(2) **True**. An order sustaining a demurrer, with or without leave to amend, is not an immediately appealable order. CCP § 904.1. Nor is it an appealable collateral order. Gail must wait to appeal from the final judgment.

(3) **False**. There can only be one final judgment in an action. The California Supreme Court invalidated a former judicial exception allowing an appeal of severed causes of action while others remained pending. Gail must wait to appeal until the court enters final judgment on all causes of action.

(4) **a.** CCP § 904.1 sets out appealable orders and judgments. An order *granting* a motion to quash service of summons is appealable under CCP § 904.1(a)(3), but not

an order *denying* the motion. An order denying a motion to quash may be reviewed upon a petition for writ of mandate under CCP § 418.10(c). The other orders and judgments in this question are expressly made appealable by section 904.1.

(5) **False**. The requirement of filing a timely notice of appeal is jurisdictional. The appellate court has no discretion to permit a late-filed appeal, even on a showing of good cause. CRC 8.104(b).

(6) **True**. The appellate court may exercise its discretion to treat an appeal from a nonappealable order as an application for an extraordinary writ if the matter involves unusual circumstances, hardship, an issue of public importance, and/or an issue of first impression.

(7) **False**. A party aggrieved by the trial court's ruling has standing to appeal. If the trial court ruled that Gail did not have standing to bring her action, she is aggrieved by the trial court decision and has standing to appeal it.

(8) **False**. The appellate court does not weigh the evidence when it applies the substantial evidence standard of review. The court's focus is on the quality of the evidence, not the quantity.

(9) **True**. Reversal requires a showing of prejudicial error, which is interpreted as a miscarriage of justice. Cal. Const., art. VI, § 13.

(10) **d.** All of the alternatives set out in this question are proper grounds for an award of sanctions. CRC 8.276.

ESSAY QUESTION

One Friday night, Clay and his friends Tai and Moe were sitting in Moe's car outside of Moe's house in San Jose, when two police officers approached the car. The officers had received a report from a neighbor that several teenagers had been unloading firearms from a car matching Moe's car's description. The teens said they had no weapons. They told the officers that they had just been talking and that Moe was about to take Tai and Clay home.

The officers ordered all three teens to get out of the car. Tai did not immediately get out of the car, and one of the officers grabbed Tai by the hair and the back of her shirt and pulled her out of the car. Clay became angry and punched the officer and then reached for the officer's gun. The two officers tackled Clay, placed him in a chokehold, and handcuffed him. The officers also handcuffed Tai and Moe and searched the car. Though the officers did not find firearms or other contraband, they took all three teens into custody and detained them overnight. Clay was charged with resisting arrest and assault on a police officer. No charges were ever filed against Tai and Moe.

All three teens have filed a civil rights lawsuit in Santa Clara County Superior Court against the City of San Jose, the police department and the individual police officers, alleging that the police engaged in impermissible profiling based on their young age and that the officers used unnecessary force to arrest and detain the teens. The teens are seeking damages from the City for the alleged mistreatment, and preliminary and permanent injunctions preventing the police department from engaging in such profiling or using extremely dangerous force to detain suspects.

The trial court granted a preliminary injunction for the plaintiffs on March 14. Tai and Moe filed a motion for summary judgment against all defendants. The court granted the motion and entered judgment for Tai and Moe on all causes of action on May 23. Clay's case remained pending. The police department wishes to appeal the issuance of the injunction and the summary judgments in favor of Tai and Moe. It filed its notice of appeal on August 12.

(1) Discuss whether the preliminary injunction and the summary judgments are appealable.

(2) Assuming the trial court's rulings are appealable, discuss:

(a) how much time the police department has to file its notice of appeal from the preliminary injunction and the summary judgment motions; and

(b) what standard(s) of review the Court of Appeal is likely to apply.

Answer to Essay Question

(1) Appealability

- Appeal from the preliminary injunction:
  - General Rule: parties may appeal final judgments.
  - CCP § 904.1(a) permits appeal of certain nonfinal orders and judgments. An order granting an injunction is an immediately appealable order. CCP § 904.1(a)(6).
- Appeal from the summary judgments for Tai and Moe:
  - Entry of summary judgment is a final appealable judgment. In contrast, the defendants would not be able to appeal from the order granting summary judgment. Instead, they would have to file a petition for extraordinary writ.

- The defendants may appeal from the summary judgment entered for Tai and Moe, even though the action remains pending against Clay. In actions involving multiple parties, the judgment is considered final if it leaves no issue for further determination as to a particular plaintiff or defendant, even if further proceedings are pending against another party.

(2)(a) Timeliness of Notice of Appeal

- CRC 8.104 governs the timing of the filing of the notice of appeal. There are no circumstances in this case that would extend the filing under CRC 8.108. Under the general rule, the police department must file its notice of appeal by the earliest of the three time limits set out in CRC 8.104(a).
- The time limits are considered to be jurisdictional.
- If either of the two alternative 60–day periods applies, the notice of appeal is filed late. If the 180–day period applies, the notice of appeal is timely.

(2)(b) Standards of Review

- The three main standards of review are de novo (independent), abuse of discretion, and substantial evidence.
- Preliminary Injunction:
    - The court exercises its discretion to issue an injunction. Thus, the issuance is reviewed under the abuse of discretion standard. Any factual determinations underlying the court's exercise of discretion are reviewed under the substantial evidence standard.
- Summary judgment:
    - A grant of summary judgment is a determination that there are no triable issues of material fact. The judgment is reviewed de novo.

*

CHAPTER 9

PRIOR ADJUDICATION

I. STARE DECISIS

Stare decisis refers to adherence to legal precedent by the courts. This judicially-created doctrine promotes certainty and predictability in the application and development of the law.

A. Binding Versus Persuasive Authority

Under the rules of stare decisis, certain court decisions have binding effect on rulings made by other courts. Those court decisions that are not considered binding precedent may nonetheless have persuasive effect on other courts considering the same issues.

1. Decisions on Matters of State Law

When deciding matters of California law, stare decisis requires that California courts of inferior jurisdiction must adhere to decisions of courts of superior jurisdiction. (See California Court System chart, Chapter 1, p. 3).

a. California Supreme Court Decisions

When California courts are considering state law issues, decisions of the California Supreme Court are binding on all inferior California courts. Auto Equity Sales, Inc. v. Superior Court, 57 Cal.2d 450, 20 Cal.Rptr. 321, 369 P.2d 937 (1962).

b. California Court of Appeal Decisions

California Court of Appeal decisions are binding on all California superior courts in the state, even those located outside of the issuing court of appeal's district or division. When different panels of the courts of appeal have issued conflicting decisions, the superior courts are free to follow whichever Court of Appeal decision they find more persuasive. California does not follow a "horizontal stare decisis" rule. One panel of the Court of

Appeal does not have to follow any other panel's decision, even if that decision came from the same appellate district or division. In re Marriage of Shaban, 88 Cal.App.4th 398, 105 Cal.Rptr.2d 863 (2001).

2. Decisions on Matters of Federal Law

U.S. Supreme Court decisions regarding federal law are binding on all California courts when the state courts are deciding a federal question. Federal circuit and district court decisions addressing federal questions are not binding on California courts, although such decisions are entitled to significant weight as persuasive authority. When there is a split of authority in the circuit courts, California state courts do not consider Ninth Circuit decisions to be any more persuasive than the decisions of other circuits. Elliot v. Albright, 209 Cal.App.3d 1028, 257 Cal.Rptr. 762 (1989).

3. *Compare Federal Procedure*

In contrast to the California practice, a circuit Court of Appeals decision is binding on only the federal district courts within that circuit. It is also binding on all subsequent panels of the particular circuit under the horizontal stare decisis rule, unless the federal appellate court decision is subsequently reversed by the circuit court en banc or by the U.S. Supreme Court. Agostini v. Felton, 521 U.S. 203, 117 S.Ct. 1997, 138 L.Ed.2d 391 (1997).

4. Illustration

California enacted a statute pertaining to bankruptcy filings. On the basis of diversity jurisdiction, a creditor challenged California's statute in federal court, claiming federal law preempted the state statute. In a 2–1 decision, the Ninth Circuit Court of Appeals ultimately agreed with the creditor that federal bankruptcy law preempted California's statute. In a later lawsuit in state court, a California Court of Appeal panel found the reasoning in the dissent from the Ninth Circuit's decision—contending that the California statute was not preempted—to be a more persuasive reading of federal law. The Court of Appeal was not bound by the Ninth Circuit's majority opinion. Credit Managers Association of California v. Countrywide Home Loans, Inc., 144 Cal.App.4th 590, 50 Cal.Rptr.3d 259 (2006).

B. Overruling Precedent

The stare decisis doctrine requires lower courts to follow prior appellate court precedent (subject to the limitations discussed above), even if a different panel of appellate justices might have reached a different result. Moradi–Shalal v. Fireman's Fund Insurance Co., 46 Cal.3d 287, 250 Cal.Rptr. 116, 758 P.2d 58 (1988). Although the California Supreme Court may overrule its prior precedent, it will do so only in limited situations.

1. Overruling Court-Created Errors or Unsound Cases

The California Supreme Court may overrule prior precedent when the Court created an error that it must correct, especially if the error is of significant concern to the community. In addition, the Court may reconsider its prior decisions if later opinions show that an earlier decision was unsound or is appropriate for reevaluation. The Court is more likely to overrule an earlier decision if "it has generated and will continue to produce inequitable results, costly multiple litigation, and unnecessary confusion." *Moradi–Shalal*, 46 Cal.3d at 297, 250 Cal.Rptr. at 121, 758 P.2d 58.

2. Factors in Court's Consideration to Overrule

In assessing whether it should overrule precedent, the California Supreme Court may consider several factors, including whether: (a) subsequent courts have been reluctant to follow the decision; (b) scholarly analysis has been critical of the decision; and (c) there have been adverse social and economic consequences of the decision.

3. *Compare Federal Procedure*

The U.S. Supreme Court has acknowledged the importance of stare decisis. While the Court does not mindlessly adhere to previous decisions, the Court will not overrule prior precedent without special justification. Patterson v. McLean Credit Union, 491 U.S. 164, 109 S.Ct. 2363, 105 L.Ed.2d 132 (1989). When the Court has overruled prior interpretations of statutes, it typically has done so because changes in legal doctrines or subsequent congressional actions have eroded the reasoning in the previous opinion. Further, the Court has departed from prior precedent when the decision proved to be unworkable or irreconcilable with other legal goals. Additionally, the Court may overrule precedent that is no longer consistent with historical understanding or principles of justice.

4. Illustration

In an opinion, the California Supreme Court held that the Insurance Code contained a private cause of action for non-customer claimants harmed by an insurance company's unfair business practices. After that decision, Plato sued Daggett for damages caused when Daggett's car collided with Plato's. Plato and Daggett settled the dispute with Daggett's insurance company. As permitted under the Supreme Court's previous holding, Plato then sued the insurance company, alleging the company engaged in unfair practices during the settlement. The California Supreme Court reexamined its decision and overruled its interpretation of the Insurance Code based on scholarly criticism, the fact that most other states had refused to adopt such a policy, the inability of lower courts to apply the decision consistently, and the increase in litigation sparked by the old rule. Moradi–Shalal v. Fireman's Fund Insurance Co., 46 Cal.3d 287, 250 Cal.Rptr. 116, 758 P.2d 58 (1988) (reversing Royal Globe Insurance Co. v. Superior Court, 23 Cal.3d 880, 153 Cal.Rptr. 842, 592 P.2d 329 (1979)).

C. Retroactivity

1. Judicial Decisions Versus Legislation

Generally, the California courts consider judicial decisions to apply retroactively and legislation to apply only prospectively. The rule of retroactive application of judicial decisions stems from Blackstone's 18th–century theory that judges "find" the law rather than "create" it. Newman v. Emerson Radio Corp., 48 Cal.3d 973, 258 Cal.Rptr. 592, 772 P.2d 1059 (1989).

a. Exception: Prospectively-Applied Judicial Decisions

There are two general exceptions to the retroactive application of judicial decisions: (1) courts need not retroactively apply the rule if doing so would create significant concerns about the effect of a new rule on the administration of justice; and (2) retroactivity may not be appropriate if the parties' reasonable reliance on the existing law would be unjustly undermined.

b. Exception: Retroactively-Applied Legislation

Legislation that affects substantive rights can apply retroactively only if the Legislature clearly states that intent. McClung v. Employment Development Department, 34 Cal.4th 467, 20 Cal.Rptr.3d 428, 99 P.3d 1015 (2004). Moreover, statutes that are silent about their retroactivity may be applied to pending litigation if the statute affects only the litigants' *procedural* (but not substantive) rights. Californians for Disability Rights v. Mervyn's, LLC, 39 Cal.4th 223, 46 Cal.Rptr.3d 57, 138 P.3d 207 (2006).

2. *Compare Federal Procedure*

Case law is generally applied retroactively in the federal courts. When deciding whether to deviate from the practice of retroactive application of court decisions, federal courts consider the following: (a) the decision must either "overrule clear past precedent on which the litigants may have relied" or decide "an issue of first impression whose resolution was not clearly foreshadowed," thus establishing a new legal principle; (b) the court must determine whether retroactivity would impede the law's operation, taking into consideration the merits of the specific case and the prior history of the legal principle; and (c) if retroactivity would lead to substantial inequitable results, the court may decline retroactive application. Chevron Oil Co. v. Huson, 404 U.S. 97, 92 S.Ct. 349, 30 L.Ed.2d 296 (1971). As in California, federal statutes generally apply prospectively only, unless Congress expressly and unequivocally indicates a contrary intent. Immigration and Naturalization Service v. St. Cyr, 533 U.S. 289, 121 S.Ct. 2271, 150 L.Ed.2d 347 (2001).

3. Illustration

In an earlier decision, the California Supreme Court interpreted a provision of California's Fair Employment and Housing Act (FEHA) to apply only to discrimination perpetrated by supervisory workers and not to discrimination perpetrated by non-supervisory co-workers. The California Legislature later amended FEHA to specifically apply the provision to discrimination perpetrated by both supervisory and non-supervisory co-workers. In the amendment, the Legislature stated that it was merely clarifying the meaning of the existing statute. Because of the strong presumption against the retroactive application of statutes, the California Supreme Court concluded that the Legislature's statement that it was clarifying state law was not sufficient to indicate legislative intent to apply the amendment retroactively. Thus, the statute only covered cases of non-supervisor discrimination that occurred after the amendment's passage. McClung v. Employment Development Department, 34 Cal.4th 467, 20 Cal.Rptr.3d 428, 99 P.3d 1015 (2004).

D. Law of the Case and Judicial Estoppel

1. Law of the Case

a. Application of Doctrine

The law of the case doctrine applies when cases are tried, appealed, retried and then appealed a second time. Once the appellate court hearing the first appeal states a rule of law essential to the decision and remands the case for further proceedings, subsequent trial and appellate courts must adhere to that rule of law in later proceedings in that case. Clemente v. State of California, 40 Cal.3d 202, 219 Cal.Rptr. 445, 707 P.2d 818 (1985). This adherence is required even if the rule of law was incorrectly decided or applied in the first appeal. The law of the case doctrine applies until the litigation and appeals are terminated. Compare the doctrines of claim and issue preclusion (see section II, below), which apply to subsequent actions.

b. Exceptions

The law of the case doctrine is a policy, not a strict requirement. As a result, there are several notable exceptions to the doctrine's application:

- Courts need not follow the law of the case doctrine when intervening changes in the law have occurred, such that prior precedent was overruled or new controlling precedent was established.
- Courts have declined to adhere to the doctrine when following it would lead to an unjust result.
- The doctrine does not apply if the issue was not addressed during the prior appeal.

2. Judicial Estoppel

Judicial estoppel is an equitable doctrine applied in the court's discretion. It is sometimes referred to as preclusion of inconsistent positions. The court invokes this doctrine when a party's inconsistent positions would result in a miscarriage of justice. Judicial estoppel applies when:

- A party has taken two positions;
- The positions were taken in judicial or quasi-judicial administrative proceedings;
- The party was successful in asserting the first position;
- The two positions are completely inconsistent; and
- The first position was not taken as a result of ignorance, fraud, or mistake.

Hanna v. Los Angeles County Sheriff's Department, 102 Cal.App.4th 887, 125 Cal.Rptr.2d 686 (2002).

3. *Compare Federal Procedure*

Federal courts also observe the law of the case and judicial estoppel doctrines. Those doctrines have essentially the same parameters as California's rules. Zedner v. United States, 547 U.S. 489, 126 S.Ct. 1976, 164 L.Ed.2d 749 (2006); Ingle v. Circuit City, Inc., 408 F.3d 592 (9th Cir. 2005).

4. Illustration

Penne filed suit against Digby in Yuba County Superior Court. The trial court granted Digby's motion for summary judgment. Penne promptly appealed from the judgment. The Court of Appeal reversed and remanded to the trial court, concluding that there were triable issues of fact that precluded summary judgment. When the trial court received the case for the second time, Digby moved for judgment on the pleadings, contending that a case on which the appellate court had relied was wrongly decided. The trial court granted Digby's motion for judgment on the pleadings. When Penne appealed this second trial court decision, the Court of Appeal again reversed, ruling that regardless of the correctness of the underlying case law, the appellate court's decision in the first appeal was the law of the case, and it governed all subsequent proceedings in the case. Yu v. Signet Bank/Virginia, 103 Cal.App.4th 298, 126 Cal.Rptr.2d 516 (2002).

II. RES JUDICATA

Res judicata is a common law doctrine barring relitigation of causes of action or issues. Res judicata promotes judicial economy, ensures repose for the parties, and strengthens the court system generally. There is no uniform terminology, in California or elsewhere, regarding the use of the term res judicata. It is here used to include both *claim preclusion* (which is sometimes alone called res judicata) and *issue preclusion* (also known as collateral estoppel).

A. Claim Preclusion

1. Requirements

There are four elements of claim preclusion:

- a final judgment on the merits in Action #1;

- the same parties or those in privity with a party in Action #2 as in Action #1;
- a judgment in Action #1 that was based on the same cause of action as that brought in Action #2; and
- the cause of action in Action #2 actually was or could have been litigated in Action #1.

Frommhagen v. Board of Supervisors, 197 Cal.App.3d 1292, 243 Cal.Rptr. 390 (1987).

a. Prior Final Judgment on the Merits

Any final judgment that reaches the legal substance of the claim is considered to be on the merits. Examples include summary judgment, default judgment, and stipulated judgment. A judgment based on procedural matters, such as subject matter jurisdiction, personal jurisdiction, venue, or involuntary dismissal under the diligent prosecution statutes, is not considered a judgment on the merits. A judgment is considered final for claim preclusion purposes upon the conclusion of any appeal taken by a party, or upon the expiration of the time for taking an appeal.

b. Parties or Privies

Claim preclusion applies only against one who was a party to the first action, or against a nonparty who was "in privity" with the party. Privity assumes a relationship between the party and nonparty that is close enough to justify the imposition of claim preclusion principles upon the nonparty. Clemmer v. Hartford Insurance Co., 22 Cal.3d 865, 151 Cal.Rptr. 285, 587 P.2d 1098 (1978). Examples of those in privity include representatives of deceased parties and successors in interest.

c. Same Cause of Action

The definition of "cause of action" is critical in claim preclusion analysis. In marked contrast to most jurisdictions, California subscribes to the "primary rights" theory of the cause of action. "A 'cause of action' is composed of a 'primary right' of the plaintiff, a corresponding 'primary duty' of the defendant, and a wrongful act by the defendant constituting a breach of that duty." Crowley v. Katleman, 8 Cal.4th 666, 681, 34 Cal.Rptr.2d 386, 393, 881 P.2d 1083 (1994). The primary right is the right to be free of the type of harm or injury caused by the defendant. In most other state jurisdictions, claims are considered to be a single cause of action if they arise out of the same transaction or occurrence, as defined by the Restatement (Second) of Judgments.

1) Determining a Primary Right

The determination of a primary right can be challenging, especially in cases involving more than one type of injury. It is a determination with significant impact, since, for claim preclusion purposes, an attempt to litigate the "same" cause of action (primary right) in a later lawsuit will be barred. However, the same set of facts may yield different primary rights, which may be vindicated in separate actions. Each primary right represents a distinct harm suffered. Whether several legal theories are pleaded, or different types of remedies are sought, is irrelevant. What matters is whether the defendant violated the plaintiff's right to be free from the particular sort of injury suffered. Grisham v. Philip Morris U.S.A., Inc., 40 Cal.4th 623, 54 Cal.Rptr.3d 735, 151 P.3d 1151 (2007).

2) Declaratory Relief

When a party sought purely declaratory relief in Action #1, the resulting judgment does not preclude further litigation in Action #2 of the primary rights involved. CCP § 1062. If, however, the party's first action sought declaratory relief mixed with other forms of relief (such as an injunction), any resulting judgment—including the granting of declaratory relief—will preclude further litigation under the doctrine of claim preclusion. Mycogen Corp. v. Monsanto Co., 28 Cal.4th 888, 123 Cal.Rptr.2d 432, 51 P.3d 297 (2002).

3) Causes of Action Based on Both State and Federal Law

If the defendant's conduct violated both California and federal law, the question arises whether there are two primary rights, or one primary right with two legal theories. If the California and federal laws are both intended to address the same injury or harm to the plaintiff, then only one primary right is implicated.

d. Cause of Action Was or Could Have Been Litigated

A final judgment bars relitigation not only of those causes of action that were actually litigated in the first action, but also of those that could have been litigated at the same time. "If the matter was within the scope of the action, related to the subject matter and relevant to the issues, so that it *could* have been raised, the judgment is conclusive on it despite the fact that it was not in fact expressly pleaded or otherwise urged." Sutphin v. Speik, 15 Cal.2d 195, 202, 99 P.2d 652, 655 (1940) (emphasis in original). This requirement causes confusion because it seems at odds with the primary rights doctrine.

2. Claim Preclusion and Compulsory Cross-Complaints

Statutorily, a "related" cause of action that a defendant has against a plaintiff must be brought as a compulsory cross-complaint in the original action or else the defendant will be barred from bringing it as a separate lawsuit. CCP §§ 426.10, 426.30. (See Chapter 3(VI)(A)(1).) The defendant's cause of action is related if it arises out of the same transaction or occurrence as the plaintiff's cause of action. CCP § 426.10(c). This transactional approach to cross-complaints is in stark contrast to the application of the primary rights theory in other claim preclusion situations under California law.

3. Compare Federal Procedure

a. Federal Substantive Law

Federal courts applying federal substantive law usually follow the transactional definition of a claim (cause of action), not the primary rights theory. If a subsequent claim arises from the same transaction or occurrence as the first claim, its relitigation is barred. This transactional rule is also applied by the majority of states, as recommended by the Restatement (Second) of Judgments.

b. State Substantive Law

In contrast, a state law claim contained in a federal action is subject to the claim preclusion rules of the state in which the federal court sits. Semtek International Inc. v. Lockheed Martin Corp., 531 U.S. 497, 121 S.Ct. 1021, 149 L.Ed.2d 32 (2001). Thus, a California federal court sitting in diversity or exercising supplemental jurisdiction would apply California's primary rights doctrine to claims arising under state law.

4. Illustration

Patrick, a furniture maker, sued Donahue Furniture, Inc. in Sutter County Superior Court for breach of contract when Donahue failed

> to pay Patrick for a shipment of furniture pursuant to their contract. Patrick won a judgment against Donahue for $30,000. Before Patrick could enforce the judgment, Donahue filed for bankruptcy. Patrick's judgment remained unsatisfied. Seeking to enforce the judgment, Patrick filed a second lawsuit against Donahue and its shareholders. Patrick alleged that the defendants attempted to transfer and hide assets in order to prevent him from collecting on his judgment. Patrick brought tort causes of action for fraud, conversion and conspiracy. Donahue asserted that the second lawsuit was barred by claim preclusion. In applying the primary rights doctrine, the court will not bar the second lawsuit. The tort claims in the second suit relate to Patrick's right to be free from the defendants' fraudulent conduct that deprived him of the value of his judgment, while the cause of action for breach of contract in the first action seeks to vindicate a different primary right. Had the court applied the transactional test instead of the primary rights doctrine, the court might have prevented Patrick from pursuing the second lawsuit on the ground that the causes of action in both suits arise out of the same transactions and occurrences. Brenelli Amedeo, S.P.A. v. Bakara Furniture, Inc., 29 Cal.App.4th 1828, 35 Cal.Rptr.2d 348 (1994).

B. Issue Preclusion

1. Requirements

There are five elements of issue preclusion:

- an issue of law or fact in Action #2 that is identical to an issue litigated in Action #1;
- the issue was actually litigated in Action #1;
- the issue was necessary to the decision in Action #1;
- the decision in Action #1 was a final determination on the merits; and
- the party against whom preclusion is sought in Action #2 was a party or in privity with a party in Action #1.

Producers Dairy Delivery Co. v. Sentry Insurance Co., 41 Cal.3d 903, 226 Cal.Rptr. 558, 718 P.2d 920 (1986); Restatement (Second) of Judgments § 27.

a. Identical Issue

A key aspect of issue preclusion involves determining whether the issue litigated in the prior action is identical to an issue raised in the later action, regardless of how the causes of action are framed. A broad definition of the issue can subsume many smaller subissues. A narrow definition of the issue can allow relitigation of many matters that otherwise might appear nearly identical.

b. Actually Litigated

The application of the "actually litigated" requirement by California courts has led to confusion. Some courts appear to have imported the "could have been litigated" standard pertinent to claim preclusion. Torrey Pines Bank v. Superior Court, 216 Cal.App.3d 813, 265 Cal.Rptr. 217 (1989). Other opinions shed doubt on whether the "actually litigated" requirement applies to issues or legal theories. In jurisdictions outside of California that follow the Restatement (Second) of Judgments § 27, the requirement that an issue must have been previously litigated is applied strictly. Courts analyze a number of factors in making this determination, including whether the prior proceeding allowed the parties to present their case, and whether the parties had an incentive to vigorously litigate the issue.

c. Necessary to the Decision

An issue must not only have been actually litigated, but resolution of that issue also must have been "necessary" to the judgment. If the ultimate disposition of the prior action was not based on the determination of the issue, it was not necessarily decided and further litigation of that issue is not precluded. Four Star Electric, Inc. v. F & H Construction, 7 Cal.App.4th 1375, 10 Cal.Rptr.2d 1 (1992). The issue will be deemed "necessary" as long as it was not "entirely unnecessary" to the prior judgment. Lucido v. Superior Court, 51 Cal.3d 335, 342, 272 Cal.Rptr. 767, 770, 795 P.2d 1223 (1990). If the prior judgment is based on alternative grounds, many courts have followed the rule in the Restatement (Second) of Judgments § 27, comment *i*, which states that if either alternative ground is sufficient standing alone to support the judgment, the judgment is not conclusive as to either issue by itself. If the reviewing court affirms on only one of the alternative grounds, the second ground is not considered conclusively established. Newport Beach Country Club, Inc. v. Founding Members of Newport Beach Country Club, 140 Cal.App.4th 1120, 45 Cal.Rptr.3d 207 (2006).

d. Final Judgment on the Merits

The judgment in the prior action must be final and on the merits. Factors in favor of finality include whether the parties were heard on the matter, whether the court issued a reasoned opinion, and whether any potential appeal has been resolved. Sandoval v. Superior Court, 140 Cal.App.3d 932, 190 Cal.Rptr. 29 (1983). If an appeal is pending, or the time for bringing an appeal has not yet expired, the judgment is not yet final.

e. Parties or Privies

For issue preclusion to apply, a party in a subsequent action must have been the same party in the previous litigation, or must have been so closely related in interest that the party can fairly be said to have had its day in court.

2. Non-Mutual Issue Preclusion

a. Defensive Use

Issue preclusion in California may be raised defensively (by a defendant in Action #2 against a plaintiff who litigated and lost on that issue against a different party in Action #1). Bernhard v. Bank of America, 19 Cal.2d 807, 122 P.2d 892 (1942).

b. Offensive Use

The doctrine may also be asserted offensively (by a plaintiff in Action #2 against a defendant who litigated and lost on that issue against a different party in Action #1). Imen v. Glassford, 201 Cal.App.3d 898, 247 Cal.Rptr. 514 (1988). The court will scrutinize the application of offensive issue preclusion to ensure it is fair. In doing so, it will consider whether:

- the party against whom it is asserted had a full and fair opportunity to litigate;
- the party against whom it is asserted could foresee multiple suits;
- the party asserting it could not easily have been joined in the first action; and
- there are no inconsistent judgments on the record.

Id. (citing Parklane Hosiery Co. v. Shore, 439 U.S. 322, 99 S.Ct. 645, 58 L.Ed.2d 552 (1979)).

c. Preclusive Effect as to Third Parties

In the contractual arbitration context, determination of an issue in arbitration proceedings is not issue preclusive as to persons who were not signatories to the arbitration agreement, unless the parties to the arbitration agreement expressly agree to permit third parties to assert issue preclusion. Vandenberg v. Superior Court, 21 Cal.4th 815, 88 Cal.Rptr.2d 366, 982 P.2d 229 (1999). Similarly, issues that are stipulated to or are settled in Action #1 are not preclusive as to third parties in Action #2.

3. *Compare Federal Procedure*

Federal courts strictly apply the requirement that an issue must have been "actually litigated." Arizona v. California, 530 U.S. 392, 120 S.Ct. 2304, 147 L.Ed.2d 374 (2000). The fundamental elements of issue preclusion in federal practice are otherwise identical to those in California, and both defensive and offensive use of issue preclusion is allowed. Unlike California, a final federal judgment has issue preclusive effect even if an appeal is pending.

4. Illustration

Hank and Wilma agreed to divorce. The Marin County Superior Court entered a final judgment dividing the marital assets. However, Hank has a pension that, while known to both Hank and Wilma, was not addressed in the judgment of dissolution. Wilma subsequently brought suit for an accounting of Hank's assets, contending she should receive a portion of the pension. Because the precise issue of the division of the pension was not actually litigated in the previous dissolution proceeding, the doctrine of issue preclusion does not apply. Wilma may raise the issue of the pension in the accounting action. Henn v. Henn, 26 Cal.3d 323, 161 Cal.Rptr. 502, 605 P.2d 10 (1980).

SAMPLE EXAM QUESTIONS

OBJECTIVE QUESTIONS

(1) Which of the following represent(s) binding precedent on the California Court of Appeal for the First District?

a. A prior decision of the California Supreme Court;

b. A prior decision of the U.S. Court of Appeals for the Ninth Circuit;

c. A prior decision of the California Court of Appeal for the First District;

d. Both a and c.

(2) The California Supreme Court may overrule its own precedent:

a. When the Court created error that must be corrected;

b. When the precedent is unsound;

c. Never—only the U.S. Supreme Court can overrule California Supreme Court precedent;

d. Both a and b.

(3) True or False: In California, legislation is generally applied prospectively and judicial decisions retroactively, absent a judicial or legislative requirement to do otherwise.

(4) True or False: The law of the case doctrine applies to both legal and factual rulings made by an appellate court.

(5) True or False: The doctrine of judicial estoppel applies in federal courts as well as in California courts.

(6) True or False: For both claim and issue preclusion purposes in California, a judgment is considered final as soon as it is entered by the Superior Court.

(7) In California, claim preclusion bars a party from filing a lawsuit if:

a. The current cause of action arises from the same transaction, occurrence or series of transactions or occurrences as a previously litigated cause of action;

b. The plaintiff seeks to vindicate in a subsequent action the same primary right as was previously litigated;

c. A court previously issued a declaratory judgment on the matter to be litigated in the subsequent action;

d. Both b and c.

(8) A party will be unable to relitigate an issue raised in a subsequent proceeding when which of the following conditions exist(s):

a. The issue to be litigated is identical to that actually litigated and necessarily decided in the former proceeding;

b. The decision on the issue in the former proceeding is final and on the merits;

c. Preclusion is sought against a person who was a party or in privity with a party to the former proceeding;

d. All of the above.

(9) True or False: California permits defensive use of issue preclusion but not offensive use of issue preclusion.

Answers to Objective Questions

(1) **a.** The decisions of California courts of superior jurisdiction are binding on courts of inferior jurisdiction. Therefore, decisions of the California Supreme Court are binding on all California courts of appeal. A ruling issued by a California Court of Appeal panel is not binding on any subsequent appellate panel regardless of which district issued the ruling. Federal circuit court decisions (regardless of circuit) are not treated as binding authority by the California state courts.

(2) **d.** Both a and b are correct bases for the California Supreme Court to overrule its precedent.

(3) **True**. Generally, California applies judicial decisions retroactively and legislation prospectively, unless the court or Legislature indicates otherwise.

(4) **False**. Law of the case applies to rules of law, not factual determinations.

(5) **True**. The judicial estoppel doctrine is recognized in both California and federal courts.

(6) **False**. A judgment is considered final for claim and issue preclusion purposes when the appeal from the judgment is completed or the time to appeal has expired.

(7) **b.** California is in the minority of states that recognizes the primary rights doctrine, in contrast to the transactional standard used by federal courts and in many state jurisdictions. A single cause of action under the transactional standard might be considered two causes of action under the primary rights theory.

(8) **d.** This question sets out the requirements for issue preclusion in California.

(9) **False**. California permits both defensive and offensive use of issue preclusion.

ESSAY QUESTION

Sarah experienced severe abdominal pains and saw Dr. Nan in Yreka. After conducting an examination, Dr. Nan concluded that Sarah's pains were a mild digestive ailment and nothing to worry about. As it turned out, Sarah's pains were caused by an ectopic pregnancy. As a result of the pregnancy, Sarah had to have a hysterectomy. Sarah was hospitalized for three weeks. In addition to her physical injuries, Sarah suffered emotional distress.

Sarah sued Dr. Nan in Siskiyou County Superior Court for professional negligence and prevailed. The jury awarded Sarah damages based on both her physical injuries and emotional distress, and the court entered judgment. One year later, Sarah and her husband Tim decided that they wanted to have a baby. Because of Sarah's condition, the couple had to hire a surrogate and pay roughly $50,000 for the process. Sarah and Tim filed suit against Dr. Nan and the Hospital where Dr. Nan worked at the time of Sarah's initial injury (the Hospital was not a party to the first lawsuit) to recover the expenses associated with the surrogacy.

Analyze the potential claim and issue preclusion defenses Dr. Nan and the Hospital might raise in response to Sarah's and Tim's lawsuit. Discuss whether Sarah and Tim might successfully assert issue preclusion against Dr. Nan and/or the Hospital.

Answer to Essay Question

- Claim Preclusion
    - Dr. Nan and the Hospital will argue that Sarah and Tim's causes of action are barred by claim preclusion and had already been decided in the earlier lawsuit.
    - Elements of claim preclusion:

- Final judgment on the merits in the first action.

- Same plaintiffs and same defendants (or those in privity) in both first and second actions.

- Both causes of action are based on the same primary right.

- The cause of action in the second action actually was or could have been litigated in the first action.

- Final judgment on the merits of the first case:

  - There was a judgment on the merits of Sarah's personal injury and emotional distress causes of action.

  - It is probable that the time for appeal has expired.

- Same parties or privies:

  - Sarah was the plaintiff in both actions. Tim became a plaintiff in the second action. His relationship as Sarah's husband is probably one of privity.

  - Only Dr. Nan was a defendant in the first case. Thus, the Hospital may not assert claim preclusion, but it may be asserted by Dr. Nan.

  - The Hospital might argue that Dr. Nan litigated in privity with the Hospital in the first case, because she was employed there at the time. However, since the Hospital was not involved in the original trial, this argument is likely to be unsuccessful.

- Same cause of action:

  - The difference between the causes of action in the two lawsuits is the difference in the damages sought. The theory of recovery—negligence—is the same in both cases. Both cases involve recovery for injuries that Sarah sustained to her body. As such, both claims arguably involve the same "primary right" to be free of the kind of reproductive injury that Sarah suffered, making claim preclusion appropriate, at least with regard to Dr. Nan. However, some courts could reasonably interpret Sarah's claims as arising from different primary rights.

        - Under the transactional standard used in other jurisdictions, the plaintiffs' causes of action may be regarded as one.

- Issue Preclusion

    - Sarah and Tim will probably contend that the negligence issue has already been litigated and decided in the first action against Dr. Nan, and the jury's finding of negligence should be conclusive.

    - Requirements for issue preclusion:

        - Valid final judgment on the merits of the first action.

        - Same issue was actually litigated and necessarily determined in the first action.

        - Issue preclusion may only be asserted against person who was a party or in privity with a party in the first action.

        - Issue preclusion may be asserted by someone not a party in the first action:

            - Non-mutual defensive issue preclusion: permissible provided the person against whom it is asserted had a full and fair opportunity to litigate the issue.

            - Non-mutual offensive issue preclusion: permissible provided it is not unfair and:

                - The party against whom it is asserted had a full and fair opportunity to litigate.

                - The party against whom it is asserted could foresee multiple suits.

                - The party asserting it could not easily have been joined in the first action.

                - There are no inconsistent judgments on the record.

    - Valid, final judgment:

        - The judgment for Sarah in the first action was on the merits of her personal injury and emotional distress causes of action.

- It is probable that the time for appeal has expired.

- Same issues actually litigated and necessarily determined:

  - The issue litigated in the first action was the negligence of Dr. Nan, not the negligence of the Hospital. However, under a theory of vicarious liability, Dr. Nan's negligence might be attributed to the Hospital. The Hospital might be considered to be in privity with Dr. Nan.

  - The issue of negligence was essential to the judgment in the first action because it was the basis for the judgment. Dr. Nan had full motivation to litigate it vigorously the first time.

- Preclusion asserted against a person who was a party:

  - Dr. Nan was a party in the first action, so Sarah and Tim could assert issue preclusion against her. However, the Hospital was not a party in the first action. Unless the Hospital is considered to be in privity with Dr. Nan, issue preclusion against it may not be proper.

- Non-mutual application:

  - Tim was not a party to the first suit, but he might be able to assert issue preclusion against Dr. Nan because she had a full and fair opportunity to litigate in the first action. Tim could not have been joined in the first action because he had no cause of action to plead at that time.

Table of Cases

References are to pages

INDEX

References are to pages

†